Charles A. Moser is Professor of Slavic at George Washington University. His books include *Antinihilism in the Russian Novel of the 1860s* (Mouton) and *Pisemsky: A Provincial Realist* (Harvard).

D1440945

Esthetics as Nightmare

Esthetics
as
Nightmare

Russian

Literary Theory,

1855–1870

CHARLES A. MOSER

Princeton University Press

Princeton, New Jersey

PG
2944
M67
1989

Copyright © 1989
by Princeton University Press
Published by Princeton University Press,
41 William Street, Princeton, New Jersey 08540
In the United Kingdom:
Princeton University Press,
Guildford, Surrey

Library of Congress Cataloging-in-Publication Data
Moser, Charles A.
Esthetics as nightmare : Russian literary theory, 1855–1870 /
Charles A. Moser.
p.   cm.
Bibliography: p.
Includes index.
ISBN 0-691-06763-5 (alk. paper)
1. Russian literature—Philosophy. 2. Russian literature—19th century—
History and criticism. 3. Criticism. I. Title.
PG2944.M67 1989
891.7'09'003—dc 19
88-19505
CIP

Publication of this book has been aided by
a grant from the Paul Mellon Fund
of Princeton University Press

This book has been composed in Linotron Galliard

Clothbound editions of Princeton University Press books
are printed on acid-free paper, and binding materials are
chosen for strength and durability. Paperbacks although satisfactory
for personal collections, are not usually suitable for library rebinding

Printed in the United States of America
by Princeton University Press,
Princeton, New Jersey

In memory of
Ernest J. Simmons
1903–72

I consider such problems as the legitimacy of poetry amid other human activities, poetry's moral significance, contemporaneity in our day, etc. to be nightmares from which we should long since have freed ourselves forever.

—*Afanasy Fet (1859)*

The reader will no doubt decide that esthetics is my nightmare, and in this case the reader will be quite right.

—*Dmitry Pisarev (1864)*

Contents

◊

Illustrations

◊

Vasily Botkin

Nikolay Chernyshevsky

Nikolay Dobrolyubov

Alexander Druzhinin

Evgeny Edelson

Apollon Grigorev

Mikhail Katkov

Konstantin Leontev

Dmitry Pisarev

Nikolay Shelgunov

Nikolay Solovev

Varfolomey Zaytsev

Preface

◊

*E*STHETIC QUESTIONS WERE AT THE FOREFRONT
of Russian intellectual life during the fifteen years or so following the conclusion of the Crimean War and Alexander
II's accession to the throne. To be sure, the rigors of censorship had substantially abated after Nicholas I's death, which
ended what has come to be known as the "epoch of censorship terror," but it was still difficult to discuss many religious, philosophical, and especially political problems in the
public prints. As a result, many Russian intellectuals resorted to literature and literary criticism as a means of dealing with what were at bottom political questions. If a novel
or short story "accurately" depicted Russian reality, then it
could at least implicitly point to the reforms needed for the
improvement of that reality; and literary critics, while purporting to discuss those same literary works, could deal with
such reforms or changes directly. Thus some of Russia's best
minds then occupied themselves at least some of the time
with literature and literary criticism, and their political motivations go far to explain the violence of the controversies
which arose over such key documents of the period as Ivan
Turgenev's *Fathers and Sons* of 1862 and Nikolay Chernyshevsky's *What Is to Be Done?*, published the following year.

One may take the argument a step further, however, and
raise the more general problem of esthetics, though with

special reference to literature, the most intensely controversial form of art then. The riddle of the nature of art, the proper relationship between art and that reality which it depicted in some fashion, engaged not only the political passions which literature itself aroused, but in addition metaphysical ones having to do with the linkage between the ideal and the real. The disputants recognized this quite clearly at the time: as Evgeny Edelson wrote in 1867, when the debate was beginning to subside, "all the hostilities and sympathies of the contending parties were focused on this point, finding complete and unceremonious expression in the quarrel over art and esthetics."[1] Thus disputes over art during those years burned in Russia with an intensity which we in the West may find difficult to comprehend, but which also makes the period a very interesting one for investigation more than a century later, especially since many of the problems which their participants raised then in their fundamental form are still with us.

The controversy of the 1860s was the more intense also because it was even at the time perceived as conducted along liberal and conservative lines, with liberal and radical critics inclined to reject their conservative opponents' arguments out of hand, and vice versa. Upon this division was superimposed another, that between critics and writers: most of the prominent critics were political radicals, while many of the creative writers (and their number included such giants as Fedor Dostoevsky, Leo Tolstoy, Ivan Turgenev, and Ivan Goncharov) were conservative or at most moderate by political persuasion. The conservative critic Nikolay Solovev noted this as early as 1864 when he spoke of the "schism" between Russia's "most energetic thinkers" and her "most

---

[1] Evgenii Edel'son, "O znachenii iskusstva v tsivilizatsii," *Vsemirnyi trud* (January 1867), 220.

gifted artists."[2] A critic of quite different political viewpoint, Nikolay Shelgunov, who viewed literature through an obvious political prism (he denied that *War and Peace* contained anything worthwhile, for example, and ignored Dostoevsky), wrote in 1871:

> In the 1840s we had Belinsky *alone* and an entire galaxy of writers; in our day, on the other hand, we have quite a few critics and journalists who attained prominence at about the same time, but hardly a single writer of fiction.[3]

Since Shelgunov is referring to men of liberal or radical persuasion when he talks of writers and critics, he and his archrival Solovev agreed that literary criticism of the 1860s was chiefly in the hands of radicals, and creative writing under the control of conservatives. *Russky vestnik* (Russian Herald), the Moscow journal which first printed an extraordinary number of fictional works by such authors as Turgenev, Tolstoy, and Dostoevsky that have since become classics of world literature, had no critics of repute among its contributors, while the radical journals *Sovremennik* (The Contemporary) and *Russkoe slovo* (Russian Word) published highly influential critical articles, but few fictional works known to anyone except literary historians today.

The radical journals did have a few writers still worthy of attention, however, and in like manner there were among the conservatives some critics who upheld the theoretical values of art and literature. It is the aim of this book to trace the leading ideas in the controversies over art and literature in Russia from 1855 to 1870 in their various combinations and permutations, as formulated both by critics whose names are still writ large in Soviet and Western scholarship—Ni-

---

[2] Nikolai Solov'ev, "Teoriia bezobraziia," *Epokha*, no. 7 (July 1864), 12.

[3] Nikolai Shelgunov, "Sochineniia D. I. Pisareva" (intended for publication in 1871 but forbidden by the censorship), *Literaturnaia kritika* (Leningrad, 1974), 264.

kolay Chernyshevsky, Nikolay Dobrolyubov, Dmitry Pisarev—and by critics of more conservative persuasion who are often neglected in Soviet and Western research. Apollon Grigorev, to be sure, has received a fair amount of scholarly attention, but men like Evgeny Edelson, Nikolay Solovev, Efim Zarin, and others also advanced intriguing ideas, and moreover ideas whose validity should not be measured by their lack of popularity at the time, if only because they found support from contemporary creative writers who now rank among the greatest in world literature. Nor does this study limit itself to views expressed in formal literary criticism or theory: it also surveys the implicit or explicit doctrines of art and literature to be found in the fiction of that time. Art is far too important a subject to be left solely to the critics.

An examination of the leading ideas on literature and art set forth during the 1860s shows that some of the controversy over them sprang from simple misunderstanding, as N. V. Kashina remarks à propos of Dostoevsky and the radical critics with whom he conducted heated polemics.[4] Theories on art cannot in the final accounting be separated along a neat conservative-radical spectrum, although this will do as a first approximation. One of this book's primary objectives is precisely to examine some of the finer points of the polarized debate of the 1860s.

A study such as this one must have a beginning and an end. The former is relatively easy to define, for the year 1855 saw not only a change of monarchs and an outburst of political optimism, it also witnessed the publication of what is surely the most influential master's essay in literary history and the founding document of the entire esthetic debate to follow: Nikolay Chernyshevsky's *Esteticheskie otnosheniia iskusstva k deistvitelnosti* (Esthetic Relations of Art to Reality).

---

[4] N. V. Kashina, *Estetika F. M. Dostoevskogo* (Moscow, 1975), 215.

This small book defined the parameters of the entire discussion of the period, although its author claimed no special expertise in the field of esthetics, did not write a great deal more on the subject, and even virtually ceased to function as a practicing literary critic after 1859.

Indeed, as the controversy progressed its participants changed kaleidoscopically, and that is one reason why one should emphasize its ideas more than its participants, although one cannot of course disregard the latter entirely. Chernyshevsky yielded his place as leading radical critic to Nikolay Dobrolyubov, who had achieved prominence by 1859 but died a tragically early death in late 1861. By 1864 Dmitry Pisarev had raised the fallen banner of radical criticism, but he for all practical purposes left the critical arena when his journal *Russkoe slovo* was suppressed in 1866, and he died by drowning in 1868. By that time the cause of radical criticism had been partially taken up by Nikolay Shelgunov, an older man who had been associated with the Russian radical thinkers for many years but only began writing literary criticism in the latter half of the 1860s. The conservative critics, on the other hand, participated in the discussion for longer periods, but less intensely. Apollon Grigorev wrote sporadically on general esthetic topics from the controversy's inception in 1855 until his death in 1864. Evgeny Edelson wrote well but infrequently on esthetic matters, and his major statement on the subject dates from as late as 1867, not long before his untimely death in January of 1868. Nikolay Solovev first appeared in Dostoevsky's journal *Epokha* (Epoch) only in 1864, though he participated very actively in the discussion from then until 1867. In 1869 his collected esthetic writings appeared in three volumes under the title *Iskusstvo i zhizn* (Art and Life), to be extensively reviewed and rebutted by Shelgunov in 1870. After 1870 Solovev ceased to write literary criticism altogether, and Shelgunov moved mostly into other areas as the esthetic debate of the

1860s ran its course. It therefore seemed appropriate to set the upper margin of this study at 1870, the year which witnessed the final vigorous discussion of Pisarev's ideas by his staunch defender Shelgunov in a rebuttal of Pisarev's determined opponent Solovev.

In fact Dmitry Pisarev is in many ways the central figure of this study. Although I seek to encompass all critical viewpoints of importance set forth between 1855 and 1870, since both Soviet and Western scholars had written extensively on the radical critics and on the critical controversies of the later 1850s and early 1860s, I have by way of compensation here emphasized certain conservative critics such as Solovev, Edelson, and Zarin, and the years from roughly 1862 to 1870. But the principal antagonist of the conservative critics over those years was none other than Pisarev, who drew out the doctrines of radical literary criticism to their logical extremes, and thus forced his conservative opponents, his radical colleagues, and us, too, so many years later, to grapple with fundamental problems of the nature of art and reality.

Soviet scholars have traditionally been a trifle wary of Pisarev, and have paid less attention to him than they have to Chernyshevsky and Dobrolyubov, precisely because of the relentless logic of his argumentation which exposed the fundamental thrust of radical esthetic thought. Thus, for example, Pisarev's famous excoriation of Pushkin's work in its entirety was a logical development of the Chernyshevskian view of art, but it cannot be accepted by Soviet scholars who for powerful cultural reasons must revere both Chernyshevsky and Pushkin. If they are to be consistent, as Pisarev challenges them to be, they must reject either Chernyshevsky or Pushkin. Unwilling to do this, they negate the great negator himself: Pisarev.

Pisarev is not only an interesting esthetic theoretician; he is also a keen practical critic, by no means devoid of artistic sense, a lively writer and stimulating thinker, and a complex personality. He deserves careful consideration of the sort he has received only infrequently in Soviet investigations or in Western scholarship, which is sometimes unduly influenced by prevalent Soviet attitudes.

This study deals with the esthetic controversies almost exclusively within Russian boundaries. No such controversy can take place solely within the confines of a single country, of course, and the ideas of French and especially German thinkers had a substantial impact upon Russian theoreticians (there could be little reciprocal influence simply because few Europeans read Russian at the time, and relevant works were slow to be translated). The Russian critics discussed in this book participated in a general European culture and drew upon its stock of ideas in formulating their arguments. They developed few if any strikingly original ideas in the course of the discussion, but this fact is of secondary importance. Instead, the particular channels which the controversy followed within the Russian context are of interest to students of Russian culture, and the general ideas which Russian thinkers derived from the common European intellectual fund and applied to the question of the relationship between art and reality make the discussion still today of concern to anyone who deals seriously with esthetics.

The first chapter of this study offers a roughly chronological overview of the principal participants in the debates from 1855 to 1870, as well as of the major documents in which they expressed their ideas. I assume a relatively high level of knowledge of the period on the reader's part, and therefore do not discuss the biographies of well-known figures such as Chernyshevsky, Dobrolyubov, or Pisarev, except when biographical details are directly relevant to the controversy. I provide some biographical information on lesser-known figures, though even then only when they played a prominent role in the discussion. Lesser-known writers who published only one or two works are not given much biographical attention. In the first chapter I discuss primarily the particular circumstances in which a theoretical work appeared and avoid taking up its larger ideas, since I go into these in subsequent chapters.

The following chapters treat these leading ideas under three headings: Art and Rationality, Art and Morality, and Art and Reality. There is some unavoidable overlap among these divisions, but I have tried to keep it to a minimum. Although many of these ideas on art are nearly timeless, particular formulations were made at certain points in history, and I have sought to indicate the time and source for each such formulation: after all, the history of ideas has a chronology, which can be of crucial importance. Finally, to each of the three theoretical chapters I have appended an "Excursus" analyzing a literary work or literary works in the light of certain points made in that chapter and in a way appropriate to arguments made within that chapter.

Finally, I have compiled a brief bibliography in two parts. The first part is a listing of the principal editions used as primary sources, and then the journal publications which have served as primary sources. The second part lists secondary works. This listing is confined rather strictly to the most important books and articles on the specific subject of esthetics, i.e., art and literature in Russia during the period under discussion.

Small portions of this study have appeared in print earlier: "Stepan Trofimovič Verxovenskij and the Esthetics of His Time," published in the *Slavic and East European Journal* in 1985 (reprinted by permission of AATSEEL of the U.S.); and "Nihilism, Aesthetics, and 'The Idiot,' " published in *Russian Literature* in 1982. I am grateful to these publications for permission to reprint.

Finally, I should like to express my thanks to the George Washington University for a sabbatical leave in the spring of 1985 which enabled me to write most of this manuscript; to the Library of Congress, without whose extensive collections (especially of nineteenth-century Russian journals) I could not have carried out my research; to Valerye Hawkins for her typing of the original manuscript; and to Professors Hugh McLean of the University of California at Berkeley and Grigory Tamarchenko of Boston University, who were kind enough to read the manuscript at an earlier stage and give me the benefit of their comments. The faults which remain in this study are my responsibility.

Washington, D.C.
January 1988

A Note on the References

SINCE I WISHED TO MAKE THE SCHOLARLY APPARA-
tus of this study as efficient as possible, I have included page
references directly in the text when this was feasible. These
references are to collected editions, single- or multi-volume,
listed in part I of the bibliography. Thus if the text offers a
quote from Pisarev followed by (2:177), this means page 177
of volume 2 of his four-volume *Sochineniia* of 1955–56 listed
in the bibliography as the basic reference in this study.

Writings which have not been reprinted or which have
been reprinted but were unavailable to me (e.g., the works
of Nikolai Solov'ev) have been cited from the journal publications listed in part II of the bibliography ("Primary
Sources: Journal Publications"), and are given in the notes,
usually with abbreviated titles after the point of first mention.

References to publications by Efim Zarin and Nikolai
Solov'ev in *Otechestvennye zapiski* for 1865 and especially 1866
are provided by volume and page rather than by month and
page, since during that time the journal published twice
monthly instead of once a month. Each volume comprised
four issues covering two months, and was paginated con-
secutively.

Apollon Grigor'ev receives special treatment in the ap-
paratus. Although the basic text for references is his *Litera-*

turnaia kritika, published in Moscow in 1967, I have used the first volume of his *Sochineniia* published by Villanova University Press in 1970 as the source in the notes for certain articles not included in *Literaturnaia kritika*, and the journal publications as the source only for a few articles not reprinted in either volume.

In the notes and bibliography I have used the Library of Congress transliteration system without diacriticals; in the body of the text I have employed a less rigorous but more readable system of transliteration.

Esthetics as Nightmare

◊

Chapter One

The Disputants and Their Journals

T HE YEAR 1855 WAS A CRUCIAL ONE, FOR RUSSIAN history generally as well as for the development of Russian intellectual and literary life. Not only did that year witness the death of Nicholas I and the beginning of the reign of Alexander II; it also saw the issuance of two publications which intensified a relatively calm discussion of esthetic matters into what could be characterized as a debate or controversy over art and literature which would rage for some fifteen years before subsiding to a more reasonable level. It was no chance matter that the book which supplied the intellectual foundations for the radical arguments in that dispute was a discursive piece of literary and artistic scholarship: an essay presented by Nikolay Chernyshevsky (1828–89) to the faculty of St. Petersburg University in partial fulfillment of the requirements for the degree of master of arts. Its title: *The Esthetic Relations of Art to Reality*. And it was also appropriate that the publication which inspired the so-called "esthetic" critics should have been the first relatively complete edition of the works of Russia's greatest poet, Alexander Pushkin, which appeared in six volumes (with a further volume to come subsequently) under the editorship of the critic, scholar, and memoirist Pavel Annenkov (1813–87). The differing natures of these two publications very aptly symbolized the divergent viewpoints which the radical and esthetic critics would advance in the years following.

The 1850s: Defining Positions

Nikolay Chernyshevsky—who, like a number of his intellectual allies, came from a clergy family and studied in church schools before decisively rejecting religion—arrived in St. Petersburg from Saratov in May of 1853.[1] Before that point he had taught for a time in Saratov, and also acquired a family, which he had to find a means of supporting in the capital. By January 1854 he had obtained a teaching position in St. Petersburg too, but was disturbed very little when he retained it for less than a year since his real ambition was to become either a scholar or a journalist. To this end he had begun publishing in St. Petersburg newspapers and periodicals before 1853 was out, and within a mere month of his arrival had called upon the eminent Slavist Izmail Sreznevsky in order to begin the process of earning his master's degree at St. Petersburg University. He successfully passed his examinations in late 1853 and early 1854, then turned to the writing of his master's essay under the supervision of Professor Alexander Nikitenko. Nikitenko (1804–77), a self-made intellectual born a serf, a historian of Russian literature, and for many years an enlightened censor, had himself written a dissertation some twenty years earlier on a subject from esthetics (*On Creative Force in Poetry*), and thus was an appropriate mentor for Chernyshevsky.

Chernyshevsky worked very rapidly at his essay. He had begun writing by late July or early August of 1854 and produced only one text, which he did not revise. Thus he had

---

[1] This account draws upon the classic biography by Iurii Steklov, *N. G. Chernyshevskii: Ego zhizn' i deiatel'nost'. 1828–1889*. Second edition (Moscow-Leningrad, 1928), I:131–43.

completed his writing by September, and Nikitenko approved his thesis late that same month. The larger academic bureaucracy would not be hurried, however, and approved the text only some six months later, in April 1855. The thesis was printed on May 3 and publicly defended on May 10. Evidently the word spread that this was no ordinary master's essay, for a number of leading intellectual and literary figures of the day attended the defense. Among them were Pavel Annenkov—who had a way of being present on important literary occasions in Russian history—and Nikolay Shelgunov (1824–91), who had met Chernyshevsky soon after the latter's arrival in St. Petersburg and who left a detailed description of the occasion. Before this prominent audience Chernyshevsky uncompromisingly defended the major points of his argument, rather to the discomfiture of certain of his professors, who disagreed with his approach. As Chernyshevsky himself recalled the occasion afterward, he had expected to discuss substantive matters, but in fact the defense lasted only about an hour and a half and dealt with "trivialities." Nikitenko alone among his professors asked sensible questions, he thought, and the whole event was rather a formality.[2] After the defense, despite its doubts, the faculty recommended that Chernyshevsky be awarded his degree, but the minister of education at the time refused to accept their recommendation and withheld it. A new minister of education did confer it three years later, but by that time Chernyshevsky had abandoned all thought of a scholarly career and did not bother to accept it. It mattered little to him whether his contributions were officially recognized, for by 1858 he knew that the radical intelligentsia, the people he cared about, regarded itself as virtually obliged to accept the arguments he made in his essay: the volume had acquired something like the force of intellectual law, as an

---

[2] See Chernyshevsky's letter of May 16 [1855] to his family: 14:299–300.

unsympathetic commentator noted in 1866.[3] Chernyshevsky could scarcely have hoped to exert a more powerful influence on Russian society than he in fact did through this short work.

The intellectual power of Chernyshevsky's essay sprang from the simplicity of its basic principles, and that simplicity in turn derived from his monistic, unitary approach. Chernyshevsky rejected from the start of his argument any notion of philosophical dualism, any true division between the natural and the supernatural, the real and the ideal. His thought is permeated by the monistic assumption: truth is unitary; there cannot be different ways of perceiving truth, and by extension reality: there can be only one way, to which the force of reason must ultimately bring everyone. Thus when Chernyshevsky turned to the subject of art, his first concern was the elimination of dualism from esthetic thought.

Dualism in esthetic thought could manifest itself in the dichotomy of form and content, or the notion of embodying a particular idea in a certain material form, an important element in the then dominant Hegelian doctrines of esthetics as elaborated, for example, by Friedrich Theodor Vischer, who published his monumental *Aesthetik oder Wissenschaft des Schönen* in six volumes between 1846 and 1857. Chernyshevsky chose Vischer as his chief opponent, even though the *Aesthetik* had not appeared in its entirety at the time Chernyshevsky wrote.

Chernyshevsky rejected the Hegelian argument that "the beautiful is the perfect correspondence, the perfect identity between idea and image," along with the related definition of the sublime as the "preponderance of the idea over the form": both these definitions provided excellent examples of philosophical dualism. But then Chernyshevsky

[3] Konstantin Sluchevskii, *Iavleniia russkoi zhizni pod kritikoiu estetiki. II. Esteticheskie otnosheniia iskusstva k deistvitel'nosti, gospodina Ch.* (St. Petersburg, 1866), iv.

noted, Chernyshevsky applies his monistic approach to esthetics quite consistently. He rejects the dualistic Hegelian notion of the sublime as the "preponderance of idea over form" and defines the sublime as simply "that which is very much larger than anything with which we compare it." And since he does not believe in the ancients' concept of a supernatural fate—what we have regarded as fate is merely chance, he says—as an essential element of the tragic, he defines the tragic as merely "the horrible in human life."

Chernyshevsky thus held with unusual consistency to the central tenet of his essay ("the beautiful is life") and applied it to esthetic notions across the board. His intellectual audacity was breathtaking, and his work appeared at precisely the right time, at the point when the budding radical intelligentsia, nurtured on the ideas of the late Vissarion Belinsky but oppressed by the censorship since 1848, was thoroughly prepared to accept his theories and disseminate them widely. The unitary nature of his thought gave it singular power among those who sought unquestioned truth and looked for a secular ideal to be realized in the society of the future, and his followers remained extraordinarily faithful to his doctrines: they simply repeated them, without devising any significant variations upon them.

The Esthetic Relations of Art to Reality was immediately recognized as a work of importance, and not just by those who crowded the hall in May of 1855 to hear its author defend it against a cluster of hostile academics whose teaching he rejected. All those who dealt seriously with such matters realized from the start that this was a work to be reckoned with. As early as August 1855 Apollon Grigorev published a theoretical article in the journal *Moskvityanin* (The Muscovite) in which he referred to Chernyshevsky's "astounding doctrine" of art.[6] And Evgeny Edelson, who would be a ma-

---

[6] Apollon Grigor'ev, "Obozrenie nalichnykh literaturnykh deiatelei," *Moskvitianin*, no. 15–16 (August 1855), 190.

jor spokesman for the esthetic viewpoint in years to come, wrote an extensive review of the *Esthetic Relations* for *Moskvityanin*, although for various reasons it did not appear at that time. Though Edelson apparently claimed to be pleased by the appearance of an entire theoretical study devoted to esthetic problems, he dedicated his article to a careful discussion and defense of Hegelian esthetics. Edelson ended by concluding that Chernyshevsky's theory was "not successful" because his viewpoint derived from the already outmoded "Natural School" of the 1840s.[7] As time passed, however, Edelson realized how much damage that "unsuccessful theory" was causing in Russian intellectual life. Some twelve years later he spoke of Chernyshevsky's approach as one of "obvious and total contempt for any artistic activity at all," although he still recognized the contribution Chernyshevsky's essay had made to the discussion of esthetics which began at that time.[8] Ivan Turgenev condemned Chernyshevsky's ideas from the very start, terming the *Esthetic Relations* "false and harmful" in private correspondence with Vasily Botkin and Nikolay Nekrasov dating from the late summer of 1855 (Pis'ma, 2:300–01). And the editor and critic Stepan Dudyshkin (1820–66) did not care for Chernyshevsky's essay at all.[9]

Of course Chernyshevsky's theories could not have acquired the influence they did in so short a time had he not had powerful defenders as well as detractors. Mikhail Saltykov-Shchedrin was one of the most outspoken among the former: he prepared an article containing a defense of Cher-

[7] M. G. Zel'dovich, "Nesostoiavshaiasia retsenziia na 'Esteticheskie otnosheniia iskusstva k deistvitel'nosti' (N. Chernyshevskii i E. Edel'son)," *Russkaia literatura*, no. 3 (1969), 147–51.
[8] Evgenii Edel'son, "O znachenii iskusstva v tsivilizatsii," *Vsemirnyi trud* (January 1867), 218.
[9] See Boris Egorov, "S. S. Dudyshkin–kritik," *Uchenye zapiski Tartuskogo gos. universiteta*, no. 119 (1962): *Trudy po russkoi i slavianskoi filologii*, 5: 210.

nyshevsky's ideas and a further development of his theories for publication in an 1856 issue of *Russky vestnik*, the journal which in a few years would acquire a reputation as a bastion of conservatism in Russian literature and criticism. While he was at it, Saltykov criticized Pavel Annenkov's article "On the Significance of Artistic Works for Society," also published in *Russky vestnik* (February 1856), in which Annenkov opposed Chernyshevsky's viewpoint.[10]

We might have expected Annenkov to be in the thick of such a debate from the beginning, for he always managed to be at the center of Russian literary life somehow. In his earlier years he had been the man in Rome to whom Nikolay Gogol dictated the final version of *Dead Souls*, and he had been with Vissarion Belinsky when the great critic traveled in Europe just before returning home to die. He is also credited with having been the first to use the word "realism," one of the leading terms of nineteenth-century criticism. He was a close personal friend of Ivan Turgenev's, and served as a prepublication critic of many of his finest works. In the latter half of the 1850s he became one of the chief theoretical defenders of art's autonomy, against the radical doctrines which had found their most compact expression in Chernyshevsky's essay. However, those doctrines had powerful spokesmen, who succeeded not only in placing Annenkov generally on the defensive but also influenced his own thinking: as a prominent Soviet student of the criticism of the 1850s and 1860s puts it, Annenkov was always so ambivalent in his own judgments that he found it difficult to resist Chernyshevskian certitudes.[11]

Despite all this, Annenkov's greatest contribution to the

---

[10] V. E. Bograd, " 'Literaturnyi manifest' Saltykova," *Literaturnoe nasledstvo*, vol. 67 (Moscow, 1959), 281–314.

[11] Boris Egorov, "P. V. Annenkov—literator i kritik 1840–kh-1850-kh gg.", *Uchenye zapiski Tartuskogo gos. universiteta*, no. 209 (1968): *Trudy po russkoi i slavianskoi filologii. XI. Literaturovedenie*, 51–108.

debate of 1855–70 was no doubt the publication of Pushkin's works accompanied by Pushkin's biography, for it was Annenkov who brought the poet out of the relative obscurity into which he had fallen after his death in 1837 and initiated the process of providing him a place in the history of Russian literature which has remained supreme. For the esthetic critics and writers of the 1850s interpreted Pushkin's views on art as set forth in his poetry (particularly his cycle on the poet), and that poetry itself, as supporting ideas of the supremacy of art over reality, and of the artist over the common man. The radical critics in turn took Nikolay Gogol as their standard, viewing him as the creator of socially useful literature which at least implicitly called for a restructuring of society. Thus political passions were superimposed upon an artistic dispute, and the controversy over the nature of art and literature became extremely heated by the end of the 1850s.

Annenkov equipped the first volume of his edition with an essay of more than 400 pages entitled "Materials for a Biography of Alexander Sergeevich Pushkin." This work cannot at all be characterized as a brief for the esthetic viewpoint, although in the middle it does include a short segment on Pushkin's view of the poet and the poet's independence, and at the end a few words on Pushkin's importance for Russia's cultural development. But the very existence of the edition was a major factor in the debate of the times, and it is probably no chance matter that, as the attack on art's independence intensified, Yakov Isakov should have brought out, in 1859, still another collection of Pushkin's works based primarily on the Annenkov edition. Through his writings Pushkin remained a presence in the debate.

To be sure, the radical critics did not immediately recognize the importance of the publication of Pushkin's collected works: the French specialist Charles Corbet points out that at the time Chernyshevsky was quite complimentary toward Pushkin, but became much less so by 1857, when the ideological battle lines had been drawn.[12] But a man like Alexander Druzhinin (1824–64), one of the leading theoreticians of the esthetic camp, was much quicker to recognize what this publication meant for the future of Russian culture. Before 1855 was out Druzhinin had published a lengthy review of the Annenkov edition, which he hailed as "the first monument to a great writer from posterity." And he presented Pushkin as a man who at the time of his death had been moving beyond the status of a great national poet to become a "poet of all ages and nations," and who in addition displayed the correct theoretical understanding of art's independence. Pushkin, Druzhinin wrote, "was never an adherent of any theory harmful to art, no matter how brilliant and insubstantial it might have been."[13] Thus Druzhinin quickly prepared the ground for the campaign to make Pushkin the intellectual and artistic mentor of the esthetic critics, to claim Russia's greatest poet as their ally.

The American scholar George Genereux has argued that the year following the publication of Chernyshevsky's essay and Annenkov's edition of Pushkin—1856—was the "decisive year" in the esthetic debate of the 1860s. For it was in that year that Chernyshevsky published his *Essays on the Gogol Period of Russian Literature*, in which he raised the Gogolian banner against the Pushkinian one, and in that year that the esthetic critics Alexander Druzhinin and Vasily Botkin (1811–69) in their turn took up the cudgels against Chernyshevsky. Genereux holds that in 1856 the situation was still very much in flux, that this was

the year when critics formulated for the first time, lengthy, detailed, considered statements of esthetics and

[12] Charles Corbet, "Černyševskij esthéticien et critique," *Revue des études slaves*, vol. 24 (1948), 124.
[13] Aleksandr Druzhinin, "A. S. Pushkin i poslednee izdanie ego sochinenii," 7:30–82. The quotations are from pp. 32, 78, and 81.

art, of artist and critic; statements that were not partisan expressions of a political, social or philosophical nature.[14]

Genereux argues that the debate was concluded with the victory of Chernyshevsky and his followers by 1864, the year of Druzhinin's death.[15] I cannot agree that the debate was ever definitively over, in 1864 or any other year (and Druzhinin died after a long illness, during which he contributed nothing to the discussion); nor can I agree that any individual year could be so crucial to the discussion of 1855–70 as Genereux seems to believe. Still, it is true that the year 1856 did see the early stage of the esthetic debate at its height.

That year began with the publication of a major series of articles on Pushkin in *Russky vestnik* by its editor, Mikhail Katkov (1818–87). For most of his life Katkov was an editor rather than a critic or literary theoretician, but he did function regularly as a practical critic if only because as an editor he had to evaluate a great deal of fiction. So he took advantage of this opportunity to set forth a systematic theory of art in his discussion of Pushkin, whom Katkov praised as the "poet of the instant" who was "capable of elevating the basic mood of a given moment to a typical expression."[16] In any case, Katkov's attention helped in the campaign to elevate Pushkin's reputation generally.

Pushkin's supporters of the later 1850s saw in him primarily a symbol of intellectual and artistic freedom from formal and informal social and political pressures. Thus, in a major article "On the Enslavement of Art" (1859), Nikolay Akhsharumov (1819–93) declared that Pushkin stood out

---

[14] George Genereux, "The Crisis in Russian Literary Criticism: 1856—The Decisive Year," *Russian Literature Triquarterly*, no. 17 (1982), 139.

[15] Ibid.

[16] Mikhail Katkov, "Pushkin," *Russkii vestnik* (January 1856), 155–72; (February 1856), 306–24; (March 1856), 281–310. The quotation is from March, 291.

among all others by the "gigantic power of his imagination and his freedom, enslaved by nothing, bound to no theory or necessary principle."[17] In 1859 the minor poet and critic Boris Almazov (1827–76) developed this same idea in an article on Pushkin published in the literary almanac *Utro* (Morning). He maintained that Pushkin's spiritual freedom as a poet was so extraordinary that it could not be shackled even by the notion of "service to art," adding that for him Pushkin was the archetype of the poet. "It is no accident," he wrote, "that when the notion of the poet occurs to us we inevitably think of Pushkin, just as Napoleon occurs to us at the thought of a military leader and Talleyrand at the thought of a diplomat."[18]

The radical critics, however, quickly mounted a counter-attack against Pushkin, which by 1860 had reached such heights that Stepan Dudyshkin would complain dispiritedly that both the reading public and the critics were becoming increasingly indifferent to the poet's work.[19] Nikolay Dobrolyubov, for example, held that poets like Pushkin and Lermontov were of significance only for the time in which they lived and worked, and not for the periods which came after them.(4:168) Nikolay Nekrasov—who regarded Pushkin as a poetic mentor, but was personally and ideologically close to the radical critics—ceased to echo Pushkin in his poetry or refer to him in his critical articles for many years during the height of the radical campaign against him, from roughly 1857 to the early 1870s.[20] The popular radical satirical poets of the 1860s—Dmitry Minaev in particular—wrote

[17] Nikolai Akhsharumov, "O poraboshchenii iskusstva," *Otechestvennye zapiski*, no. 7 (July 1858), 310.

[18] Boris Almazov, "O poezii Pushkina," *Utro: Literaturnyi sbornik* (Moscow, 1859), 181, 149.

[19] S. S. [Dudyshkin], "Russkaia literatura. I. Kritika. Pushkin—narodnyi poet," *Otechestvennye zapiski*, no. 4 (April 1860), section 3, 69.

[20] See Kornei Chukovskii, *Pushkin i Nekrasov* (Moscow, 1949).

frequent parodies of Pushkin's verse which had the cumu-
lative effect of diminishing his standing in the eyes of society
generally. But the radical assault against Pushkin's reputation reached its zenith with Dmitry Pisarev's article of 1865,
"Pushkin and Belinsky," one of the most skillful and all-in-
clusive critiques ever written by a major critic against a major poet of his own nation. We shall discuss this article in
more detail below.

No matter how powerful an artistic presence Pushkin
was in the mid-1850s, though, he could no longer speak for
himself: he had to be interpreted by contemporary critics.
And his editor, Annenkov, supplied a great deal of this interpretation, particularly in 1856. For example, in his article
"On the Significance of Artistic Works for Society" (1856)
Annenkov praised Pushkin and argued that the reading of
his work could provide great benefits to contemporary society. He also defended the role of pure art in society, and
criticized Gogol for succumbing to excessive didacticism in
his last years: "exhortation is an abstract definition of an object," he wrote, "and not its depiction."[21] Thus Annenkov
came down firmly on the side of Pushkin against the later
Gogol, and against the interpretation of Gogol by the later
Belinsky, even though he had been a personal friend of both
Belinsky and Gogol.

The next month Annenkov elaborated upon his understanding of the proper role of art in a piece for *Sovremennik*,
a major intellectual journal originally founded by Pushkin
but which by 1856 was moving into Chernyshevsky's orbit
and would not be open much longer to those who viewed
art as did Annenkov. In this article, a review of Sergey Aksakov's recently published *Family Chronicle*, Annenkov used

---

[21] Pavel Annenkov, *Vospominaniia i kriticheskie ocherki* (St. Petersburg, 1879),
2:[1]–22. In this edition the original title is altered to the colorless "Staraia i novaia
kritika." The quotation is from p. 22.

Aksakov's masterpiece of calmly epic recollection and description as the basis for his formulation of several general conclusions on literature.[22] Indeed the *Family Chronicle* appeared at a very appropriate time for the esthetic discussion of the 1850s. Radical critics like Dobrolyubov read it as an unconscious condemnation of the serfdom on which rested the social order of the time it described, while the esthetic critics viewed it as a work of dispassionate literary art which on the whole affirmed the reality which it depicted.[23]

At this point Annenkov was joined by two other defenders of esthetic principles who took issue with Chernyshevsky and his ideas. One was Druzhinin, who had welcomed Annenkov's edition of Pushkin the year before and who had been long associated with *Sovremennik* until Chernyshevsky began to take control of it in 1856–57. Under these circumstances Druzhinin shifted to the journal *Biblioteka dlya chteniya* (Library for Reading) as his platform beginning in late 1856. Although he did not succeed in making it a truly successful publication, it did serve as an important outlet for the ideas of the esthetic camp until his failing health compelled him to relinquish ownership to Aleksey Pisemsky around 1860. He then retired from the field until his death in 1864, at the age of thirty-nine.[24]

Druzhinin liked to think of himself as the author of humorous feuilletons, for which he became well known especially during the early 1850s, but he was also an editor and a defender of esthetic values. His finest single contribution to

---

[22] Annenkov, "S. T. Aksakov i ego 'Semeinaia khronika'," ibid., 109–31 (first published in *Sovremennik* for March 1856).

[23] See Andrew Durkin, *Sergei Aksakov and Russian Pastoral* (New Brunswick, N.J., 1983), 4–5.

[24] On Druzhinin, see Derek Offord, "Druzhinin and the 'Pushkin School' of Russian Literature," in *Poetry, Prose and Public Opinion: Aspects of Russia 1850–1970. Essays Presented in Memory of Dr. N. E. Andreyev*, ed. William Harrison and Avril Pyman (Letchworth, England, 1984), 19–42.

the general theory of literary criticism was his response to Chernyshevsky's *Essays on the Gogol Period* entitled "Criticism of the Gogol Period in Russian Literature and Our Attitude Toward It" (1856)(7:189–242). Druzhinin took as his epigraph a very Pushkinian quotation from Nekrasov as a means of needling Nekrasov, by then the editor of *Sovremennik*. Druzhinin next offered a critique of Belinsky's legacy, upon which the radical critics drew so heavily, and followed that up with a spirited defense of the artist's intellectual independence and a brief against didacticism in art. Gogol, Druzhinin said, had indeed often been didactic, but in 1856 one read him, not for his didacticism, but for the poetry of his writing, that poetry which ensured his immortality in Russian literature (7:234).

Druzhinin's staunch ally in the debates of 1856–57 was Vasily Botkin, a Moscow merchant of independent means who had once, like Annenkov, been close to Belinsky. He had begun publishing as far back as 1836, and his chief interests lay in esthetic problems of literature, art, and especially music. He worked mostly behind the scenes, however, writing little himself; and at his death he left large bequests to various cultural organizations.

Botkin's major contribution to the debate during these years was a review of Afanasy Fet's poetry. It appeared in *Sovremennik* for January 1857, one of the very last articles by a member of the esthetic camp to come out in that journal.[25] The first of the article's two parts summarized Botkin's theoretical views on art, while the second analyzed Fet's verse. Botkin and Fet together (Fet was married to Botkin's sister) represented a fairly extreme esthetic point of view: both of them felt that art should be concerned only with beauty, and held that beauty was an even more basic component of real-

---

[25] Vasilii Botkin, "Stikhotvoreniia A. A. Feta," *Sovremennik*, No. 1 (January 1857), section 3, 1-17 (part 1 only).

ity than material things or economic relationships. Botkin, in short, confronted Chernyshevsky's ideas on reality, art, and their interconnections quite directly. However, this attempt to confound the enemy on his home ground (*Sovremennik*) bore no permanent fruit. From approximately that point until the government suppressed it permanently in 1866, *Sovremennik* would be the major platform for the radical critics.

As Chernyshevsky extended his control over *Sovremennik* in 1856–57, the esthetic critics made an abortive attempt to head him off by offering another candidate as the magazine's chief critic. That candidate was Apollon Grigorev (1822–64), whom one of his disciples after his death called the "founder of scientific criticism" in Russia.[26] Grigorev had been the leading critic of the distinguished journal *Moskvityanin*: when it ceased publication in 1856, Grigorev lost a principal outlet for his writing. He would make good that loss (though only partially) when Fedor Dostoevsky and his brother Mikhail organized *Vremya* (Time) and *Epokha* (Epoch) in St. Petersburg during the first half of the 1860s.

Grigorev was an interesting if eclectic literary critic, one ready to take his ideas wherever he found them but also willing to acknowledge his intellectual indebtedness openly. Among Russian critics, Belinsky exerted the most direct and profound influence upon him,[27] but he also admired Schelling, taking from him such basic notions as that of the cognitive power of art and its superiority to analytic reasoning. Grigorev's swan song, "Paradoxes of Organic Criticism"

---

[26] Dmitrii Averkiev, "Apollon Aleksandrovich Grigor'ev," *Epokha*, no. 9 (September 1864), 6.

[27] On this subject, see Victor Terras, *Belinskij and Russian Literary Criticism: The Heritage of Organic Aesthetics* (Madison, Wis., 1974), 214–22. This study traces Belinsky's influence on several other critics treated here as well, including Chernyshevsky, Dobrolyubov, and Pisarev.

(1864), reduces in large part to a recapitulation of Victor Hugo's critical ideas. And, as Victor Terras has shown, Grigorev had a strong intellectual affinity for the thought of Thomas Carlyle.[28] Both became conservatives, Terras writes, through their "historical and organic view of human life" and their dislike of abstract theory; both were great moralizers; both distinguished between genius and talent; both admired the heroic in history; and both developed a convoluted prose style which diminished their influence. Grigorev thus served as a conduit for some of the best critical thought of Russia and the West to the mind of such a writer as Fedor Dostoevsky, and also to a few critics—especially Nikolay Strakhov—who formed the semblance of a critical school in his wake.

Unfortunately, when contemporary critics divided into two warring camps, instead of joining the esthetic camp (to which he was by far the closer) and seeking to lead it, Grigorev adopted an independent stance and sought to develop a critical "third way," a policy which deprived him of some natural allies whose support he needed. He would have had difficulty in mobilizing those allies even in the best possible case, for he had a prickly personality, drank to excess, and was rather unreliable in such practical matters as meeting deadlines. Still, he took a very active part in the esthetic discussions from their beginning in 1855 right down to his untimely death at the age of forty-two in 1864.

One of Grigorev's initial contributions to the discussion, an article entitled "On Truth and Sincerity in Art," appeared in March 1856 in the Slavophile journal *Russkaya beseda* (Russian Conversation).[29] In this piece Grigorev dealt with

---

[28] Victor Terras, "Apollon Grigoriev's Organic Criticism and Its Western Sources," in *Western Philosophical Systems in Russian Literature*, ed. Anthony Mlikotin (Los Angeles, [1979]), 79. The beginning of this article contains a good outline of Grigorev's critical theories.

[29] The full title is "O pravde i iskrennosti v iskusstve. Po povodu odnogo este-

a number of theoretical questions, including problems of morality and the ideal in literature, matters in which Fet and Botkin never took much interest.

Grigorev returned to the fray with an article for the January 1858 issue of Druzhinin's *Biblioteka dlya chteniya*, entitled "A Critical View of the Foundations, Significance and Methods of Contemporary Artistic Criticism" and dedicated to the poet Apollon Maykov, who would later become one of Fedor Dostoevsky's closest confidants.[30] In this piece Grigorev discussed the distinguishing characteristics of the approaches he termed "purely artistic criticism" (the esthetic camp) and "historical criticism" (the radical camp), and then asserted his own independence by counterposing to each approach his doctrines of "organic criticism."

Grigorev's name is very closely associated with the tradition of "organic criticism," and thus it is not surprising that in the next year he would seek to elaborate on certain details of that doctrine in "A Few Words on the Laws and Terminology of Organic Criticism."[31] His readers were puzzled by some of the critical terminology which Grigorev employed, so he set out to explain it and demonstrate its logical derivation from an organic understanding of art and literary criticism. But he was as unfortunate as ever in his timing: the article appeared in *Russkoe slovo* for May 1859, or during the brief period when that journal was under the control of Grigorev's friends. It then very quickly fell under the sway of Dmitry Pisarev and his allies, and was linked with that radical grouping thereafter in the history of Russian literature.

---

ticheskogo voprosa. Pis'mo k A. S. Khomiakovu." I have used the text in Grigorev's *Sochineniia*, vol. 1 (Kritika) (Villanova, 1970), 127–200.

[30] Apollon Grigor'ev, "Kriticheskii vzgliad na osnovy, znachenie i priemy sovremennoi kritiki iskusstva," *Biblioteka dlia chteniia*, no. 1 (January 1858), 1–42.

[31] Grigor'ev, "Neskol'ko slov o zakonakh i terminakh organicheskoi kritiki," *Russkoe slovo*, no. 5 (May 1859), 1–19. Cited here from *Sochineniia*, 201–42.

All during this time the radical critics were quite active themselves. In January 1858 Chernyshevsky took to the pages of *Sovremennik* to issue a blast against Turgenev's short story "Asya." Entitled "A Russian at a Rendezvous," this article was one of the last pieces of literary criticism he would publish before he handed over control of the journal's critical section to his disciple Nikolay Dobrolyubov. In this article Chernyshevsky criticized Turgenev for dealing exclusively with private passions in "Asya" when important social problems were crying out for literary treatment. Annenkov reacted to what he called that "remarkable article" of Chernyshevsky's with an essay of his own published in *Ateney* (Athenaeum) the same year under the title "The Literary Type of the Weak Man."[32] But where Chernyshevsky in his article had discussed "Asya" quite concretely, Annenkov in his offered a rather abstract analysis of a particular social and psychological type interwoven with general comments on art, almost without any reference to Turgenev's short story.

In 1859 Annenkov published a critical article on Turgenev's *A Nest of Gentlefolk*, in the August issue of *Russky vestnik*,[33] a piece which included a few general comments on art; and also a review of Pisemsky's best novel, *A Thousand Souls*, published in *Ateney* in the early part of the year.[34] These articles are of interest not only for what they tell us of Annenkov's development of his earlier ideas, but also because they display at least the indirect influence of the ideas of Chernyshevsky and his followers on the social significance of art. Here Annenkov maintains that literature must benefit society and rejects the phrase "art for art's sake," which the radical critics were using as a cudgel to beat their opponents

[32] Pavel Annenkov, "Literaturnyi tip slabogo cheloveka," 2:149–72.
[33] Annenkov, "Nashe obshchestvo v *Dvorianskom gnezde* Turgeneva," ibid., 194–221.
[34] Annekov, "Delovoi roman v nashei literature," ibid., 173–93.

with at the time. Simultaneously, however, he affirms his belief in the importance of art and in its autonomy. In short, Annenkov, like Turgenev, found some of the radicals' social and political doctrines quite attractive, but he disagreed with their artistic ideas, partly for purely personal reasons, as the Soviet specialist Boris Egorov has noted.[35]

Other esthetic critics defended their principles more stoutly than Annenkov. Among them was Nikolay Akhsharumov. When his essay "On the Enslavement of Art" appeared in the July 1858 issue of *Otechestvennye zapiski* (Fatherland Notes), its intellectually unsteady editor Stepan Dudyshkin appended to it a comment declaring his disagreement with certain of its conclusions but speaking of the favorable impression made by its author's "warm and honest convictions." The article was an impassioned defense of art's independence, a brief for its uselessness, and an essay on the importance of freedom for art and the artist during a period of art's "melancholy and unavoidable enslavement."[36] Afanasy Fet gave voice to similarly intransigent notions in a review of Fedor Tyutchev's verse dedicated to Grigorev and published in the February 1859 issue of *Russkoe slovo*. In this essay, his principal coherent statement on art, he argued that art should be concerned solely with beauty, and not at all with social utility.[37] After the appearance of this piece Fet largely ceased to publish critical articles and therefore participated no further publicly in the critical discussion. It seemed as though something had gone out of his convictions. Only when Chernyshevsky published his novel *What Is to Be Done?* in 1863 did Fet and Botkin set out to write a withering response, but their review in the end amounted

---

[35] Egorov, "P. V. Annenkov," 95, 98.
[36] Akhsharumov, "O poraboshchenii iskusstva," 326.
[37] Afanasii Fet, "O stikhotvoreniiakh F. Tiutcheva. A. A. Grigor'evu," *Russkoe slovo*, no. 2 (February 1859), 63–84.

to little more than a detailed plot summary conjoined to a few rather lame comments. The article was so weak that even *Russky vestnik* rejected it for publication at the time, and it first appeared only in 1936 as a document primarily of interest to specialists in literary history.[38]

By the end of the 1850s, then, the esthetic camp was in some disarray. There were men of conviction among the esthetic critics—Akhsharumov, Fet, Botkin—but they were not very prolific and did not have a large following. More moderate critics like Grigorev were too independent and too subtle to exert major intellectual influence, while Druzhinin and Annenkov had either ceased to publish or become uncertain of their own convictions. In addition to all this, the radical cause found a powerful voice beginning in approximately 1858: that of Nikolay Dobrolyubov.

Though Dobrolyubov had arrived in the capital in 1856, when he was but twenty, he spent some time under Chernyshevsky's tutelage and only began to make an independent mark on Russian criticism toward the end of 1858. In the two short years allotted him before he began to succumb to the illness which would carry him off at the age of only twenty-five in November 1861, Dobrolyubov made an indelible impression upon Russian culture. Both Soviet and Western scholars are compelled to deal with the assessments of contemporary writing that he handed down at the time, even if they reject them: Dobrolyubov's interpretations simply cannot be ignored.

Dobrolyubov was not one to write grand theoretical articles on literature. His most famous pieces are devoted to concrete analyses of outstanding contemporary works by such authors as Ivan Goncharov, Ivan Turgenev, and Alex-

[38] "Neizdannaia stat'ia A. A. Feta o romane N. G. Chernyshevskogo 'Chto delat'?'" Introductory article by Iurii Steklov, publication and notes by G. Volkov, in *Literaturnoe nasledstvo*, no. 25–26 (Moscow, 1936), 477–544.

ander Ostrovsky, but in the course of producing these analyses he occasionally included theoretical or polemical passages from which one may extract the outlines of his theory of art, as we shall attempt to do in subsequent chapters of this study.

In the initial portion of one of his most influential articles—"What Is Oblomovism?", published in *Sovremennik* for May 1859—Dobrolyubov needles the esthetic critics first by declaring his inability to produce "esthetic" criticism and then by launching into a very effective "esthetic" interpretation of *Oblomov* and its author's literary talent. But that temporary detour does not deflect him from his main purpose, which is to write a detailed critique of the society which could have engendered such a hapless, although in many ways also attractive, character as Oblomov. Dobrolyubov merely uses literature here as an excuse to discuss the existing social order, which he thinks is quite accurately reflected in the novel: in a sense the radical critic considers the novel more real than the reality upon which it is based.

Similarly, when Dobrolyubov published an overview of Ostrovsky's work under the title "The Kingdom of Darkness" in July 1859, he again started it with a list of esthetic criticisms to which Ostrovsky's plays might be liable, but then decided he would leave such matters to critics like Boris Almazov and Nikolay Akhsharumov; then he launched into a brief but interesting digression on the "relationship of artistic talent to a writer's abstract ideas." All this demonstrates that, if critics like Annenkov and Grigorev acceded to certain arguments from the radical camp, the converse was also true: even Dobrolyubov sometimes acknowledged his opponents' concerns. In fact, at one point in "What Is Oblomovism?" he even went so far as to speak of "art's eternal demands"(4:312), a phrase lifted directly from the vocabulary of the esthetic critics.

To be sure, Dobrolyubov before long became increas-

ingly hostile to his antagonists' ideas. In his discussion of
On the Eve, "When Will the Real Day Come?", Dobrolyubov starts out by dismissing "esthetic criticism" as "something indulged in by sensitive young ladies," and then offering a parody on an "esthetic" discussion of a work of
Turgenev's (6:96). And in another treatment of Ostrovsky,
"A Ray of Light in the Kingdom of Darkness" (October
1860), dealing with his prize-winning play *The Storm*, Dobrolyubov mounts a sustained assault on the old-fashioned
critics who recognize the beautiful on the basis of rules formulated in outmoded esthetics textbooks. Dobrolyubov exclaims in mock surprise about those who believe that criticism consists merely in the application of well-established
rules to new works of art:

> We are astounded at the way in which these estimable
> individuals insist upon assigning to criticism such an in-
> significant and degrading role. For if one limits criticism
> to the application of "eternal and general" laws of art to
> particular and shortlived phenomena, why then one con-
> demns art to stagnation, and gives criticism the purely
> bureaucratic function of policing the field! (6:292)

For his part, Dobrolyubov thought the literary critic's work
much more vital than that: he himself provided a remarkable
example of what one might term cooperation between critic
and writer in the establishment of set interpretations of particular works. The best instance of this is provided by Ivan
Goncharov, who did not sympathize with Dobrolyubov's
theoretical notions of art in the slightest. But in an article of
1879 on the subject of his novel *The Precipice* (1869), Goncharov commented that an artist sometimes becomes so en-
grossed in the images of his work that "he may himself comprehend their meaning only with the assistance of a subtle
critical interpreter like Belinsky or Dobrolyubov."[39] Gon-

---

[39] Ivan Goncharov, "Luchshe pozdno, chem nikogda": 8:70. For a good over-

charov believed he knew whereof he spoke. In his lifetime he published three novels: *A Common Story* of 1847; *Oblomov* in 1859; and *The Precipice* in 1869. Belinsky had welcomed and made the reputation of *A Common Story*; Dobrolyubov had established the standard reading of *Oblomov*; but no critic was available to render similar service when *The Precipice* appeared. Goncharov attributed the low repute of his third novel to just this lack of a nurturing critic, and the radical critics, for their own reasons, agreed with him. In 1870 Nikolay Shelgunov, looking back on men like Dobrolyubov whom he termed "critic-journalists," argued that Russia would have no sensible literature at all if such figures had not existed:

> All our artists would wander off along various paths, be-
> cause it is only the critic-journalists who show them the
> way. Who guided our novelists—Turgenev, Dostoev-
> sky, Goncharov, Pisemsky, and all the other writers of
> more recent years? They were guided by Belinsky, Dob-
> rolyubov, Pisarev. Novelists merely collect the firewood
> and stoke the engine of life, but the critic-journalist is
> the driver.[40]

On this interpretation the critic is clearly superior to the writer: the latter supplies only raw material for the critic to inject into the consciousness of society. Dobrolyubov exemplified the radical intelligentsia's ideal of the literary critic better than anyone else, and that fact helps to explain his continuing influence upon our views of several principal nineteenth-century writers, including Ostrovsky and Goncharov.

At about the time of Dobrolyubov's ascendancy—in

---

view of Goncharov's theories, see Milton Ehre, "Ivan Goncharov on Art, Literature, and the Novel," *Slavic Review*, vol. 29, no. 2 (June 1970), 203–18.

[40] Nikolai Shelgunov, "Dvoedushie esteticheskogo konservatizma," *Delo*, no. 10 (October 1870), 54–55.

1860, to be exact—an intelligently modulated voice joined
the discussion of esthetic principles, the voice of a man now
little remembered in the history of Russian literature
though he was a sensitive critic who enjoyed the respect of
those who knew him or read his works: Evgeny Edelson
(1824–68). After growing up in Ryazan, Edelson entered
Moscow University, where he became a Hegelian and also
fell under the influence of Mikhail Katkov, then in the midst
of a brief academic career before turning to journalism.
When the gathering European political storm prevented
him from going abroad in 1847, he joined a group of young
writers and critics gathered about *Moskvityanin*, a group
which included Ostrovsky, Grigorev, and Almazov. In the
latter half of the 1850s, when *Moskvityanin* was no more, he
published in such journals as *Russkaya beseda* and *Biblioteka
dlya chteniya* (when the latter was on its last financial legs, he
made an unsuccessful attempt to salvage it by means of a
personal loan). He then moved on through *Otechestvennye
zapiski* and *Vsemirny trud* (World Labor) before finding an
appropriate intellectual home with the *Zhurnal Ministerstva
narodnogo prosveshcheniya* (Journal of the Ministry of Education). Soon after taking up a position there, however, he
died suddenly, in January 1868, at the age of only forty-three.
The anonymous author of his obituary in the *Zhurnal Ministerstva narodnogo prosveshcheniya* recalled him as "a most
attractive individual, always prepared to do anyone a serious
favor, always pleasant, indulgent, and modest."[41] His literary
criticism reflects that same character. In fact, he was if anything too gentle for the polemical time in which he lived,
which may explain why he had no critical followers even

---

[41] I have drawn biographical data on Edelson from the article on him by
B. Grekov in the *Russkii biograficheskii slovar'* (St. Petersburg, 1912), vol. 24; and the
anonymous obituary article "Evgenii Nikolaevich Edel'son (Nekrolog)," *Zhurnal
Ministerstva narodnogo prosveshcheniia* (January 1868), 117–21.

though he came closer than any other critic to writing and publishing over the entire period from 1855 to 1870.

Edelson's first important general esthetic statement appeared rather late, in the October 1860 issue of *Biblioteka dlya chteniya*, under the title "On Poetry."[42] Disturbed by the concerted attacks on poetry then being launched by the radicals—"poetry has perhaps never before been subjected to such peril of losing its weight and independence as it is at the present moment," he wrote at the outset of his essay— Edelson came to the defense, not so much of poetry, as of fantasy and the poetic imagination. "On Poetry" was a systematic, sober statement on the necessity for artistic independence, replete with quotations from German theoreticians, one which looked forward to the even more detailed defense of art which Edelson would publish in 1867, the last full year of his life.

The 1860s: The Lines Drawn Firmer

On February 19, 1861, Tsar Alexander II emancipated the serfs of the Russian Empire. That single act in and of itself made 1861 the central year of nineteenth-century Russian history. It was also a year of intellectual and political ferment which led to a further hardening of the cultural lines which had begun to form during 1859 and 1860. Although Dobrolyubov went abroad in early 1860 in a vain attempt to recover his health, the radical critics clearly held the upper hand in the debate. Annenkov, Druzhinin, Fet, and Botkin had largely fallen silent, and once the theoreticians had retreated they were followed by the lyric poets—the most "socially useless" and therefore most vulnerable of writers— who ceased to publish in the generally antipoetic atmos-

[42] Evgenii Edel'son, "O poezii," *Biblioteka dlia chteniia*, no. 10 (October 1860), [1]–32.

phere of the day.[43] The times as it were demanded a new set
of participants in the debate, and they were forthcoming, as
it happened. Now several of them were themselves writers,
mostly of more "esthetic" persuasion.

It was a curious anomaly of the situation of the 1860s in
Russia that, although the radical groups enjoyed clear superiority in the field of literary criticism (especially in the
decade's earlier years), the finest writers disagreed with radical doctrine, and made that disagreement known in their
works. After the publication of *Fathers and Sons* in February
1862, there came into existence a substantial body of prose
fiction now known by the generic term of "antinihilist novels," works which depicted the doctrines and personalities of
the radical younger generation in either a neutral or a negative light.[44] The authors of antinihilist novels could make
their sympathies known, say, through discussions of artistic
questions involving radical characters, or by making an artist the central hero of a work. Furthermore, quite often authors of antinihilist fiction came under such strenuous attack
that they published statements in their own defense in
which they were almost obliged to deal with fundamental
esthetic questions.

Thus not only were the ideological demarcation lines
more clearly drawn in the 1860s than they had been in the
1850s—when Fet and Botkin could still publish in *Sovremennik* and Saltykov could defend Chernyshevsky's ideas in *Russky vestnik*—but the discussion ceased to be almost exclusively the province of professional critics and journalists and
moved more broadly into the pages of creative literature.
Indeed, even if the radical critics had succeeded in driving

[43] For a more detailed discussion of this point, see Charles A. Moser, "Poets
and Poetry in an Antipoetic Age," *Slavic Review*, vol. 28, no. 1 (March 1969), 48–
62.
[44] On this subject, see Charles A. Moser, *Antinihilism in the Russian Novel of the
1860's* (The Hague, 1964).

all their critical opponents from the field, the rejection of their ideas by such literary lights as Turgenev, Dostoevsky, Tolstoy, Leskov, Goncharov, and Pisemsky would still have restored balance to the discussion.

One of these major writers was Fedor Dostoevsky, who arrived in the capital in late 1859 after a decade in prison and exile, began publishing his prison memoirs *Notes from the House of the Dead* in 1860, and in 1861 started bringing out the journal *Vremya* in collaboration with his brother Mikhail. Having no prominent critics on his staff with the exception of Apollon Grigorev, in 1861 Dostoevsky wrote what was for him an unusually large number of critical essays, of which the most instructive one, "Mr. —bov and the Problem of Art," dealt with Dobrolyubov, who commonly signed his pieces "N. —bov." In this discussion, which appeared in February, Dostoevsky noted that the "problem of art" had divided society into "two hostile camps," whose theoretical viewpoints he then summarized before offering his own synthesis, in a Grigorevian mold, based on the notion of art as an "organic whole" (18:72, 94). Dostoevsky's solution was not widely accepted, and in fact he was such a born polemicist that it was unnatural for him to serve as a reconciler of differences, especially in a field so close to him as esthetics. Still, Dostoevsky's journals *Vremya*—until it was suppressed in the aftermath of the Polish insurrection of early 1863—and *Epokha* (1864–65) provided a much needed platform for critics like Grigorev and his ally Nikolay Strakhov (1828–96) to propound their views of art.

By this time the groupings in Russian journalism were well established. *Sovremennik* remained the most influential radical organ (though suspended for a few months in 1862) until it was definitively closed down following Dmitry Karakozov's attempt on Alexander II's life in April 1866. *Sovremennik* held this position even though after Dobrolyubov's death its critical section came under the control of the pedestrian Maksim Antonovich (1835–1908). Sharing Cherny-shevsky's and Dobrolyubov's ecclesiastical background, Antonovich came from Kharkov province to study at the St. Petersburg Seminary before abandoning any thought of entering the church. He began to publish critical articles in *Sovremennik* in 1859, and from the time of Dobrolyubov's death in 1861 down to the journal's suppression in 1866 was the chief intellectual heir to Chernyshevsky and Dobrolyubov and a leading opponent of the esthetic critics to his right and the radical heresies propounded by Dmitry Pisarev to his left. By the middle of the decade, however, Antonovich had quarreled with Nekrasov, still *Sovremennik*'s publisher, and left the critical arena to dedicate himself for the most part to geological work. He did not participate further in the literary discussion of the latter half of the decade, and published critical articles only very rarely thereafter.

Antonovich's rival for the literary leadership of the radical camp, the man who best expressed the viewpoint of the radical intelligentsia of the 1860s, was Dmitry Pisarev (1840–68), a complicated personality and ingenious critic, who died at twenty-eight. The Soviet scholar Semyon Konkin has divided his brief career into four segments.[45] During the first of these (1859–60) Pisarev contributed articles of a relatively ordinary sort to *Rassvet* (Dawn), a magazine for young ladies. This was followed by a transitional period in 1861–63, when Pisarev and the journal with which he was closely associated, *Russkoe slovo*, had not yet become uncompromisingly radical in their approach. During the third period (1864–66), while confined to the Sts. Peter and Paul prison in St. Petersburg as a political subversive, he contributed to *Russkoe slovo* regular articles in which he expressed the extremes of his doctrine and through which he attained

[45] Semen Konkin, *Esteticheskie i literaturno-kriticheskie vzgliady Pisareva* (Saransk, 1973), 22.

the zenith of his intellectual influence. Finally, in 1867–68, when Pisarev was formally at liberty but seemed broken by his prison experience (he had a history of nervous disorder in any case), he published desultory contributions to *Delo* (The Cause) and *Otechestvennye zapiski*, the successor journals to *Russkoe slovo* and *Sovremennik*, respectively.

Soviet specialists in Russian literary history find it difficult to deal with Pisarev. Although he obviously developed the critical thought of Chernyshevsky and Dobrolyubov, he was willing to take certain of their implicit ideas to explicit extremes, and formulate conclusions from which his predecessors might have recoiled. There is, then, a tendency among Soviet scholars to treat Pisarev as an interesting but not entirely respectable figure in the field of literary criticism. Nikolay Shelgunov, however, had a rather different view of the matter. He had known all the radical theoreticians personally, and after Pisarev's death he himself came forward as their collective heir although he was older than any of them. In a melancholy article intended for publication in 1871 he wrote that young people in the provinces had unhappily divided into Dobrolyubovite and Pisarevian factions when there should have been no difference of principle at all between them. "The younger generation," he said then, "could not see that just as Dobrolyubov was Belinsky's heir, so Pisarev continued and developed Dobrolyubov's work."[46] Fate, he maintained, had sent Russia an immediate successor (Pisarev) to the critic so untimely taken from her (Dobrolyubov), but the younger generation would not accept him (260).

Though much less sympathetic to radical doctrines than was Shelgunov, the modern French scholar Charles Corbet considers it quite self-evident that Pisarev simply took Chernyshevsky's ideas to their logical conclusion, and believes

[46] Shelgunov, "Sochineniia D. I. Pisareva," 253, 256.

that it is wrong to distinguish sharply between the two in order to dismiss Pisarev as a "nihilist."[47] Pisarev himself was not entirely consistent on the entire matter. In one of his greatest articles he contended that he had done nothing more than develop two of Belinsky's leading ideas: "that art must not serve as its own aim and that life is higher than art" (3:366–67). But then on another occasion Pisarev said that, just as Dobrolyubov would no doubt have disagreed with Belinsky on nearly everything, so also he, Pisarev, parted company with Dobrolyubov on most matters (3:35). However, one may discount this as a characteristically Pisarevian exaggeration of the differences between himself and his predecessors, stemming from his conviction that there was no such thing as logical development (*priemstvennost*) in literary or intellectual history. He could also, of course, point to his deep disagreements with Chernyshevsky and Antonovich over the interpretation of *Fathers and Sons* as well as his violent quarrel of 1864–65 with Antonovich on esthetic questions—and yet, despite this, it seems most accurate to say that such differences were more tactical than fundamental; that, on the whole, a direct though not entirely straight ideological line runs from the later Belinsky through Chernyshevsky and Dobrolyubov down to Pisarev.

Pisarev had a considerable following, not only among the younger generation but among his ideological opponents as well, at least in the first half of the 1860s. Dostoevsky's friend and ally Nikolay Strakhov wrote in early 1862 that Pisarev was the fruit of the seeds Chernyshevsky had planted, the "most expressive phenomenon of our contemporary literature, in whom its deepest secrets are revealed";[48] and in 1864 Apollon Grigorev singled out Pisarev as the "only gifted person" among the "theoreticians," his name

[47] Corbet, "Černyševskij esthéticien," 122, n.4.
[48] Nikolai Strakhov, "Primer apatii," *Iz istorii literaturnogo nigilizma 1861–1865* (St. Petersburg, 1890), 103, 102.

for the radical critics.[49] A recent student of Chernyshevsky, Grigory Tamarchenko, has written that Pisarev was the only contemporary critic perceptive enough to grasp the genre of *What Is to Be Done?* upon its appearance.[50] Pisarev had also welcomed *Fathers and Sons* when it came out, and published a sensitive critical appreciation of it ("Bazarov") which is still reprinted in anthologies of critical essays on Turgenev. Thus especially from 1862 to 1864 Pisarev displayed a remarkable critical talent and literary sensitivity, not only in his readiness to accept innovative works like *Fathers and Sons* and *What Is to Be Done?* on their own terms, but also in such things as his feel for language and his willingness to submit to literary influences in his own life.

Pisarev was certainly the finest stylist of all the mid-century radical critics: even readers of the late twentieth century can still respond to the literary and artistic energies of his prose. Yakov Polonsky (1819–98), a poet who struggled artistically against the antipoetic atmosphere of the 1860s created by Pisarev and his followers but who nonetheless sympathized with much of their philosophy, used to analyze the esthetic sources of Pisarev's hold over contemporary minds. Thus in a personal letter of 1867 to Konstantin Sluchevsky, Polonsky argued that Pisarev influenced his readers largely through the brilliance of his language.[51] Polonsky reflected at even greater length on the problem of Pisarev in a curious essay of 1867 for *Otechestvennye zapiski* entitled "Prosaic Flowers of Poetic Seeds," an article with which Nekrasov found himself in strong disagreement but which he published simply as a personal favor to the author.[52] Polonsky

---

[49] Apollon Grigor'ev, "Paradoksy organicheskoi kritiki," *Epokha*, no. 5 (May 1864), 267.

[50] Grigorii Tamarchenko, *Chernyshevskii-romanist* (Leningrad, 1976), 258.

[51] See the letter in *Shchukinskii sbornik*, no. 7 (Moscow, 1907), 335.

[52] Iakov Polonskii, "Prozaicheskie tsvety poeticheskikh semian," *Otechestvennye zapiski* (April 1867, book 2), 714–49.

begins by declaring that he is one of "Pisarev's admirers," and by purporting to address himself to those who also respect Pisarev greatly. But then he goes on to argue that the Pisarev of the mid-1860s is merely developing a number of liberal notions which poets—including Polonsky himself—had propounded many years before. If one reads the minor post-Pushkin poets, Polonsky claims, one will see that "Pisarev in many respects is nothing more than a prose flowering of poetic seeds scattered throughout their lyric compositions." From that fact it follows that "poetry is not nonsense," despite Pisarev's claims to the contrary, for his own ideas are derived from poetic sources![53] On another level, Polonsky makes the astute observation that Pisarev is quite good as a practicing critic, but he usually goes astray when he must deal with literary theory.[54] Polonsky is confident, though, that Pisarev will overcome his present errors:

> If Pisarev is fated to develop and move forward, which is quite conceivable in view of his unusual capabilities, then in time he will himself regard his present writings as mere experiments or as attempts at theories intensely held but not yet developed fully.[55]

However, the sober assessments and accurate comments on Pisarev to be found in Polonsky's lengthy discussion—published only a year before the critic's tragic death, at a time when his star was already setting—are embedded in semi-hysterical polemics and self-justifying argumentation which weaken their force substantially.

The fact that Pisarev had a good literary background and a sense of literary values may be detected from the considerable number of acknowledged and unacknowledged literary quotations to be found in his critical writings. Probably

[53] Ibid., 721–22.
[54] Ibid., 734.
[55] Ibid., 748.

the most important single source of literary quotation in Pisarev is Griboedov's *Woe from Wit*, which the critic cited constantly, both on a conscious level because he approved of its social message, and on a subconscious level because he recognized if only intuitively the artistic power of this classic poetic work.

Pisarev's defense of *Fathers and Sons* provides another instance of his sensitivity to literature. In his lengthy study "Bazarov," which appeared only a month after the book came out, Pisarev concentrated his attention upon Bazarov, whom he accepted as a remarkably accurate portrayal of the best in the younger generation. "Turgenev himself will never be a Bazarov," Pisarev wrote, "but he has peered within this type and come to understand him more precisely than any of our young realists ever will" (2:26). Indeed, Pisarev's acceptance of Bazarov was so straightforward as to create a permanent rift between him and the *Sovremennik* group, which denounced Turgenev's hero as a slander on the younger generation and attacked Pisarev strongly for his temerity in disagreeing. Despite all this, Pisarev remained faithful to his literary ideal. In a major article of 1864 he called Bazarov his "favorite" (*lyubimets*) (3:21), and added that he had adopted Bazarov as a personal model because "this image was created without the slightest intention of flattering our realists" (3:86), which meant it was a genuinely objective depiction, the sort Pisarev always sought in literature. In 1865 Pisarev was still maintaining, very much against Antonovich's viewpoint, that Bazarov was "no slander and no caricature, but an absolutely accurate collection of realistic tendencies" (3:294). To this, however, we must add an observation made later by Nikolay Shelgunov, who pointed out very accurately that Pisarev remained faithful to his own conception of the image of Bazarov, and that was not the same as Turgenev's:

In [Bazarov] there was reflected a sharp turn in Russian
thought which Pisarev came forward to interpret. For
that reason the Pisarevian Bazarov does not resemble the
Turgenevian one. Pisarev's Bazarov amounts to his own
conception and his more mature thought, purified and
filtered through Pisarev's own philosophy. (271)

Still, however one interprets Pisarev's attitude toward *Fathers and Sons*, it is clear that this work of imaginative literature had a profound impact upon the leading radical critic
of the 1860s.

In fact the image of Bazarov was so powerful that it focused the entire controversy which erupted after 1862: his
image summed up the literary and intellectual development
of the radical generation which had occurred up to the time
of the novel's appearance, and also defined that development which would follow, both in literature and in life, especially the former: for Bazarov exerted a considerable impact on literary development after 1862, and especially on the
antinihilist novel. For our purposes at this stage, Goncharov's *The Precipice* (1869) provides a characteristic example of
the antinihilist novel, especially through one of its major
personages, the radical Mark Volokhov. In a review of *The
Precipice* published within the year of its appearance, Nikolay Shelgunov first maintained that Mark constituted the
"entire essence" of the novel, and then went on to claim that
"Bazarov serves as Mark's prototype": that is, one fictional
personage, rather than an actually existing individual, serves
as the prototype for another fictional character (221). In this
instance Shelgunov no doubt intended to belittle Mark's
significance by identifying him as a literary concoction based
upon yet another literary concoction, and not upon anything real. But in fact he also had an esthetic point: literary
works do influence other literary works which follow them.
And they can mold reality itself, an observation on which

most contemporary observers were agreed in the instance of
Fathers and Sons.

The year of that novel's publication—1862—was a time
of political instability. After the emancipation of the serfs
unrest had spread throughout the country to the point at
which St. Petersburg University had been closed down in
the fall of 1861 because of student disturbances. The intellectual ferment crested in the winter and spring of 1862. In an
effort to suppress it, the authorities suspended both *Sovremennik* and *Russkoe slovo* for several months and arrested Pisarev (on July 2) and Chernyshevsky (on July 7), confining
both of them to the Sts. Peter and Paul Fortress. In May
1864 Chernyshevsky was sent into Siberian exile while Pisarev remained in prison, from which he would be released
only in late 1866. These acts of official repression did not
silence the radical camp immediately, but in the long run
they had their effect, even though the two journals were permitted to resume publishing after some six months and remained loyal to their radical principles. The political turmoil
subsided effectively only after the outbreak of the Polish insurrection in early 1863 swung public opinion sharply to the
government's side.

The reaction to *Fathers and Sons* from Chernyshevsky,
Antonovich, and other members of the *Sovremennik* group
was suprisingly negative. Antonovich, the spokesman for
the group, published a lengthy review of the novel only a
month after its appearance, taking as his title ("An Asmodeus of Our Time") the name of an obscure antiradical
novel of 1858 by the conservative journalist and author Vik-
tor Askochensky. Antonovich denounced the book as nothing more than a "moral and philosophical tract" which was
"absolutely unsatisfactory from the artistic point of
view" (36). Aware that Turgenev was very much against didacticism in literature, Antonovich decried *Fathers and Sons*
as a ghastly example of didactic fiction: Turgenev's charac-

ters, he declared, were all "abstract ideas and various tendencies personified and given proper names," and Bazarov
in particular was nothing more than the embodiment of the
"so-called negative tendency" in Russian society (37). In
short, *Fathers and Sons* was not at all artistic, but rather a
"didactic novel, a genuine scientific tract," the sort of work
one might never have expected to be written by the "chief
representative . . . of pure art for art's sake," as Antonovich
chose to label him (44). Furthermore, Antonovich went on,
if one examined the book's ideas, the novel turned out to be
ideologically as faulty as it was artistically inept. In support
of this conclusion Antonovich offered an extensive plot
summary which demonstrated more than anything else how
ludicrously he had misunderstood the book, and he insisted
on viewing Bazarov as a demonic figure, some sort of Asmodeus who had no link at all with contemporary reality.

Turgenev was astounded by the public's misinterpreta-
tions of his novel. In a personal letter of the time he commented that most readers had failed to grasp his intentions
in the book: only Dostoevsky and Botkin (both relatively
conservative in their esthetic theories, we should note) had
understood what he meant to say. Then Turgenev had to
contend with a long critique of the novel from a group of
Russian students at Heidelberg University led by Konstantin Sluchevsky contained in a letter, no longer extant, to
which he responded with a letter of April 1862 from Paris
(4:379–82). Here he proclaimed his solidarity with Bazarov,
although one may suspect that he was exaggerating somewhat in view of his audience. Later, as the decade drew to a
close and Turgenev hoped that the passions *Fathers and Sons*
had once aroused had subsided, he wrote that he agreed
with all of Bazarov's views except those having to do with
art. Though that qualification may at first seem minor, it in
fact is a major one, for Turgenev had a very inclusive theory
of art which had many points of contact with his overall phi-

losophy of life. However, the most important fact for our purposes here is that, indirectly and directly, through *Fathers and Sons* Turgenev injected the contemporary debate over literature and esthetics into the realm of artistic literature.

The following year, 1863, saw the appearance of two works of imaginative literature which contributed to the ongoing discussion of esthetic matters: Aleksey Pisemsky's *Vzbalamuchennoe more (Troubled Seas)* and especially Nikolay Chernyshevsky's *What Is to Be Done?*

Though Chernyshevsky's transmogrification from critic to novelist was unexpected, there was some logic to it. He was intelligent enough to realize that he lacked artistic talent, in all probability; and in addition he believed that art was no more than a temporary concession to human frailty, one which would be withdrawn in the ideal society of the future. But he lived at the present moment, and just as he had utilized the accepted vocabulary of esthetics in writing *The Esthetic Relations of Art to Reality*, so he also realized he would have to yield ground to artistic literature if he wished to communicate his message to the general public. He was shrewd enough to see that, although the radical literary theoreticians were for the time being triumphant in the early 1860s, there were few truly talented radical fiction writers to advance the cause. Chernyshevsky had done what he could to encourage the creation of imaginative literature which would incorporate positive images of the radical generation for which he spoke, but with only limited success: those radical writers who were productive were more interested in condemning the shortcomings of the existing order than in pointing the way to a positive future one. Then came the bombshell of *Fathers and Sons*, which Chernyshevsky viewed as a major blow against his campaign for revolutionary political objectives: indeed Bazarov's powerful image had even succeeded in misleading that considerable portion of the left intelligentsia under Pisarev's influence. In fact Pisarev seemed bewildered by the situation, and had concluded his fine essay "Bazarov" with something very like an appeal for guidance:

> So what is to be done? Are we to infect ourselves on purpose in order to have the satisfaction of dying beautifully and peacefully [as Bazarov does]? No! What are we to do, then? We must live as long as we can, eat dry bread if we lack roast beef, be with women if we cannot love a woman, and generally stop dreaming of orange trees and palms when there is nothing but snowdrifts and frozen tundra under our feet. (2:50)

Since no one else would accept the responsibility of replying to Pisarev's "what is to be done?" Chernyshevsky decided to react at one stroke both to *Fathers and Sons* and to Pisarev's insistent question with a novel of his own, taking his title from Pisarev and the names of certain characters from Turgenev. Since no one else would, he would point the way to the society of the future through a work of imaginative literature.

Chernyshevsky wrote his first and most outstanding novel while incarcerated in the Sts. Peter and Paul Fortress, waiting for his fate to be decided. He did have some personal motivations for attempting the book. Among the most important was apparently the desire to discover whether he possessed any "poetic talent" as a writer, for he was considering becoming a professional novelist. In a draft foreword to a projected novel written after *What Is to Be Done?* he mused: "I have neither the desire nor the intention of being a novelist by trade unless I am persuaded I have poetic talent. If I had realized I lacked that, I would not have published a second novel" (12:682). It is certainly paradoxical that after the success of *What Is to Be Done?* the man who up to that point had been the most determined foe of imaginative literature in Russia should have thought seriously of becoming a "novelist by trade."

Dated April 4, 1863, *What Is to Be Done?* was published serially in *Sovremennik* from March through May 1863, and exerted an enormous influence on the entire subsequent development of the Russian intelligentsia. It was certainly an appropriate response on the political and philosophical, if not artistic, levels to *Fathers and Sons*, as its author had hoped. Chernyshevsky must have had several ideological objectives in mind in writing it. For one thing, he wished to eclipse Bazarov as the image of the radical in the minds of Russian readers with Rakhmetov, an extraordinary individual dedicated entirely to the cause of the people and progressive ideas and with but one small frailty: he smoked cigars. For another, as novelists have always done traditionally, he wished to deal with affairs of the heart, although in this case within the framework of what we would now call a feminist novel. Thus his central character is a woman, Vera Pavlovna, who marries Lopukhov partly in order to escape the legal authority of her parents; and when she falls in love with another progressive young man, Kirsanov, her husband fakes suicide to enable her to find happiness in her new love. Later he returns to the scene and all live together harmoniously, without jealousy or recrimination, as Chernyshevsky's "new men" were very much wont to do. And finally, Chernyshevsky's was a social novel containing a blueprint of the economic organization of the future society: Vera Pavlovna organizes a sewing shop for a group of young women who work together cooperatively, setting a fine fictional example which young radicals of the day tried to emulate in reality, though with little success.

Aside from writing a book designed to project a new image of the radical, demonstrate the enlightened relationships between the sexes prevailing within the younger generation even at that moment, and point the way to the future

economic organization of society, Chernyshevsky also
wanted to apply certain of his theories on the linkage between art and reality. This is a topic to which we shall return
below.

Aleksey Pisemsky's lengthy *Troubled Seas* made a more
modest contribution to the esthetic discussions of these
days. After assuming the editorship of *Biblioteka dlya chteniya* upon Druzhinin's illness, Pisemsky had run very much
afoul of the radical intelligentsia in 1861–62 and abandoned
St. Petersburg for Moscow. There he published *Troubled
Seas* in *Russky vestnik* from March through August 1863, almost concurrently with *What Is to Be Done?* Pisemsky conceived of the book as a portrait of "contemporary Russia," a
vast canvas depicting representatives of the major social currents of the day, including especially typical figures of the
younger generation, with which he disagreed deeply. Pisemsky had little taste for theoretical formulations, and we
find few of them in either his fiction or his correspondence.
One exception to this rule occurs in this novel's concluding
paragraph, in which Pisemsky advanced the proposition
that his book was a truthful representation of contemporary
falsehood:

> May the future historian read our tale with attention and
> trust: we present to him a faithful, although incomplete,
> picture of the morals of our time, and if not all of Russia
> is mirrored in it, at least all her falsehood has been care-
> fully collected herein. (4:549)

Even the conservatively inclined critics, however, had difficulty in accepting such an approach, and excoriated Pisemsky roundly for his book. Apollon Grigorev declared that
Troubled Seas had exposed Pisemsky as an obscurantist of the
highest order; Pavel Annenkov felt that Pisemsky had failed
to create a conceptual framework within which the novel

could be contained; and Evgeny Edelson criticized the book for its openly polemical character.[56]

In 1864 the controversy over literature and esthetics continued on the pages of works of imaginative literature. Dostoevsky's *Zapiski iz podpol'ia (Notes from Underground)*, which appeared in the January–February and April issues of *Epokha*, constituted an indirect contribution to the Turgenev-Chernyshevsky polemic, although more in the philosophical and ethical sphere than the artistic one. Where esthetics are concerned, a more relevant work for our purposes is the obscure *V svoem kraiu (In One's Own Land)*, published in the May, June, and August 1864 issues of *Otechestvennye zapiski*. Its author, Konstantin Leontev (1831–91), was a very original figure in Russian intellectual history. Born in Kaluga, he studied medicine at Moscow University and then worked as a physician during the Crimean War and afterward. From 1856 through about 1866 he published novels, short stories, and some literary criticism, in *Otechestvennye zapiski* for the most part. From 1863 to 1873 he served as a consular officer in various cities of the Ottoman Empire. Thereafter Leontev followed a religious vocation, and ended his life as a monk at a leading Orthodox monastery.

Around 1860 Leontev was fascinated by esthetic questions. He worked out a philosophy of esthetic immoralism: founded on the assumption that esthetic criteria rather than moral ones possessed the most general validity for mankind, it held as well that the ideal to be striven for was unity in variety. Leontev placed many of these ideas and others which sprang from them in the mouth of his character Milkeev from *In One's Own Land*, and contributed to the es-

[56] On the critical reaction, see Charles A. Moser, *Pisemsky: A Provincial Realist* (Cambridge, Mass. 1969), 128–29. See also Evgenii Edel'son, "Russkaia literatura. Vzbalamuchennoe more," *Biblioteka dlia chteniia*, no. 11 (November 1863), 1–26; no. 12 (December 1863), [1]–21.

thetic discussion of the day both through Milkeev and through his own writings, although they were not widely read or noted at the time.

Several other events of importance for the esthetic debate took place in 1864 in addition to these publications and Chernyshevsky's banishment to Siberia. Alexander Druzhinin, inactive for some time, died on January 19, as did Apollon Grigorev on September 25, soon after he had been released from debtors prison through the good offices of an anonymous benefactress. His death was a severe loss to the literary intelligentsia grouped around Dostoevsky's journals. Pisarev a few months later called him the "last major representative of Russian idealism" and paid tribute to the sincerity with which Grigorev had argued his beliefs, but he also remarked that Grigorev's recently published correspondence showed he had realized that his ideas "were outdated, they had no future, and they would probably never be resurrected" (3:251–52). Pisarev proved a poor prophet here, for the Symbolists at the turn of the twentieth century treated Grigorev's ideas with great respect, and he has since been accorded a significant place in the history of Russian critical thought. Much later—in 1876, on the occasion of the publication of the first volume of an edition of Grigorev's works under Strakhov's editorship which was never completed—Nikolay Shelgunov took a more than dim view of him. This was the way Shelgunov put it:

> No doubt the people of the historical school [Grigorev's term for the radical critics of the 1860s] have made mistakes; no doubt the people of the historical school have contradicted one another generation after generation; but in those contradictions and constant alterations of ways of thinking, as well as in the changes of their forms of life—or at least in their efforts to attain them—there was life, whereas Grigorev preached death. (366)

That assessment may seem to us excessively harsh, but Shelgunov maintained then that Grigorev's contribution to the discussion of literary theory in his day had been entirely negative, and therefore readers of 1876 had no reason at all to applaud the appearance of this volume of his writings.

Shortly before he died Grigorev made what turned out to be a final attempt at a systematic exposition of his critical views. Referring to certain disagreements he had had recently with Dostoevsky on the subject of Russian literature, and therefore "on art generally," he cast this piece ("Paradoxes of Organic Criticism") in the form of "letters to F. M. Dostoevsky."[57] Characteristically, from the very start he launched into a series of digressions, which—though of intrinsic interest—were connected only tangentially with organic criticism, and certainly were not arranged in systematic fashion. At the end of the article he indicates there are greater things ahead: "Up to this point everything is the tale-teller's introduction, while the tale is yet to come." And with that his last major article concluded, as Grigorev prepared yet once again to make the case for his interpretation of literature. It was a very appropriate exit.

With Chernyshevsky and Grigorev gone, then, and Dostoevsky and Turgenev retired into temporary silence (Turgenev) or creative writing and unrelenting editorial work (Dostoevsky), the stage was open for a new cast of characters. Antonovich continued to speak for the radical camp, to be sure, but now he was deprived of a principal ally in Chernyshevsky, and was thrown onto the defensive by a newly energized Dmitry Pisarev writing from a prison cell. From 1864 to 1866 Pisarev become more interested in theoretical questions and less concerned with practical criticism, some-

---

[57] Apollon Grigor'ev, "Paradoksy organicheskoi kritiki," *Epokha*, no. 5 (May 1864), 255–73; no. 6 (June 1864), 264–77.

what more doctrinaire and considerably more outrageous than he had been before.

In the September, October, and November 1864 issues of *Russkoe slovo* Pisarev published a major statement under the title "An Unresolved Question," now more generally known as "Realisty" ("Realists"). Here he expounded some of his most extreme esthetic doctrines: the epigraph to this book from Pisarev is taken from that article. Drawing the ideas of Chernyshevsky and Dobrolyubov out to their logical extremes, he proclaimed his "total indifference" to art in all its forms except for literature (3:114). (In a later article he wrote, for instance, that music "can touch us, agitate us, make us melancholy or gay, but it cannot even attempt to persuade us or dissuade us of something," as literature can [3:479]: and Pisarev believed determinedly that art should have that intellectual purpose.) But the critic thought that even literature eventually would vanish from the face of the earth as a useless human activity which merely delayed the resolution of mankind's genuine problems.

The power of such extreme opinions as Pisarev's often enough engenders an opposite if not equal reaction, and something of the sort occurred in this instance. During 1864 there appeared for the first time in the pages of *Epokha* a young man from the provinces named Nikolay Solovev (1831–74). He published his first article, "Theory of Ugliness," in the July issues; then, with Dostoevsky's encouragement, he followed this up with "Theory of Usefulness and Advantage" in the November issue and "Fruitless Prolificacy" in December.

We know very little about Solovev's background except that, like Leontev, he worked as a physician before turning to esthetic questions in the heat of the battle in the 1860s, and that he ceased writing on esthetic questions after his collected critical writings appeared in three volumes in 1869 under the title *Art and Life*.[58] At that point he had but five years left to live.

From the very beginning Solovev followed a clear theoretical line. His principal argument, set forth in his first article, "Theory of Ugliness," was that ethical conceptions should be linked to esthetic feeling rather than intellectual calculation (as the radicals maintained) or religious revelation (as the traditionalists argued). Over the next few years he would develop this central idea and others stemming from it with great consistency in his critical writings.

In addition, Solovev deliberately and consciously thrust himself forward as the esthetic camp's champion against Pisarev. There was, after all, no one else who could take on this task: Grigorev was dead, Dostoevsky would soon go abroad to escape his creditors, Edelson published only infrequently and was no polemicist in any case. Thus, for example, Solovev designed his article "Fruitless Prolificacy" of December 1864 as a polemic response to Pisarev's just completed series of articles "An Unresolved Question." Pisarev soon recognized Solovev as a major opponent and mentioned him from time to time, ordinarily very unflatteringly, in his articles of 1865–66. He included a critique of one of Solovev's pieces in his own very polemical "Stroll Through the Gardens of Russian Literature" (1865), commenting sarcastically on the "inconceivable chaos [that] reigns in the flourgrinding establishment which, out of politeness, we call Mr. Solovev's head" (3:286); in another article of 1865 he berated Solovev as an "improbably weakminded sort" as he dedicated nearly an entire page to a polemic against him (3:437); and in a third piece of that same year he denounced

Solovev as a "pitiful pygmy" because the latter disagreed
with his interpretation of Nikolay Pomyalovsky (3:417).
Solovev lacked Pisarev's polemical gifts, but did his best
to return blow for blow. One of his most common tactics
was to refer to Pisarev or his ideas as in some way "comic,"
a word which generally infuriated the radicals. Later in 1865,
when discussing the running dispute between Antonovich
and Pisarev which Dostoevsky dubbed the "schism among
the nihilists," Solovev remarked that when *Sovremennik* had
begun to beat a sensible retreat from the absurdities to
which its doctrines led, it had found its way blocked by Pisarev, "the best expression of those ridiculous notions at
which the tendency created by *Sovremennik* has arrived."[59] As
a rule, though, Solovev preferred discussing ideas to assault-
ing individuals, as Shelgunov recognized in 1870 when he
commenced a long review of *Art and Life* with the remark
that Solovev was a serious opponent and it behooved the
radicals to discover why, though he began from the same
premises as they did, he arrived at such different conclusions.[60] But the debate over esthetics in the mid-1860s did
often enough assume an unpleasantly personal tinge, and
that was mostly the result of Pisarev's intolerance of princi-
pled opponents both on the right (Solovev) and on the left
(Antonovich).

Antonovich sometimes attacked Pisarev quite sharply,
especially after the appearance of "Realists." In an article de-
monstratively entitled "Pseudorealists" (*Sovremennik* for
July 1865) Antonovich proclaimed his intention of repairing
the damage done to the "true image of realism" by the "Bazarovian realists," those who had adopted Bazarov as their
model and had scarcely known what they believed until Tur-

[59] Nikolai Solov'ev, "Ob otnoshenii estestvovedeniia k iskusstvu," *Otechestvennye zapiski* (November 1865), 134.
[60] Shelgunov, "Dvoedushie," [41].

genev simplified radical doctrine sufficiently for their under-standing in *Fathers and Sons*. Extremists, he wrote, like those "blockheaded adherents of realism" Pisarev and his *Russkoe slovo* associate Varfolomey Zaytsev, could do great damage to sensible doctrines of the sort which Antonovich now came forward to defend.[61] Pisarev replied with a detailed ref-utation of Antonovich's arguments entitled "We Shall See!" and published in the September issue of *Russkoe slovo*. Though not so ferocious as he could be when assailing his opponents on the right, Pisarev still defended his positions stoutly, though when it was all over he declared that he would not continue the argument with the *Sovremennik* critic further unless Antonovich did something unusually outrageous.

Pisarev had himself been outrageous enough during the early months of 1865. In his well-known potpourri of March, "A Stroll Through the Gardens of Russian Literature," he had composed an epitaph of sorts for Apollon Grigorev; at-tacked his new critical opponent Solovev; pronounced anathemas against his political enemies in literature such as Nikolay Leskov (who had published his antinihilist novel *Nekuda [No Way Out]* in 1864) and Pisemsky, whom he still could not forgive for such broadsides as *Troubled Seas*; and formulated rather extreme theoretical statements on litera-ture and art. He was preparing the way for one of the most controversial essays he ever published: "Pushkin and Belin-sky," which came out in the April and June issues of *Russkoe slovo*.

Since he clearly understood the issues at stake in the con-troversies over literature and art in his day, the *enfant terrible* of radical criticism must have known for some time that eventually he would have to confront that mightiest cham-

[61] See the text of the article in Maksim Antonovich, *Literaturno-kriticheskie stat'i*, 243–86.

pion of esthetic doctrine, Alexander Pushkin. He undertook this task in one of the greatest of nineteenth-century Russian polemics, an essay which still today is capable of unsettling Pushkin's admirers, especially by its relentless onslaught against his lyric poetry.

Pisarev began with a lengthy discussion of *Eugene Onegin*, because Belinsky had designated it as Pushkin's most serious and important work. He focused his attention on Onegin, much as he had done with Bazarov in his discussion of *Fathers and Sons*. Pushkin could have examined the social roots of Onegin's personal malaise, Pisarev thought, but he refused to, instead raising each of Onegin's moral failings to a "law of nature." Furthermore, the poem had no intellectual content: Pushkin did not describe any of the arguments and discussions in which he tells us Onegin participated since, Pisarev was persuaded, he had not the slightest idea of what a "serious argument leading to thought" might be. Pisarev thus regarded the poem as not even neutral, but positively harmful in its impact:

> Exalting in this fashion in the eyes of the reading public certain types and traits of character which are low, banal, and worthless in themselves, Pushkin employs all the powers of his talent to dull that social consciousness which a true poet should stimulate and guide through his writings. (3:330)

Eugene Onegin, Pisarev thought, did more than merely accept reality: it was a "vivid and brilliant apotheosis of a most melancholy and senseless status quo" (3:357). In this formulation, then, Pisarev defined very precisely a principal point of contention between the radical view of art and the esthetic view: Pisarev rejected social reality as "senseless," while Pushkin accepted it, with all its imperfections, and found it beautiful.

After dispensing with *Eugene Onegin* Pisarev turned to

Pushkin's lyric poetry. Here he employed the notoriously unfair device of recasting Pushkin's poems as prose paraphrases, and then decreeing that the ideas contained within them are intellectually and politically contemptible. "No one else among Russian poets," Pisarev announced, "can inspire his readers with such limitless indifference to the people's sufferings, such profound contempt for honest poverty, and such systematic rejection of useful work as Pushkin" (3:400). Therefore, in the critic's opinion, Pushkin's influence upon his readers was highly undesirable.

Pisarev concluded "Pushkin and Belinsky" with a peroration on the subject of Pushkin's famous poem "Pamyatnik" ("The Monument") which is worth extensive quotation for the extremity of its rhetoric and because it is a good sample of the article as a whole:

> "I shall be immortal," Pushkin says, "because I aroused kindly feelings with my lyre." "Excuse us, Mr. Pushkin," thinking realists will say, "but what exactly are those kindly feelings which you have aroused? Loyalty to childhood friends and close associates? Do such feelings really need arousal? Are there truly people on this earth incapable of loving their friends? And do you mean to say that such stonehearted people—if they actually exist—will become tender and loving at the sound of your lyre? Love for beautiful women? Love for fine champagne? Contempt for useful work? Respect for aristocratic idleness? Indifference to the interests of society? Intellectual timidity and stagnation in all basic questions of one's view of the world? The best of all these *kindly feelings* aroused by the sounds of your lyre is, of course, love for beautiful women. There is in fact nothing wrong with this feeling; but in the first place one might note that it is fairly powerful in and of itself, without any artificial stimulation; and in the second place, you must admit that the organizers of the latest St. Petersburg dancing lessons can arouse and direct this feeling incom-

parably more successfully than the sounds of your lyre.
And as for all those other *kindly feelings*, it would be
much preferable if you did not arouse them at all."
(3:414)

While engaged in demolishing Pushkin's reputation, Pisarev felt that in all fairness he should criticize Belinsky as
well, since the latter had been Pushkin's leading advocate,
particularly in the 1840s, when he extolled *Eugene Onegin* as
an "encyclopedia of Russian life." Pisarev differed sharply
with his predecessor in his evaluation of Pushkin's works in
particular, and to a lesser degree in his general views on art,
but he dealt with Belinsky much more gently than with the
poet. We should not berate Belinsky too harshly for his contradictions and illogicalities, he wrote, because Belinsky
"stands on the dividing line between two contradictory
views of the world" (3:379), and therefore it was inescapable
that he should suffer from a certain intellectual confusion.

Concluding Arguments

The year 1865 was a major one for the entire esthetic debate
between 1855 and 1870: after 1865 that debate slowly subsided, and it is no accident that the most contemporary of
writers, Dostoevsky, should seriously have considered giv-
ing the most ideological of his novels, *Crime and Punishment*, the title *1865*. This year was important not only because
of the energies which Pisarev injected into the discussion
then, but also because it saw the publication or republica-
tion of two major statements on esthetics, one by Chernyshevsky, the other by Pierre-Joseph Proudhon (1809–65).

The radical intelligentsia has long had a well-cultivated
sense of its own history, and therefore it welcomed a second
edition of the *Esthetic Relations of Art to Reality* published on
the tenth anniversary of its first appearance by Alexander
Pypin, a scholar and minor journalist associated with *Sovre-*

mennik. The first edition had been printed as a mere adjunct to the formal defense of the essay, and in only 400 copies, as Chernyshevsky wrote at the time to his family. Of those 400 copies, he had given away more than 100 to people at the university and to friends, he said; he worried over whether he could sell the 250 or so he had left through local bookstores (we might note parenthetically that Chernyshevsky found the book in which he mounted his assault on esthetics pleasing esthetically: "the brochure is quite decent in appearance," he wrote, "and the typeface and the paper are nice.")[62] The small number of copies makes it all the more astonishing that his ideas should have achieved the preeminence they did within one short decade. But Pypin and his associates no doubt felt that it was desirable to make the text much more generally available than it had been up to that time; and beyond that, on the symbolic level they wished to mark the tenth anniversary of its appearance, to celebrate the intellectual victories it had won in the intervening period, and to pay tribute to its author, sent into exile the previous year in part for his commitment to the ideas it contained.

The appearance of the second edition of the *Esthetic Relations* in early 1865 stimulated new discussion of its arguments, although this time from a different historical perspective. Maksim Antonovich, probably wishing to sustain the *Sovremennik* group's claim to be Chernyshevsky's intellectual heirs, published a substantial review of the essay in the March *Sovremennik*.[63] He began by noting that this "little-known but quite remarkable work" had first codified the views which by 1865 had attained "almost exclusive mastery in our literature." It is true, he said, that Chernyshevsky's style of exposition was a bit dry, and disciples of his like

---

[62] Letter to his family of May 3, 1855: 14:297–98.
[63] Antonovich, "Sovremennaia esteticheskaia teoriia," 196–242.

Dobrolyubov had developed his thought in a more lively manner; but by now his doctrines were so widely accepted that some (here Antonovich had Pisarev and Zaytsev in mind) even took them to extremes (196–98). Antonovich then devoted the bulk of his article to an exposition of his own understanding of the nature of art. That understanding drew heavily on Chernyshevsky's ideas and even developed some of them further, but it also defended in principle the importance of art in human affairs and its right to exist, even against the logical pressure of certain of Chernyshevsky's doctrines themselves. Indeed the tension here was sufficiently palpable that two years later Evgeny Edelson wrote that Antonovich had brought down the wrath of *Russkoe slovo* upon himself for undertaking the logically impossible task of defending both art and Chernyshevsky's ideas at the same time.[64]

Russkoe slovo quickly contested Antonovich's claim to be Chernyshevsky's genuine successor. The first treatment of the second edition of the *Esthetic Relations* came from the pen of Varfolomey Zaytsev (1842–82), who had begun publishing in *Russkoe slovo* in 1863 after arriving in St. Petersburg from his native Kostroma. He was only an occasional literary critic, for his main interests were not literary, but his viewpoint was fully as radical as Pisarev's, and less subtle. In 1866 he was jailed for four months for influencing young minds to their detriment, in the official view, and in 1869 went abroad to dedicate the remainder of his life to radical emigré politics.

Zaytsev published his commentary on the *Esthetic Relations* in the April 1865 issue of *Russkoe slovo*. The piece was, among other things, a polemic against Antonovich's interpretation of Chernyshevsky's ideas: Zaytsev was unkind enough to lump Antonovich together with the "esthetes"

---

[64] Edel'son, "O znachenii iskusstva" (January 1867), 222–23.

whom he regarded as his implacable enemies. Zaytsev affirmed that the *Esthetic Relations* elaborated the theory of art "which we [the *Russkoe slovo* group] are following," and argued that Chernyshevsky clearly believed that art "must decline to the degree that human beings become ever more perfect, and that art deserves total and ruthless negation."[65] Zaytsev thus supported Pisarev in maintaining that *Russkoe slovo* was the true guardian of the Chernyshevskian heritage in the field of esthetics.

Of course it fell to Pisarev to make the journal's chief statement on this issue, which he did in May in a brief, impassioned, and justly famous article entitled "The Destruction of Esthetics" (3:418–35). In order to bolster his case Pisarev, so to speak, rescued Chernyshevsky from himself, maintaining that when he first presented his novel theories he was compelled to couch his argument in traditional terms simply in order to be understood. By 1865 there was no more need for such subterfuge: through the "outmoded" terminology, the thicket of Chernyshevsky's language, one could now see that "the author obviously had in mind, not the establishment of a new esthetic theory, but rather the extirpation of the old theory, indeed the eradication of all esthetic theory generally" (3:420). Pisarev maintained that Chernyshevsky's fundamental definition of the beautiful as life "clearly demonstrates that the author, as a thinking man, was absolutely indifferent to the beautiful in the narrow and generally accepted meaning of that word" (3:422). Then Pisarev went on to formulate a statement very closely associated with his name ever since: given Chernyshevsky's definition of the beautiful, "esthetics, to our great satisfaction, vanishes in physiology and hygiene" (3:423). That statement

[65] Varfolomei Zaitsev, [Review of the 1865 edition of *Esteticheskie otnosheniia*], *Izbrannye sochineniia* (Moscow, 1934), 1:328–41. The quotes are from pp. 328 and 331.

was a trifle cryptic as well as controversial, and so aroused considerable misunderstanding. In a reply to Antonovich published later in 1865, Pisarev clarified his thought by saying that "esthetics is being transformed into a part of physiology and hygiene in exactly the same way alchemy was transformed into chemistry and astrology into astronomy" (3:464). In other words, Pisarev viewed esthetics as a pseudoscience of the beautiful: whatever little there might be within it of value would be absorbed into genuine science, and the rest discarded.

At the end of "The Destruction of Esthetics" Pisarev remarked that the Russian reading public had now developed to the point where it debated only the intellectual content of a literary work, that which was of interest to a thinking man, just as Chernyshevsky had advocated in the *Esthetic Relations*. But no one even remembered that Chernyshevsky was the source of this attitude: the very fact that this viewpoint had so thoroughly penetrated the public mind demonstrated that esthetics could no longer make any scientific claims at all (3:434–35).

One can understand why Antonovich and his group should have been displeased with essays like Pisarev's and Zaytsev's: with the power of logic and youthful vigor they confirmed the worst fears of the radicals' opponents when they accused the radicals of wishing to eliminate art altogether in the ideal future society and even in the present imperfect one: this was much the sort of thing Bazarov had said, and for which Antonovich had condemned his creator so roundly. And indeed the *Sovremennik* circle had hesitated before the implications of its own doctrines. Dobrolyubov, for example, had written some verse, although not very much; Chernyshevsky in time moderated his views on art to the extent of becoming a writer of prose fiction; and Antonovich as a theoretician defended the status of art in society against the attacks of his more extreme colleagues. For their part, neither Zaytsev nor Pisarev ever succumbed to the temptation of writing poetry or fiction; toward the end of its existence *Russkoe slovo* eliminated poetry from its pages altogether, and may have planned to do the same for prose fiction. *Russkoe slovo* thus became a living theoretical reproach to *Sovremennik*.

Pisarev's esthetic opponent Nikolay Solovev came out with a series of five articles in 1865 under the general title "The Problem of Art" (published in *Otechestvennye zapiski* from May through August), largely inspired by the second edition of Chernyshevsky's essay. Solovev had grand ambitions: he thought of himself as summoned not only to crush Pisarev's arguments, but also to sweep Chernyshevsky's ideas from the boards. But he was sufficiently realistic to recognize the magnitude of the enemy's achievement and the difficulty of undoing it: "Art," he wrote in his first article, "has never encountered such a powerful opponent as the author of the *Esthetic Relations*." It was quite "improbable," he wrote in his second instalment, that the "ideas of this work [the *Esthetic Relations*] should have had such success," and he pointed out that the entire "theory of ugliness" which he had criticized in the very first article he published in *Epokha* in 1864 had derived from Chernyshevsky's thought.[66] But Solovev was a determined optimist: he asserted that the debate over esthetics had not yet been settled, as he wrote in the introduction to his first article. If the battle up to that time had gone against the advocates of art's independence, he believed, that was because her defense had been inadequate, and many artists had even fallen silent instead of speaking up for their beliefs.[67] The new critic proposed to

---

[66] Nikolai Solov'ev, "Vopros ob iskusstve," *Otechestvennye zapiski*: Article 1 (May 1865), section 1, 307–34; Article 2 (June 1865), 468–92; Article 3 (July 1865), 58–86; Article 4 (August 1865), 416–44; Article 5 (August 1865), 626–55. The quotations are from June, 479, and May, 308.

[67] Ibid., May, 307.

eliminate that shortcoming, and indeed he did work strenuously to that end for the next two years or so.

In addition to the second edition of the *Esthetic Relations*, 1865 also saw the publication of a Russian translation
of Pierre-Joseph Proudhon's *Du principe de l'art et de sa destination sociale*. This work by the celebrated French radical
social philosopher had been published in Paris very quickly
after his death, and almost as rapidly translated into Russian
under the title *Iskusstvo: Ego osnovaniya i obshchestvennoe naznachenie*. The translation was evidently done by a collective
of translators organized by the book's editor, the radical sat-
irist and poet Nikolay Kurochkin, for the moderately
lengthy work (which according to Kurochkin's foreword
had undergone four printings in Paris during the first few
months of the year) appeared in Russian before 1865 was
out.

In his four-page introduction to the translation, dated
September 27, Kurochkin remarked on what he considered
an artificial revival of esthetic criticism over the last two or
three years. Though he found that revival personally dis-
tressing, he was convinced it would not last:

> It does not matter if nearsighted or corrupt individuals
> celebrate the supposed resurrection in our literature of
> the theory of "art for art's sake," the number of whose
> cheap adepts has so increased among us these last few
> years, when journalism was in such an unenviable situa-
> tion; their unnatural triumph will not last long; in the
> sphere of thought everything which is rotten and dead
> ends in death, while only that which is healthy and pow-
> erful in its truthfulness has a right to life.[68]

Elsewhere in his introduction Kurochkin remarked that
much of the content of Proudhon's book would not be new

---

[68] Nikolai Kurochkin, "Predislovie," to P. Zh. Prudon, *Iskusstvo: Ego osnovaniia
i obshchestvennoe naznachenie* (St. Petersburg, 1865), iii.

to the Russian reader, who had been raised on the traditions of Belinsky, Chernyshevsky, and Dobrolyubov (Kurochkin conspicuously omitted Pisarev from this lineage), but since esthetics had been the focus of such lively dispute in recent times, "certain portions of the book here presented may be considered the last word in our disputes and polemics."[69] Thus Kurochkin sought to use Proudhon's final work, written on a topic on which he himself admitted he had little expertise, as the authority which would finally settle disputes raging far from Paris.

Proudhon dealt with general esthetic questions for the most part in the initial chapters of his book, and what he said there coincided very well with the Russian radicals' opinions on art; but much of the remainder of his book was given over to a discussion of the painting of his friend Gustav Courbet, whom he supported chiefly for political and not artistic reasons. Still, Proudhon's treatise had a certain impact on Russian esthetic thought, and the Russian radicals were intelligent in recognizing him as an ally and bringing his work out in St. Petersburg so promptly.

That central year of 1865 saw the publication of still other writings of importance for the historical development of the esthetic controversy. Chernyshevsky had seen to the publication of Dobrolyubov's collected works in 1862, immediately following the critic's death, but a new edition of Dobrolyubov's works in 1865 reinforced the power of Dobrolyubov's ideas in the continuing debate. For its part the esthetic group found sustenance in an eight-volume edition of Druzhinin's writings which began to appear in 1865. However, the edition did not reach its more interesting volumes until 1867, when it was too late for them to have much effect on the controversy. Since that time Dobrolyubov's

[69] Ibid., ii, iii.

collected works have been reissued frequently, and Druzhinin's not at all, until very recently.

Thus the esthetic critics did a poorer job than the radical
camp in 1865 in promoting their champions of the past, but
Nikolay Solovev continued to work to fill the gap in contemporary criticism. In addition to his extensive series of
articles on "The Problem of Art," he brought out a piece
entitled "Criticism of Criticism" in the September *Otechestvennye zapiski*. Solovev designed the essay as a rebuttal of
Pisarev's "Pushkin and Belinsky," in which, as Solovev saw
it, the radical critic had attacked "the firmest truths and literary convictions which are entirely settled."[70] The first part
of the article is a polemic against Pisarev, while the second
part argues Solovev's claim to the Belinskian critical legacy,
in another contribution to the ongoing debate as to which
critic or group could be considered the most genuine heir of
the great critic. Soon thereafter, in the November and December issues of *Otechestvennye zapiski*, Solovev published a
series of four articles on the topic "On the Relations of Natural Science to Art," with the declared objective of demonstrating that "science and art are equally mutually support-
ive and can logically coexist in the mind of any fully
developed individual."[71] With his scientific and medical
background Solovev was well qualified to attempt this task,
and his series of essays was in fact an interesting attempt to
link esthetic doctrine to the rational findings of natural science.

At this point Solovev's was not a solitary voice, for *Otechestvennye zapiski* sheltered a kindred critical soul in the person of Efim Zarin (1829–92), who published under the pseu-

[70] Nikolai Solov'ev, "Kritika kritiki," *Otechestvennye zapiski*, No. 9 (September 1865), 284.

[71] Solov'ev, "Ob otnoshenii estestvovedeniia k iskusstvu," *Otechestvennye zapiski* (November 1865), 132–46, 302–26; (December 1865), 435–54, 679–702. The quote is from November 1865, 132.

donym "Incognito." Born in Penza province and educated at a theological seminary and academy, in 1858 he had published a translation of Byron's *Manfred* in *Biblioteka dlya chteniya*. Probably in that same year he moved to the capital, where he printed more translations in *Biblioteka dlya chteniya* and began writing criticism first for that journal, then for *Otechestvennye zapiski*. Though he was not particularly well known, he does seem to have attracted some attention as a critic and esthetic theoretician, although he vanished from the journalistic arena after a burst of activity in 1865–66.

Some of Zarin's chief contributions to the discussion in 1865 bore rather general titles, as, for example, "On the Quality and Quantity of Progress in the Contemporary Movement of Our Literature" (February), or "Verba novissima" (July), which was both an analysis of the *Sovremennik-Russkoe slovo* dispute and a polemic in its own right. The following year Zarin contributed a detailed two-part study of Proudhon's esthetic theories to *Otechestvennye zapiski*.[72]

When Stepan Dudyshkin, the editor of *Otechestvennye zapiski*, died in September 1866, not long after the permanent suppression of *Russkoe slovo* and *Sovremennik*, Nikolay Nekrasov and his allies gained control of *Otechestvennye zapiski* and transformed it into a continuation of *Sovremennik*. As a consequence of this turn of events, Zarin seems to have abandoned journalism, and even so determined a figure as Solovev had to cast about for new publishing outlets, although he did print a series of articles entitled "Labor and Enjoyment" during the transition to radical control of the journal.[73] In these articles, however, he dealt very little with purely esthetic problems and moved instead toward more

[72] Incognito [E. Zarin], "Prudon ob iskusstve," *Otechestvennye zapiski*, vol. 168 (1866), 123–44, 361–79.

[73] Nikolai Solov'ev, "Trud i naslazhdenie," *Otechestvennye zapiski*, vol. 165 (1866), 655–78; vol. 166 (1866), 562–83; vol. 167 (1866), 125–49.

general philosophical and even sociological questions, such as women's place in society and the role of the family.

As for *Russkoe slovo*, its political situation had begun to appear precarious as early as late 1865. By 1866 even Pisarev's contributions were appearing rather irregularly, and lacked the impact they had enjoyed in the previous two years. Then too, with the disturbing political events of 1866 public attention tended to swing toward political questions, and away from theoretical esthetic problems.

The debate continued, nevertheless, though at a lower level, and attracted new participants. One was Konstantin Sluchevsky (1837–1904), who made minor contributions to it in late 1866 and early 1867. Of aristocratic origin, Sluchevsky was educated at military schools but then resigned from the military in 1861 to study in Paris, Berlin, and Heidelberg, by which time he had already published poetry in *Sovremennik* and *Otechestvennye zapiski*. In the early 1860s Sluchevsky evidently oscillated between the radical and the esthetic camps. Not only did he publish verse in the two journals just mentioned, which were on opposite sides of the esthetic divide, he was also the person who wrote to Turgenev in the spring of 1862 in the name of Russian students at Heidelberg to raise some unsettling points about *Fathers and Sons*, points which Turgenev found quite remarkable for their radical naivete. Some time passed, however, and Sluchevsky returned to Russia from abroad around September of 1866. There he threw himself into the esthetic controversy with a series of three pamphlets under the general title *Phenomena of Russian Life Under Esthetic Criticism*.[74] The first booklet (1866) was devoted to Proudhon's theories of art; the second (also 1866) dealt with *The Esthetic Relations of Art to Reality*; and the third (February 1867) bore the subtitle "How Pisarev Has Been Destroying

---

[74] *Iavleniia russkoi zhizni pod kritikoiu estetiki.*

Esthetics." Though in his introduction to the first booklet
Sluchevsky claimed that his six-year absence from Russia enabled him to analyze all that had occurred in that time quite
objectively, in fact he took a very partisan approach to contemporary developments and radical intellectuals such as
Proudhon, Chernyshevsky, and especially Pisarev, whom,
following Solovev's lead, he dubbed a "comic phenomenon" in contemporary Russian society.

Unhappily Sluchevsky's pamphlets of 1866–67 consisted
mostly either of simple summaries of his opponents' views
or of sheer polemics, and therefore engendered little response. That disappointed him, as he admitted himself in
the introduction to his third pamphlet. The booklets contain a few scattered points which support the esthetic viewpoint, but on the whole they are not very original or particularly stimulating. Much later, in 1878, Sluchevsky would
return to writing poetry, and finally acquire a reputation as
a poet.

By comparison with 1865, the esthetic debate of 1867 was
rather gentle. By this time *Otechestvennye zapiski* was firmly
radical, while *Russkoe slovo* was reincarnated in *Delo*, founded
in 1866. Since *Russky vestnik* was inhospitable to literary criticism and came out in Moscow in any case, the esthetic critics migrated for a time to *Vsemirny trud*, which began to
appear in 1867.

Vsemirny trud got off to a good start by publishing a
serious analysis of the entire question of art in a larger philosophical and historical context by Evgeny Edelson under
the title "On the Significance of Art in Civilization."[75] At the
beginning of his essay Edelson commented that although
there had been protests in the past against the established
intellectual order, in the 1860s the assaults against it were

organized more rapidly and mounted at many more points than ever before. Writers, he said, had become a "special caste" with a vested interest in protest; and since the initial appearance of the *Esthetic Relations* they had even begun to question the value of art itself. Still, Edelson went on, it was only very recently that critics had gone so far as to negate art entirely, and it was in response to this extreme and disturbing development that Edelson had decided to set down his reflections on the vital role art had always played in the development of human civilization. Edelson's essay remains perhaps the best general analysis of the esthetic question to have come from the esthetic critics from 1855 to 1870. But precisely because it was a serious work not written in particularly lively language, it failed to attract the attention it deserved at the time of its publication or since. When it appeared Edelson had less than a year to live, and it became his final statement on the role and meaning of art in his day.

At this same time Nikolay Solovev was also concluding his arguments. He began his article "Principles of Life" in *Vsemirny trud* for January 1867 with a declaration that Russia was in the grip of an intellectual crisis, and that it was now vitally important to reach a clear understanding of that "colossal blunder which a significant portion of our society has made" in the esthetic realm, partly because the adherents of truth and art in recent years had defended their principles so ineptly.[76] In that January article, followed by "Vanity of Vanities" in February and "Ideals" in March,[77] Solovev reformulated his basic esthetic principles and extended them into the sphere of sociology, in which he was taking an increasing interest. With these articles Solovev concluded what he had to say on the subject of art and life except for

[76] Nikolai Solov'ev, "Printsipy zhizni," *Vsemirnyi trud* (January 1867), [137]–41.
[77] Solov'ev, "Sueta suet," *Vsemirnyi trud* (February 1867), [167]–202; "Idealy," *Vsemirnyi trud* (March 1867), [157]–93.

an extended series of pieces on the Russian folksong, a series with only tenuous links to the discussion in which he had been such a central participant since 1864.

The next year, 1868, saw the deaths of Evgeny Edelson in January and of Dmitry Pisarev in July, while Nikolay Solovev apparently published nothing more on the subject of esthetics. Thus it happened that Pisarev, the most energetic and interesting of the radical critics; Edelson, the most sober and erudite of the esthetic critics; and Solovev, the most active of the esthetic critics—all either died or ceased to publish in 1868 as the debate drew to a close.

Something should be said about the position of Leo Tolstoy in the esthetic and ideological quarrels of the period 1855–70, a time when he was a looming literary presence even though he took no direct part in the esthetic disputes of the day, especially during the 1860s. This did not mean that he lacked interest in the subject, for in his own very good time he would publish an entire treatise on esthetics: *What Is Art?*, completed in 1897. Although quite Tolstoyan in its arguments, *What Is Art?* had deep roots in the disputes of 1855–70 but appeared much too late to exert any direct influence on the debate which is the subject of this study. Consequently Leo Tolstoy's name is rarely mentioned here except as the author of literary works to which certain critics addressed themselves.

Although superficially it might even seem that Tolstoy retreated from the ideological battles of the 1860s into his private world (for a time in the early 1860s he abandoned literature in order to devote himself to educating peasant children on his estate), in fact this is not so. In 1863–64, for example, he wrote an antinihilist play, *An Infected Family*, intended to rebut ideas of the type advanced in *What Is to Be Done?* He never published or staged the play, however, and instead turned his attention to the historical novel which would become *War and Peace* (1869).

In its own, Tolstoyan, way, *War and Peace* subverted many of the accepted notions of the 1860s—in a personal letter Turgenev remarked that the novel was "based on hostility toward intellect, knowledge, and consciousness"[78]—but it did so in a grand manner which requires quite particular analysis. To be sure, one discovers in Tolstoy's fiction occasional passages in which he offers views of art which he would later develop in more detail in *What Is Art?* An example of this is the description of Natasha Rostova's first visit to the opera in *War and Peace*: when she sees the artificial stage sets and the singers' costumes, the narrator tells us, "all this was so mannered, false, and unnatural that she could not make up her mind whether to be embarrassed for the performers or laugh at them."[79] In the portion of *Anna Karenina* dealing with the painter Mikhailov, Tolstoy has him ruminate that the greatest possible technical skill displayed in a work of art cannot compensate for a lack of well-defined content.[80]

Thus Tolstoy by no means entirely avoided the esthetic debate of the 1860s, and was clearly interested in its major points, but many years would pass before he formulated his thoughts on art in any systematic way.

The last significant contribution to the long controversy of 1855–70 was made in 1870 on behalf of the radical camp by Nikolay Shelgunov, now its leading critic, who had made contact with *Russkoe slovo* very soon after its founding, and also contributed to *Sovremennik*. Shelgunov improved his radical credentials, if that were necessary, in the revolutionary spring of 1862, when he was arrested for distributing revolutionary proclamations, kept in confinement for more than two years, and then exiled to the provinces. Rather like

---

[78] Letter to I. P. Borisov of August 12/24, 1870: 8:270.
[79] Lev Tolstoi, *Sobranie sochinenii*, 20 vols. (Moscow, 1960–65), 5:361.
[80] Ibid., 9:50.

Pisarev, who composed many of his most influential articles in prison, Shelgunov wrote from distant exile during the latter years of the 1860s. He was permitted to return to the capital only in the late 1870s.

Shelgunov wrote on quite varied subjects, and was a literary critic only incidentally. He functioned as a literary critic most actively in the last years of the 1860s, during his tenure with *Delo*. When Solovev's critical articles appeared in 1869 under the title *Art and Life*, it was Shelgunov who rose to defend the radical critical tradition against this "preacher of esthetic conservatism," it was Shelgunov who set out to unmask the corrupt conservative motivations behind these "fruitless efforts of individualism to distract people from life—efforts duplicitously camouflaged by science, love for one's neighbor, and morality." Shelgunov's instrument for that purpose was his article of October 1870 entitled "The Duplicity of Esthetic Conservatism."[81]

This article demonstrates that by 1870 the radical critics had begun to look at esthetic questions primarily in political terms. Certainly political considerations were behind Shelgunov's declaration in "The Duplicity of Esthetic Conservatism" that conservatives were individualists who lacked any comprehension of history or of the struggle of ideas. "Thinking they are serving the common good," he wrote, "[the peaceful esthetes] serve individualism instead. They go directly counter to the idea of the collectivity which powers the chariot of contemporary history."[82] Shelgunov's literary assessments were entirely determined by his political convictions, which meant that they were so doctrinaire that it was almost impossible for the esthetic critics to conduct a discussion with him on philosophical and esthetic grounds.

Before the critical debate ended, however, the discussion

[81] Shelgunov, "Dvoedushie," 42, 70.
[82] Ibid., 68–69.

did flow in some interesting byways of creative literature which are worth noting. One of them is to be found in Dostoevsky's *Idiot*, published in *Russky vestnik* in 1868: it will be discussed from this perspective below. Another major novel of the 1860s—Goncharov's *Obryv (The Precipice)* of 1869—is one of the few longer works of nineteenth-century Russian literature to have an artist as its central hero. At this remove in time we forget about Raysky the artist because he has been rather overshadowed by a much less central figure, the nihilist Mark Volokhov, a fact reflected in the title of an early translation of the novel into French: *Marc le nihiliste*. While he was writing the book Goncharov considered calling it *The Artist*, a title which would clearly have emphasized art's importance to the novel. Raysky is a throwback to the artistic idealists of the 1840s with whom Goncharov felt a strong affinity. He is dedicated to all the arts: he wants to paint, sketch, and write himself, he appreciates music and sculpture, and defends the esthetic ideal with unflagging vigor throughout the book. At one point he speaks of his portrait of a beautiful woman as embodying an "ideal of strict beauty and pride; she is a goddess, though an Olympian one . . . not of this world!" (5:134). To be sure, Raysky is by no means entirely positive: he makes rather a fool of himself in his relations with the heroine Vera; he is a dilettante; even his artistic convictions are old-fashioned and romantic. And yet it is indicative that precisely in the 1860s Goncharov should have sought to create a major character dedicated with all his being to artistic ideals. It seems reasonable to regard both Raysky as a character and *The Precipice* as a whole as major contributions of Goncharov's to the defense of art in the 1860s.

It might be added that a number of prose writers of the 1860s and several poets—including Aleksey Konstantinovich Tolstoy in particular—made strong statements in verse, occasionally in published articles, and more frequently in private correspondence, in defense of the rights of art, and especially in defense of poetry. Such statements may not have had much resonance at the time, but they are worth examination in this study for what they tell us about contemporary attitudes toward art.

A General Assessment of the Period

The Russian discussion of the esthetic question and the relationship between art and reality did not begin in 1855, of course, nor did it end in 1870. Vissarion Belinsky did much in the 1840s to articulate the major questions which would be debated so heatedly from 1855 to 1870. He in turn drew upon the work of critics who had gone before him, but his was surely the most prominent intellectual presence in the controversy of 1855–70, as may be seen from the fact that almost all its participants sought to claim him as their intellectual forebear. And indeed he was so protean that nearly all of them had some justification for their arguments: in 1865 even Nikolay Solovev declared that he was one of Belinsky's "admirers," and rose to defend him against Pisarev's criticisms in "Pushkin and Belinsky."[83] The radical camp was quite correct in drawing intellectual sustenance from the Belinsky of about 1844–45, but the esthetic critics, too, could justifiably look to the Belinsky of some other phase of the several he traversed during his lifetime, or else proclaim their faith that, had Belinsky lived longer, he would have adopted views more in accord with theirs, as he seemed to be doing at the very end of his life.

The discussion of art certainly did not cease after 1870, although it did subside for a time. The radical view of art and literature predominated in Russian culture until near the century's end, when a new generation of critics rejected

---

[83] Solov'ev, "Vopros ob iskusstve" (June 1865), 483.

much of the consensus forged in the 1860s and revived many ideas advanced by the esthetic critics at that time.

The years from 1855 to 1870, however, are an era of very special interest, for it was then that a large number of intellectuals of considerable distinction raised fundamental points having to do with the nature of art and literature, and did so with such emotional commitment that the controversy reached a level of intensity unusual even for Russia. Curiously enough, adherents of each of the contending groups felt besieged and outnumbered, a fact which lent the entire discussion a nightmarish quality to which both Pisarev and Fet attest from opposite ends of the philosophical spectrum.

The two key words of the discussion were "art" and "esthetics," although they meant very different things to different theoreticians. In 1855 Chernyshevsky's *Esthetic Relations of Art to Reality* was thrust into an environment clearly dominated by people who rejected his approach. Although it presented itself as a new esthetic doctrine, the more intelligent among its adherents and detractors realized that it was in fact a fundamental assault on the very idea of art. That was unprecedented in their experience, and therefore quite alarming to the esthetic critics. By January 1857 Botkin was speaking of a general European tendency to denigrate literature: even Prosper Mérimée, he said, had published an article in which he argued that poetry could exist only in primitive societies. "The dominant tendency of our time," he wrote then, "is primarily a practical and businesslike one."[84]

A bit earlier, in 1856, Botkin's ally Druzhinin had claimed that all criticism could be divided into two camps: the "artistic," which upheld the "slogan of pure art for art's sake"; and the "didactic," which "sought to influence human morals, way of life and concepts through direct instruction"

[84] Botkin, "Stikhotvoreniia Feta," I, 2.

(7:214). That notion of two hostile views of art soon spread throughout society, and most people at the time felt that everyone must subscribe to one of two views of art so mutually exclusive as to permit no bridging of the gap between them. By 1861 Dostoevsky was speaking of precisely those "two hostile camps" into which the "problem of art" had split the contemporary conversation, although Dostoevsky used the concept of "freedom" as the instrument of division where Druzhinin had spoken of "didacticism." Casting the argument in the form of a dialogue, as was his wont, Dostoevsky wrote that one group was the "party of the defenders of freedom and complete independence of art," whereas the other "party" held that "art must serve mankind through direct, unmediated, and practical utility, and even a utility defined by circumstances": there were occasions, this party believed, when the artist must place his obligation to society above his dedication to artistic liberty purely out of moral considerations (18:74–75).

Dostoevsky's formulation of the problem is noteworthy in two respects. First, just as Botkin and Druzhinin had done earlier, Dostoevsky incorrectly assumes that no one seriously questions art's right to existence: he believes both camps agree on that point but differ on the subject of art's moral function in society. Second, he seeks a way out of this bifurcation, and finds it in his celebrated story of an imaginary poet who on the day of the catastrophic Lisbon earthquake writes a purely personal lyric poem in the style of Fet, without any reference to the city's sufferings. Dostoevsky conjectures that the enraged citizenry would instantly execute the poet for his moral blindness, and with perfect justification; but he also believes that when thirty to fifty years have passed that same people might well erect a monument to him, to his poetry, and even to that particular poem. "Consequently," Dostoevsky concludes, "it is not art which is at fault, but rather the poet who abused his art at the precise moment when people had no use for it" (18:75–76). Dostoevsky thus distinguished between art as an abstract ideal and the artist, who as a human being bears certain moral obligations toward his fellow men. Such a reconciliation of the two positions was ingenious, even rather persuasive, but it was also far too subtle to have much effect given the polemics of that time.

Writing only a year later, Apollon Grigorev categorically accepted the dichotomous view of the esthetic dispute, although, like Dostoevsky, he yearned to close the gap between the two theories of art with his "organic" doctrines. "Actually," he wrote then,

> there can be only two views of life (and therefore of art). First is the *utilitarian* view, belief in theory, belief in the progress of humanity in the abstract, a view which in the final accounting destroys nationalities, art, philosophy, and history; and there is the *ideal* view, belief in life and in its inexhaustible infinity along with the acknowledgement of the eternity of everything.[85]

In fact, however, in Grigorev's opinion such a choice as this was no choice at all for most people. Grigorev believed that the radical view of life ineluctably led to art's destruction if it was carried through to its logical conclusion: "Art is dead, or at least *should* be dead as an unnecessary thing—this is the last word of nihilism," as he wrote earlier in this same article of 1862.[86] Grigorev would return to this point in his valedictory of 1864 when he argued that the "one-sidedly historical view" of the left Hegelians logically gave rise to such things as Pisarev's thoroughgoing negation of art on the basis of Belinsky's doctrines.[87]

---

[85] Apollon Grigor'ev, "Nigilizm v iskusstve," *Vremia*, no. 8 (August 1862), "Kriticheskoe obozrenie," 59.

[86] Ibid., 57.

[87] Grigor'ev, "Paradoksy" (May 1864), 263–64.

To be sure, by the time Grigorev wrote this Chernyshevsky and his colleagues on *Sovremennik* were reassuring
their antagonists that they had no intention at all of elimi-
nating art from the future society they envisaged. That attitude may have had a good deal to do with their violent rejection of Bazarov, who did negate art openly. But, as we
have already seen in part, Pisarev and his allies provided sub-
stance to the nightmares of the esthetic critics. Zaytsev, for
instance, wrote in his review of the 1865 edition of the *Esthetic Relations* that if one demanded social utility of art,
then poetry in particular had no right to exist because "all
the Racines and Goethes in the world were never of the
slightest use to anyone" (1:336). In like manner, if one demanded beauty of art, then

> the realist affirms that outside reality there is nothing
> genuinely beautiful, that reality satisfies the human de-
> sire for the beautiful completely. This affirmation is the
> equivalent of a negation of art, since it completely dem-
> onstrates art's total uselessness. (1:328)

Pisarev was nearly as intransigent on this point as Zaytsev,
although he permitted himself a few inconsistencies in his
argument. In "Realists" (1864) Pisarev wrote that the realists
understand art very well, but do not respect it (3:13). On a
later occasion he said that intellectually mankind was moving toward the realization that it could get alone quite well
without any art at all (3:62). One of his principal arguments
against art was an economic one: Pisarev held that certain
forms of art demanded a substantial material investment beyond the means of an impoverished contemporary society
which had to place its resources into the growing of food
and the development of industry (3:491). In fact the economic requirements of the day were so pressing, Pisarev
thought, that people should not devote even their free time

to enjoying the beauties of nature, but use it instead for necessary rest after working as much as possible.

On the other hand, Pisarev was not always consistent in his extremism in this area: for example, he would make certain concessions to literature among the arts, since he thought it gave substantial returns for relatively little investment (3:479–81). On another occasion he wrote that "realist criticism" did not envision the abolition of art in all its forms: it objected only when young people who might have entered upon economically productive careers were beguiled into taking up painting or music when they lacked talent for these activities and could have made much larger contributions to society by working in other areas (3:299). One may wonder whether Pisarev would have granted art the right of existence in a future society of economic plenty, or whether he would have adhered to the more rigid doctrines of a Zaytsev.

It is beyond dispute that the viewpoints of Pisarev, Zaytsev, and their followers, conjoined with the subsequent politicization of the entire question of art as illustrated in Shelgunov's writings, gave ample justification to the esthetic critics for their belief that the radicals in fact simply negated art altogether. That attitude emerged clearly in such writings as a passage from the antinihilist novel *Panurgovo stado (Panurge's Herd)* of 1869 by Vsevolod Krestovsky. After one of the characters denigrates the Polish poet Adam Mickiewicz, whose work a second character is reading, a third, a radical personage, launches into an ideological and political oration against art which reads in part:

> All those Murillos and Raphaels and other scoundrels paint angels and Madonnas and heroes surrounded by gods when right under their noses they have swarms of jolly little scenes like famine, poverty, mass ignorance, slavery, and tyranny, and these swine—just look at

them!—prefer to dwell in the heavens! Art, my friend,
can only exist at the courts of tyrants! . . . A normally
developed and free people will not and should not have
any art! And if you insist on producing art, then you
should be stuck in an insane asylum or a reformatory![88]

This is a crude statement on the political essence of art, an
argument which holds that art has existed in the past thanks
only to society's political misorganization, and therefore
that art will cease to exist once the political structure of society is set right.

The word "art," however, did not arouse such unremit-
ting antipathy within Pisarev as did the word "esthetics." He
believed the so-called esthetic feeling was not inborn, but
rather socially determined: "What we like instinctively," he
wrote in 1864, "we like simply because we have become accustomed to it" (3:61). Pisarev regarded esthetics as a deeply
conservative social phenomenon which worked against
everything he supported politically: on the one side he saw
"esthetics, instinct, routine, habit," on the other "realism,
consciousness, analysis, criticism, and intellectual progress"
(3:61). In short, a commitment to esthetic values was an
expression of that intellectual stagnation which Pisarev felt
surrounded him in contemporary society, and therefore it
was to be rejected root and branch. "The reader will no
doubt decide that esthetics is my nightmare," he wrote in
"Realists":

> Esthetics and realism are indeed in a state of irreconcila-
> ble hostility, and realism must destroy esthetics at the
> root, for at present it is poisoning and making nonsense
> out of all branches of our scientific activity, starting with
> the highest spheres of scientific work and ending with
> the most ordinary relationships between men and

---

[88] Vsevolod Krestovskii, *Krovavyi puf: Panurgovo stado*, in *Sobranie sochinenii*
(St. Petersburg, 1899–1905), 3:197.

women. . . . Esthetics is the most stable element of intellectual stagnation and the firmest enemy of intellectual
progress. (3:58)

Pisarev regarded esthetics as something like an infection
which damaged otherwise normal individuals. The realist,
he wrote, recognizes that Russian society has desperate need
of knowledge and facts, but facts interpreted within a meaningful context. Unfortunately, many people are so infected
by esthetic attitudes that they "read even serious articles and
books as if they were stories or poems" (3:69–72). Pisarev
believed that the defenders of esthetics were either stupid or
dishonest, and he could only pity a society which regarded
them as authorities in any way (3:92). In his sweepingly polemical "Stroll Through the Gardens of Russian Literature"
(1865) Pisarev mounted a merciless and fundamentally political attack on the "esthetes," but its central passage betrayed
a certain desperation, as if the critic felt he were surrounded
by innumerable defenders of pure art set upon upholding a
society which was stifling him:

> In order to distract people from serious meditation, in
> order to divert their gaze from the idiocies of life both
> large and small, in order to conceal from them the gen-
> uine necessities of this age and this nation, the writer
> must draw his readers away into a tiny little world of
> purely personal joys and purely personal griefs; . . . he
> must surround his small tales with charming descrip-
> tions of moonlit nights, summer evenings, passionate ec-
> stasies, and luxuriant bosoms; and the main thing is that
> while he is at it he must carefully conceal from his reader
> that unbreakable link connecting the fate of the individ-
> ual personality with the condition of society as a whole.
> (3:271)

Pisarev evidently believed that Russian writers too frequently succeeded in playing upon their readers' natural in-
clinations to concern themselves with personal matters

rather than larger social questions which Pisarev regarded as genuinely pressing. In political terms, the uncommitted artist distracted his readers when they should be dealing with a dreadful social reality crying out for revolutionary change (Pisarev's opponent Solovev agreed with him on this score: in 1867 he wrote that "art is the enemy of revolution just as it is the enemy of war"[89]). Thus esthetics was a nightmare for Pisarev because it sustained what he saw from his vantage point in the dungeons of the Sts. Peter and Paul Fortress as a nightmarish reality.

But the esthetic camp also felt as though trapped in a nightmare during the controversy of 1855–70. For the first time in civilized history, it seemed to them, art's very right to exist had been brought into question. They knew that art had been one of civilization's mainstays, which is why Evgeny Edelson couched his great defense of art "On the Significance of Art in Civilization" in those terms: he sought to define the "role of art in the development of civilization," and then demonstrate that it was "necesssary" for the development of civilization, from which it surely followed that art was of "use" to society. When we undertake such an investigation, he said,

> everywhere we will discover both the unconscious and the purposeless character of art as far as the carrying out of its historical task is concerned, and the eternal, unfading beauty of its highest achievements, and their irresistible esthetic impact on people of other ages, as well as, finally, the great importance of art as a civilizing element.[90]

The appeal to civilization was perhaps the most fundamental argument the esthetic thinkers could make, but to their horror they found that certain elements within the radical

[89] Solov'ev, "Printsipy zhizni," 174.
[90] Edel'son, "O znachenii iskusstva" (February 1867), 316.

camp negated even civilization: had not Bazarov quarreled with Pavel Petrovich on this very point? The esthetic critics found it truly appalling to face opponents who even rejected the ideal of civilization, and the more timid among them became demoralized, especially when it seemed to them that the radical critics were carrying the intellectual day.

The poets turned out to be most susceptible to demoralization in the 1860s, for lyric poetry bore the brunt of the radical attack on literature. In 1865 Solovev commented that the radicals had in fact succeeded by that time in suppressing poetry, though they had accomplished this in an unexpected manner: people like Dobrolyubov and the radical satirists Nikolay Kurochkin and Dmitry Minaev had destroyed poetry by producing it themselves "without any natural talent."[91] That is not a very persuasive explanation, and yet in the mid-1860s there did prevail an antipoetic attitude in society which severely intimidated such souls as Yakov Polonsky. In a dispirited letter of 1869 to Turgenev, Polonsky described the way a minor critic of the time and a friend of his had reneged on a promise to publish an article in his defense. "It is extremely difficult for me to write about you," the critic had told Polonsky,

> in such a manner as to tell the truth without at the same time arousing the wrath of the party which cannot stand poetry and which will certainly leave me without work or anything to eat if I should praise you or look on you as a poet seriously rather than jokingly. What can you do about all this? This party possesses such power because all of society is the same way. Do you think a poet means anything in the Russian society of our day? He does not. He's a cipher and nothing more. It's barbarous. It is total ignorance, all that is very true, but when in Rome you

<hr>

[91] Solov'ev, "Vopros ob iskusstve" (August 1865), 643.

must do as the Romans do. If I think in European fashion, I will starve in Russia—nobody will employ me.[92]

In this instance Polonsky and his friend accepted what might be termed a social view of art in agreeing that the critic could not oppose the antipoetic current of the day since he depended upon individuals of antipoetic persuasion for his mundane livelihood, but other members of the esthetic camp sought more metaphysical sources of reassurance in similar circumstances. Apollon Grigorev, for instance, wrote shortly before his death that "thought, science, art, nationalities, history," all such things were not mere social epiphenomena but rather the "eternal and organic work of just as eternal forces which inhere in man as an organism."[93] And in a personal letter of 1869 Aleksey Tolstoy upbraided his friend Boleslav Markevich for wavering in his fidelity to art. After quoting two well-known lines from Pushkin, Tolstoy exclaimed:

> No matter how these verses are interpreted by animals like Pisarev, may God have mercy on him [Pisarev was dead by this time], the interpreters will remain animals and Pushkin will remain a poet *forever*. Poetry, the beautiful, love for beauty—all these things, my friend, are not a matter of fashion or convention.[94]

And it was also the firm Tolstoy who in 1868 had assured Polonsky that all the radicals' efforts to destroy art were doomed to failure: "Destroying art," said one poet to the other, "is just as easy as forbidding a man to breathe on the pretext that this is a luxury for which he cannot afford the time."[95]

[92] Letter from Polonsky to Turgenev of December 27, 1869/January 8, 1870, in *Literaturnoe nasledstvo*, vol. 73, book 2 (Moscow, 1964), 228.

[93] Grigor'ev, "Paradoksy" (May 1864), 268.

[94] Letter of November 7, 1869, in A. K. Tolstoi, *Sobranie sochinenii* (Moscow, 1963–64), 4:318–19.

[95] Letter of December 20, 1868: ibid., 249.

Finally, in addition to those who sought a metaphysical basis for their belief in art's durability, a man like Nikolay Solovev cast the argument for art in the radicals' own terms. His essays of 1865, "On the Relations of Natural Science to Art," contained his principal attempt to demonstrate that esthetic feeling was grounded in the physical nature of things. When he applied this approach to music, for instance, he argued that "the reason for our sense of harmony is purely physical and not psychological, as people used to think, and one should seek it in the theory of sound itself."[96] He dealt with light and color from the physical point of view, analyzing emotional reactions to various colors and forms. Recommending a book by Adolph Zeising, *Neue Lehre von den Proportionen des menschlichen Körpers*, Solovev wrote:

> Anyone who has read this book must agree that the impact of natural forms upon our esthetic sense is subjected to the same sorts of laws as the impact of sound and light, the only difference being that in the case of sound time is the most important factor, while space plays the chief role in the case of forms.[97]

After some further discussion of forms in nature, including observations on nature's entirely esthetic use of symmetry, Solovev ended with a rhetorical question:

> If the basis [of the arts] is so closely connected with the nature of things and the structure of the human organism, then how can we possibly suppose that the arts are of no progressive significance?[98]

Thus Solovev deliberately disregarded metaphysical criteria and made his argument on the basis of the physical reality

---

[96] Solov'ev, "Ob otnoshenii estestvovedeniia k iskusstvu" (November 1865, book 2), 307.

[97] Ibid., 318.

[98] Ibid., 326.

of organic nature. The radical critics did not accept his conclusions, but his reasoning ran very much along their lines, for they consistently appealed to the authority of natural science.

Eventually the esthetic nightmare dissipated as the participants in the controversy withdrew from it or passed from the scene one by one, and passions subsided. Each side felt much beleaguered by the other, though, and each thought of itself as in absolute opposition to the other. But when we analyze the leading ideas of the time closely we shall discover that, although there were serious differences between the radical and esthetic critics, the dividing line between them was often blurred: many of those who thought of themselves as sworn opponents actually had substantial areas of agreement. Now, at a remove of considerably more than a century, it is possible to examine the leading concepts of that controversy dispassionately, to define genuine areas of disagreement, and to trace the interpenetrations of thought which made the polemics of 1855–70 into a true discussion on occasion, when representatives of each side altered their positions in response to the arguments of the other.

In the following chapters, as in this one, the terms "radical camp" and "esthetic camp" (or slight variants) will be employed as a shorthand designation for those who held that art and literature had a primarily social function, on the one hand, and for those who believed that art had its own autonomous sphere. Neither camp was fully united, as the bitter arguments between Pisarev and Antonovich, say, or Fet and Turgenev amply demonstrate, and it is a major objective of this study to follow through individual variations on those great themes which resounded through the entire discussion of the period. And yet it is a helpful oversimplification to speak of two major parties to the discussion of art and literature over the years from 1855 to 1870. Such an oversimplification provides the overarching structure which permits us fruitfully to examine the intertwinings and over-lappings of individual esthetic arguments without causing the analysis to descend unduly to the level of each individual participant. By adopting such an approach we shall arrive, I think, not only at an understanding of a major episode in the history of the Russian intelligentsia, but also at a more subtle comprehension of the nature of art and the creative process generally—for many of the issues which Russian critics debated between 1855 and 1870 are still with us today.

Chapter Two

Art and Rationality

THE DEBATE OVER LITERATURE AND ESTHETICS in Russia between 1855 and 1870 raised many issues which interwine in such complex ways that it is no easy matter to sort them out for logical analysis. But much of the discussion centered upon the large question of art and reason: what should be the place of reason, logic, understanding, and analytical knowledge in art, and particularly in works of imaginative literature? What sort of cognition should the reader expect to derive from the reading of literary works, and what intellectual approach should the writer take toward his subject?

Artistic and Scientific Knowledge

As a first approximation, it may be said that the radical critics in principle rejected any distinction between the role of the intellect in art and its function in any other sphere of human endeavor, including scholarly and scientific writing: in short, they worked for the unification of literature with all other forms of writing and rational discourse. The esthetic critics, on the other hand, sought to distinguish between scientific thought and thought in artistic works generally or literary works in particular. But there were many

shades of opinion on this question among the critics who
dealt with it.

Afanasy Fet and Dmitry Pisarev occupied the extreme
positions on this central issue of reason in art. Fet, the most
musical of Russian lyric poets, denied the intellect any place
in poetry at all. By its very nature music cannot "make an
argument," for it does not use words; in similar fashion lyric
poetry often acts directly upon the emotions, without the
mediation of rational argument, especially in the forms that
Fet favored. Fet would take this viewpoint to something of
an extreme though both Goethe and Pushkin had said similar things long before him when he used to claim in private
conversation that "in our work genuine nonsense is genuine
truth," or that his "muse babbles nothing but absurdities."[1]
This was simply a poet's way of holding that lyric poetry
should be founded upon feeling and emotion rather than
reason, that it was not the lyric poet's place to offer rational
argument or analytical thought.

In his not very numerous published statements on literary theory Fet did not go quite so far as he used to in conversation toward denying the intellect any place in literature, but he still remained on the distant edge of the esthetic
camp on this question. In his chief statement, his review of
Tyutchev's verse published in 1859, Fet argued that the artist
should deal only with beauty as his central concern.[2] He
then applied this approach, rather ingeniously, to thought
in literature:

> [J]ust as poetry itself is a reproduction not of an object
> in its entirety, but only of its beauty, so poetic thought
> merely reflects philosophical thought, and reflects only

[1] Boris Bukhshtab, "Esteticheskie vzgliady Feta," *Literaturnaia ucheba*, no. 12
(1936), 42.
[2] Fet, "O stikhotvoreniiakh Tiutcheva," 64.

its beauty at that; poetry is not at all concerned with its
other aspects.[3]

Only in this very special sense, then, would Fet grant that
rational "thought" had any place in art. Pavel Annenkov in
a programmatic article of 1856 had advanced an analogous
idea when he remarked that among the finest gifts Pushkin
had to offer his reader was the "elegance of his way of thinking" (2:14). And there is something to that notion. Even in
our day mathematicians often speak of a mathematical proof
as "elegant," and chess players can derive purely esthetic
pleasure from a series of moves, for intellectual processes
subject to the strictest of rational rules are quite capable of
providing esthetic satisfaction to the beholder.

During the early 1860s Turgenev and Fet, close personal
friends at the time, often discussed esthetic questions in
their correspondence. In his letters Fet reiterated and developed further his arguments against philosophical thought in
literature, a point on which Turgenev strongly disagreed
with him. "I have always protested," Turgenev wrote to Fet
in 1860, "against your rectilinear and mathematical abstract
thinking, and I've even wondered how it could coexist with
your poetic nature."[4] Turgenev thought it paradoxical that
Fet could arrive, through highly abstract analysis, at a position of opposition to the intellect in art. Thus in 1865 he
wrote Fet on the subject of the theories Leo Tolstoy sought
to advance through his fiction (later on Turgenev would
criticize Tolstoy for what he considered the latter's excessive
dedication to theory):

> In your constant fear of ratiocination (*rassuditelnost*),
> there is a great deal more of that very same ratiocination

[3] Ibid., 68.
[4] Letter of July 16/28, 1860: 4:108.

of which you are so frightened than of any other feeling.
It's time to quit praising Shakespeare for being a fool, as
you do; that's just as nonsensical as to claim that some
Russian peasant, in between a couple of belches, as if in
a dream, has enuciated civilization's final word.[5]

Fet was at least consistent. If he developed an abstract an-
titheoretical theory, as Turgenev believed, he firmly adhered
to that doctrine in his poetic practice, and provided the radical critics ample justification for citing his verse time and
again as a horrible example of poetry containing no thought
at all. But the intransigent Fet did not mind: he firmly believed that poetry should not deal with thought.

In the same year and the same journal in which Fet set
forth his views in an essay on Tyutchev, yet another poet,
Yakov Polonsky, utilized a piece on the minor poet Lev Mey
to establish a position on the role of thought in poetry quite
similar to Fet's. "Not every feeling and not every thought
can be transformed into poetic feeling or poetic thought,"
Polonsky wrote. "For the lyric poet the soul is his material,
just as marble is the sculptor's material, and the value of his
verse depends just as much on the solidity of his material as
it does on his working of it."[6] Polonsky maintained that
philosophical thought must be transmuted in some unspec-
ified way in order to become poetic thought: the two types
of thought could not be equated, but Polonsky was not at
all clear on how they differed.

In his day Vissarion Belinsky had formulated a famous
distinction between the philosophical thinker, who reasons
discursively, and the artist, who thinks in images. Nearly all
the participants in the discussion of 1855–70 began from this
distinction, although generally speaking the esthetic camp

---

[5] Letter of October 10/22, 1865: 6:28.
[6] [Iakov Polonskii], "Stikhotvoreniia Meia," *Russkoe slovo*, no. 1 (1859), section "Kritika," 77.

sought to develop it further while the radical camp wished to overcome it and unify the two modes of thought: the radical critic perceived himself as a discursive analyst of literary works based upon images. Occasionally things worked the other way around: one could think discursively using images. Even the radical critics—Dobrolyubov in particular—could insert brief stories, in fact miniature literary works, into their critical articles for the purpose of making a point, usually a political one. Turgenev was capable of casting literary criticism in the form of images, and did so occasionally in his correspondence. Once he used quite an unpleasant image to express his distaste for Chernyshevsky's personal and literary style, including that of *What Is to Be Done?*:

> Willy-nilly I see Mr. Chernyshevsky as a naked, toothless old man, who sometimes lisps like an infant, waggling his unwashed bottom as an added attraction, and sometimes swears like a coachman, belching and snuffling.[7]

In a letter to Annenkov of a few years later Turgenev provided a fine example of critical thinking in images when speaking of Goncharov's *The Precipice* (Goncharov and Turgenev were on quite bad terms at the time):

> His style itself, which once so entranced me, now appears to me in the form of a smoothly shaven, handsomely deathly face of a bureaucrat with sideburns extended in a thin line from the ears to the corners of the mouth.[8]

Despite these examples, in general one finds relatively few instances of incursions of thinking in images into the realm of discursive critical analysis.

Aside from Fet in his more extreme moments, few es-

---

[7] Letter to N. V. Shcherban' of June 2/14, 1863: 5:129.
[8] Letter of January 12/24, 1869: 7:278.

thetic critics denied the importance of intellect (*um*) for the artist. At the very beginning of the controversy, in 1855, Apollon Grigorev had criticized the preceding few years as a time when "intellect (*um*) in verse was placed above talent," when readers demanded that poetry express social protest and nothing else. He erroneously considered that at that point Russian criticism had moved beyond that historical stage.[9] Though Grigorev believed in thought in literature, he also held that it should play a subordinate role, perhaps a very subordinate one. Annenkov, on the other hand, writing at nearly the same time, emphasized the interconnection between art and intellect: "Only in the garb of art," he declared in early 1856, "only in artistic form can the intelligent (*umny*) word and the noble aspiration find their way to people's hearts" (2:19). Earlier in that same article Annenkov had criticized certain members of the older literary school who had placed undue stress upon "art for itself" and maintained that literature could be produced "without knowledge, without science, without a lively sense of contemporary reality." That had given their antagonists an opening for the charge that they altogether denied the importance of the intellect for art when in fact, Annenkov was persuaded, no artist could create truly effectively without a firm understanding of his subject (2:7–8).

Goncharov—who always remained artistically and philosophically rooted in the 1840s—reverted to Belinsky's conception of the artist as thinker in images when he asked in 1879: "What is the intellect in art? It is the ability to create an image" (8:107). By this definition Goncharov simply absorbed the concept of intellect in art into the idea of artistic talent, or the ability to create literary images. He saw the artistic intellect as something different altogether from the discursive intellect.

⁹ Grigor'ev, "Obozrenie," 175.

Fet's idea of the relationship between image and thought in a work of art differed from Goncharov's. Fet not only distinguished between image and idea, he also believed there was an inescapable tension between them, deriving from the fact that, in Fet's view, artistic thought should be as "general" as possible, while an image should be particular. That tension, however, was a creative one. "The image by its specificity and thought by its generality and limitlessness," he argued, "stimulate the soul of the observer to fill in what is left unsaid, to undertake new creative acts."[10] Such a tension could not arise if, as Goncharov held, the image were inextricably connected with thought in a work of art.

On this issue there were some areas of agreement between the radical and esthetic camps. In particular, both groups agreed that the thought contained in a literary work should emerge of itself, without forcing. In one of his characteristically succinct formulations based on Belinsky's ideas, Dobrolyubov distinguished very well between the two types of thought for the ultimate purpose of unifying them:

> The thinker (*myslitel*), noting, say, that people are dissatisfied with their present situation, weighs all the facts and seeks to discover new principles which could satisfy the demands now coming into existence. The poet and literary man, noting that same dissatisfaction, depicts it in such lively fashion that general attention is attracted to it, and this in itself leads people to understand what precisely is needed. The result is the same, and the importance of the two, the thinker and the poet, should be the same. . . . (6:310)

Dobrolyubov held that the artist need not preach to his readers at all, for the realistic depiction of a situation would

[10] Fet, "O stikhotvoreniiakh Tiutcheva," 70.

lead readers automatically to the appropriate conclusions. That position is in principle quite close to the one adopted by a leading defender of art's autonomy, Aleksey Tolstoy, who argued in a private letter of 1870 that art can effectively demonstrate something only when its primary aim lies elsewhere. "Anything you wish to prove," he said,

> can be successfully proven only when *you abandon the desire to prove something*; . . . a work of art as such bears within itself the best demonstration of all those truths which can never be proven by those who sit down at their desks intending to set them forth in an artistic work.[11]

Tolstoy had written with considerable heat in a letter of some two years before that if he held certain views—if he hated despotism, for instance—then they would quite naturally emerge in any work of art he produced for art's sake: this would happen unavoidably, but it could not be forced intentionally. "It's not my fault," he wrote to his friend Boleslav Markevich at the time, "if it is obvious from something I have written out of love for art that despotism is an evil. So much the worse for despotism."[12] Here the central question was one of ordering. The artist could not take as his first priority the desire to score an intellectual point: he could succeed in that only if he first sought artistic truth. It was paradoxical, but it was so.

From the beginning Annenkov had always felt the intellect rightly understood had its place in art, and by 1863 he had shifted even further in this direction under the pressure of radical argumentation. Both he and Turgenev were reasonable men, and tended to regard art as a very inclusive phenomenon. Altering the notion of intellect slightly to that of "concepts" (*ponyatiya*), Annenkov realized that if intellect

---

[11] Letter to Boleslav Markevich of January 11, 1870: 4:342–43.
[12] Ibid., 4:246.

was important for literature, concepts could be incorporated into fiction only with great care. Thus he criticized Nikolay Pomyalovsky for starting from bare concepts in his short novel *Molotov*. "Concepts," he said, "may be used as the foundation of worthwhile literary works only if they are creatively embodied in images, and not merely personified, as they are with [Pomyalovsky]."[13] From there he went on to maintain that Oblomov and Bazarov were two examples of the successful "embodiment of concepts in images": that was one reason why, in his opinion, the two figures displayed such moral similarities. But it is so difficult to embody concepts in images, we may conjecture Annenkov would have said, that it is preferable for the artist to found his artistic work directly upon images. We might note, incidentally, that Turgenev did not agree with Annenkov's reading of Bazarov as the successful embodiment of concepts. "I have never taken *ideas* as my starting point," he wrote to Polonsky in 1869, "but always images" (6:328).

In this same series of articles of 1863, Annenkov discussed the works of Mikhail Saltykov-Shchedrin, a radical who preached the central significance of thought in literature. In his interpretation of Saltykov, Annenkov regards thought as superior to mere facts in literature:

Facts, no matter how dreadful they may be and no matter how skillfully they may be grouped, are still not everything in the world: more dreadful and more important than they is the thought which engenders those facts; and it is precisely with this human thought that Shchedrin deals with such love and special artistry.[14]

As Annenkov sees it, facts have no objective existence of their own, and therefore one cannot extract "thought" from them; rather it is thought, or the human intellect, which en-

[13] Annenkov, "Russkaia belletristika v 1863 g.": 2:246–47.
[14] Ibid., 2:279.

ables us to recognize facts, and Saltykov deals precisely with these thought processes. Since Saltykov takes his themes from the social and political relations of the world about him, he deals especially with the interrelationship between facts and their interpretation in the human mind.

Annenkov's analysis may well have been too subtle for the practical-minded Saltykov. Indeed he had used Annenkov as something of a whipping boy in a theoretical article of 1856, accusing him of believing that art was a source of knowledge through "contemplation" (*sozertsanie*) rather than "analysis." He also condemned critics like Annenkov for "excluding everything achieved through analysis from the realm of art," and berated the esthetic critics for distinguishing between analysis as the basis of scientific knowledge and contemplation as the foundation of art. Over against them Saltykov argued that mankind had need of both synthetic and analytic thought. "The powers characteristic of the artist's work and the scholar's work are essentially one and the same," he declared, "and artistic thought, in reality, is nothing but general human thought."[15] Saltykov, then, apparently denied that any useful knowledge could be obtained through contemplation, and argued for the identity of artistic and scientific thought. But he made the comparison between the two types of thought in a particular order: by holding that artistic thought was the same as scientific thought, and not vice versa, he asserted the primacy of scientific thought in all human endeavor, including art. At the conclusion of his article Saltykov made an explicit commitment to the centrality of "thought" in art:

> In the first place, we demand of art that it be permeated with thought, and thought which is exclusively contemporary.

[15] Bograd, " 'Literaturnyi manifest,' " 292.

In the second place, the artist must be completely sympathetic to this idea [the thought], for otherwise he will not embrace it completely, he will be unable to express it in living forms accessible to all.[16]

Saltykov would thus have rejected the approach of, say, a Dostoevsky, whose "polyphonic" novels deliberately set certain ideas against their opposites in intellectual conflict. Saltykov preached a very narrow and political definition of thought: not only must it be up-to-date, but an author must be personally committed to the ideas in his work. Saltykov considered ideas too serious to be juggled by authors for their own amusement. In 1864 Pisarev would expand on Saltykov's point, and define "thought" in literature quite openly as political in character: "the chief aim of human thought," he wrote, "is to strive for human prosperity" (3:29). And as the esthetic discussion drew to an end, Nikolay Shelgunov would extend that political definition from thought to thinker in a review of Pisarev's works originally scheduled for publication in 1871. One segment of that unpublished article dealt with the question of intellect, and who may rightfully claim to be intelligent. Shelgunov believed that intelligence should be defined politically, and had nothing to do with the profundity of a person's logical analyses:

> Only a man who thinks along lines leading to the common good may be considered genuinely intelligent. No matter how powerful the logic of backwardness may be, such logic is nevertheless not intelligence. (278)

If thought were to be judged by political criteria, and if works of fiction were to be judged by the thought they contained, then literature, in Shelgunov's eyes, was to be judged on political grounds. But the radical critic masked this truth

---

[16] Ibid., 295–96.

by pretending to discuss the intellectual content of literature. Thus in reviewing *The Precipice* in 1869, Shelgunov began by discussing Belinsky's ideas, for Belinsky had welcomed Goncharov's first novel on grounds much like those on which Shelgunov now condemned his third more than twenty years later. Belinsky had quite correctly recognized that Goncharov at the time had written with an "ideal of pure art" before his eyes, much as he had continued to do in the 1860s; but Belinsky had been wrong in distinguishing "poetic creation from conscious thought" (216). "The measure of a talent is not the power of its poetic creativity," Shelgunov wrote quite straightforwardly, "but rather the power of the thought inspiring it, the power of its progressive social utility" (217). In all the annals of the debates of the 1860s it is difficult to discover a more overtly political definition of literary worth.

Anyone who valued "conscious thought" above all else would naturally admire natural science as the most consistent codification of rational knowledge, and indeed the relationship between science and art—or scientific thought and artistic thought—was an important topic in the esthetic controversy of the 1860s.

The radical critics—who expected science eventually to resolve all the problems of human society—believed that scientific thought was the ideal to which all other varieties of thought should aspire, although they disagreed as to whether it was either possible or desirable for artistic thought to be entirely subsumed under scientific thought. In the *Esthetic Relations* Chernyshevsky wrote that when an artist passes true judgment on the reality he is depicting, he "becomes a thinker, and a work of art, while remaining within the sphere of art, acquires scientific significance" (2:86). In this instance Chernyshevsky may have included the phrase "while remaining within the sphere of art" as merely a temporary concession to the sentiments of his au dience, for very likely he actually thought it desirable for artistic work to approach scientific precision as its goal. This interpretation clarifies a comment which Pisarev threw out in "Pushkin and Belinsky" of 1865. In his articles of those years Pisarev was fond of quoting Griboedov's *Woe from Wit*, surely one of the most poetic works of Russian literature. However, although the work's artistic qualities may have attracted Pisarev at the unconscious level, consciously he admired it primarily as a work of sociology. "In his analysis of Russian life," Pisarev said, "Griboedov reached the furthest extreme beyond which a poet cannot proceed without ceasing to be a poet and being transformed into a scholarly researcher" (3:362). No doubt Pisarev considered this a high compliment, to say that a poet wrote almost as well as a scientist. In an article of 1865 Pisarev had distinguished between himself and Belinsky by saying: "Belinsky's criticism worshipped sacred art. Realist criticism worships sacred science" (3:300). Pisarev drew a very clear line between art and science. Some thought them very closely related, he commented in the same article, but he considered them "hostile to each other," pointing out that many historical figures, recognizing this difference instinctively if not overtly, had suppressed scientific thinking at the same time they encouraged art (3:290). For the time being, Pisarev argued in one of his most famous formulations, the best thing art could do was to popularize the achievements of those on the scientific frontiers among the reading masses (3:129). "A popularizer," he said, "must necessarily be a literary artist, and the highest, most magnificent and most humane obligation of art consists of coalescing with science" (3:131). One may interpret this sentence as temporally divided: for the moment an artist should dedicate himself to publicizing scientific achievements, but in the ideal society of the future art will simply be absorbed into science as the superior form of knowledge.

Maksim Antonovich shared Pisarev's admiration for scientific thought, but he could not go along with Pisarev's total antipathy for art, and so in 1865 he offered a formulation which envisioned the preservation of both realms' autonomy. "The rational, that is scientific enjoyment of the beautiful in nature," he maintained,

> is the highest enjoyment, and consequently the highest calling of art should consist in a reproduction of reality which is artistic in form and scientific in precision.[17]

Pisarev had advocated something similar when he summoned art to popularize science, but for him this was merely a way station on the road to the victory of science over art, while Antonovich created a rather illogical dream of the "rational enjoyment of the beautiful."

The esthetic critics, while not distinguishing absolutely between scientific and artistic knowledge, still stressed the differences between them, and for the most part valued artistic knowledge at least as highly, if not more highly, than scientific knowledge, although there were some who broke ranks. Boris Almazov, for instance, in his article of 1859 on Pushkin's poetry, remarked that the realms of the statesman, scientist, or philosopher should be kept distinct from that of the artist, and added that "science and philosophy are more important for society than the arts, and humanity has greater need of them for its development than it does of the beautiful."[18] Most esthetic critics of that day, however, were fully persuaded that art possessed its own independent value.

In his Pushkin articles of 1856, for example, Mikhail Katkov offered some instructive interpretations of the distinction between scientific thought and poetry, which he defined as "cognitive thought directed toward [the under-

[17] Antonovich, "Sovremennaia esteticheskaia teoriia," 221.
[18] Almazov, "O poezii Pushkina," 155.

standing] of everything not subject to abstract thinking." After having analyzed this distinction, he declared that artistic thought moved "on the borderline between abstract generalization and the living phenomenon," adding that "artistic generalization does not destroy a phenomenon's individuality, but rather elevates it to the typical."[19]

Evgeny Edelson likewise gave some thought to the relationship between art and science. In "On Poetry" (1860) he went so far as to defend fantasy, or poetic imagination, against the claims of scientific cognition (Polonsky noted, much later, that Zaytsev had defined fantasy as "immature thought," which demonstrated once again that the radical critics viewed art purely in terms of its intellectual content).[20] Edelson argued not only that fantasy had a right to exist, but even that it was superior to scientific thought. "Fantasy," he wrote,

> comprehends all the laws based on spatial and temporal relations and subject to direct observation; it forms its picture of reality by taking account of these laws. Science comprehends a relatively small portion of these laws, but it does so consciously: it brings these laws into a rational system, links them together with hypotheses which attempt to explain the totality of phenomena.[21]

Edelson then argued that at any particular point in history artistic knowledge was necessarily more extensive than scientific knowledge could possibly be, though the latter was more precise. From this it followed that the artistic comprehension of reality was in the philosophical sense larger than scientific knowledge, and therefore more valuable to humanity. We should not attempt, of course, to get along without either form of knowledge, for neither logic nor

---

[19] Katkov, "Pushkin" (January 1856), 165–66, 166ff., 168.
[20] Polonskii, "Prozaicheskie tsvety," 737.
[21] Edel'son, "O poezii," 16–17.

imagination alone enables us to comprehend the world
fully. "In essence," Edelson wrote, "all fictions—for example
those of Greek mythology—have had just as much logical
value for their time as they have poetic value."[22] In his final
statement on art, his series of writings on art's significance
for civilization (1867), Edelson reiterated his conviction that
art provides knowledge of a different character than does
science.[23]

Pavel Annenkov, writing in 1856, had argued similarly
that although truth was one, our methods of apprehending
it could be quite various, though of equal worth. "The truth
of nature," he said, "like the truth of life, is expressed in science by *law* and *thought*; those same truths appear in art in
the form of *images* and *feelings*" (2:9). And Nikolay Solovev,
that scientist turned literary critic, maintained in 1864 that
art and science may not legitimately be divorced, for they
are but parts of an identical striving toward the interpretation of reality:

> The artist or the poet capable of perceiving types or char-
> acters or accurately sketching various circles and layers
> of society with all the ideas and interests which agitate
> them performs just as great a service for society as does
> a scientist who makes a discovery. The artist's vocation
> is not to popularize science [as Pisarev had argued], but
> to explain life.[24]

Since the two forms of cognition were so nearly identical,
Solovev felt there should be no hostility between them:
everyone would benefit from both scientific knowledge and
the more intuitive knowledge provided by art. Neither one
should be eliminated in favor of the other.

The preceding discussion shows that most participants

[22] Ibid., 27.
[23] Edel'son, "O znachenii iskusstva" (March 1867), 122.
[24] Solov'ev, "Teoriia bezobraziia," 8.

in the debate of the 1860s were agreed that scientific and artistic cognition differed in nature to some extent. Literally no one advocated the suppression of scientific knowledge, and only a few (including Pisarev) occasionally made statements which could be taken as advocating the elimination of artistic knowledge. Though the radical camp generally considered scientific knowledge superior to artistic cognition, while the esthetic critics thought the two equal, or occasionally artistic knowledge superior to scientific knowledge, the majority in both camps believed there was no basic conflict between the two categories of knowledge, and that they should coexist harmoniously.

The Polemics of Knowledge

When critics spoke of scientific or artistic knowledge they employed terms with no negative connotations in the public mind. But there were other words linked to the notion of cognition which did arouse negative reactions from the public when the esthetic critics threw them into the discussion: these were such terms as "theory," "tendency," and especially "didacticism" in art. Even the radical critics disavowed such terms as these.

The word "theory" in a literary context was associated with bloodless abstractions, preconceived, procrustean doctrines which deliberately distort the artistic depiction of reality. The esthetic critics enthusiastically berated their opponents as devotees of theory, much of it taken from the later Belinsky, who, as Nikolay Akhsharumov put it in 1858, had been "entirely permeated with theories, from his head to the tips of his toes; he was a pedagogue and mentor in the full sense of that word."[25] Their dedication to theory made the radicals' literary criticism—not to mention their

---

[25] Akhsharumov, "O poraboshchenii iskusstva," 322.

creative literature—abstract and cerebral, divorced from life; it also prevented them from pursuing the truth wherever it might lead. Grigorev was particularly sensitive to the damage theory had done to literary criticism. For him the word "theory" and its derivatives always carried exceedingly negative overtones, as he made clear when in 1864 he looked back on his longstanding opposition to "theory with its narrow concept of life and with its despotism prepared to resort to terror."[26] At the time he wrote these words the era of political terror initiated after the Karakozov attempt was still in the future, so Grigorev spoke of intellectual despotism and the intellectual terror it engendered—but perhaps he presciently foresaw the physical terror which was rooted within that intellectual despotism.

Turgenev was at one with the esthetic critics in his aversion to theory in literature, although for some reason he recognized it less readily among radical writers than he did among others. He always tended to condemn excessive theorizing in literature as Slavophilism, because that was the most derisory label he had at his command. He was an especially stern critic of Tolstoy's predilection for sweeping historical generalizations of the sort so prominent in *War and Peace*. Though he recognized Tolstoy's extraordinary artistic talent from the very beginning, he also considered him intellectually hobbled and spiritually enslaved by his theories. "It's terrible," he wrote in private correspondence,

> when a self-taught man, especially of Tolstoy's sort, sets out to philosophize: he will inevitably get on some hobbyhorse, think up some single system which will apparently explain everything quite simply—such as historical fatalism, for example—and then he just writes away! (7:122)

[26] Grigor'ev, "Paradoksy" (May 1864), 256.

On the other hand, some in the radical camp—such as Pisarev—were not at all frightened by the word "theory." In "Realists" (1864) Pisarev scolded his allies quite roundly for running away from the battle: "When their opponents present [the realists] with extreme conclusions," he wrote, "which are the natural and logical result of their own premises, why then our realists are frequently embarrassed, retreat, and look for excuses" (3:13). The realists should be willing to work out the logical consequences of their doctrines, and Pisarev for one was prepared to accept them unhesitatingly. For if, as he firmly believed, his premises were correct, then he should not fear any conclusions which could properly be drawn from them, even though they might be politically inexpedient.

Another term with which the esthetic critics belabored their antagonists was "tendency." Aleksey Tolstoy wrote very vigorously on this subject in 1869 to the publisher Mikhail Stasyulevich:

> God preserve me from any *tendency* in literature, whether old or new. . . . To what *tendency* did Dante, Shakespeare, Goethe, or Homer adhere? The old or the new? One must have a tendency in life, and then it will find expression in literature of itself. (4:324)

But Nikolay Shelgunov, as Pisarev had done before him, was ready to defend even a term like this one in his capacity as consistent radical thinker. The esthetic critics, Shelgunov wrote in 1870, sought to exclude any tendency from literature, and they had their ideological reasons for adopting such a position, "since a tendency is precisely the thread which links the artistic depiction of life to the stream of real life."[27] Shelgunov understood that this case provided an example of the way various labels, some of them negative,

---

[27] Shelgunov, "Dvoedushie," 69.

could be attached to closely related concepts: he proposed to examine the concept rather than the label, and when necessary to accept the label despite its connotational baggage.

The "didactic" tag was the most powerful one the esthetic critics had at their disposal, for it attracted all the uncommitted to their side. Very early on, in 1857, Vasily Botkin had denounced any hint of didacticism in literature. Writers are entirely free, he admitted, to create deliberately didactic works, but such writings "may be called instructive, useful, whatever you like, but not poetic."[28] In his programmatic articles of 1856 Mikhail Katkov also denounced the writer who adopts a theoretical and didactic stance. "If Pushkin had tried to put across any sort of thought in his sketches of old Russian life," he declared, "if he had wanted to try proving anything through them, why then the truth of his depiction would have vanished, we would not have gotten the truth of life."[29] Although Botkin in the article just mentioned had disputed this view, Annenkov had declared in that same year of 1856 that Gogol had succumbed to the lure of didacticism in his writing at the end of his life. "Preaching," Annenkov said, "is the abstract definition of an object, and not its depiction: it works by different means and for a different purpose" (2:22). Druzhinin, as a good Russian nationalist, attributed the decline of artistic literature in his day to the pernicious influence of "neo-German didactics." Druzhinin agreed with Annenkov and others that the late Gogol had been excessively didactic, but thought he would live on in Russian literature nevertheless through the power of his artistry (7:225, 229–34). A few years later, in 1863, Fet sneered at the radical demand for "didacticism" in literature as merely a "bast tail" to be pinned on the donkey of a literary work:

[28] Botkin, "Stikhotvoreniia Feta," 16.
[29] Katkov, "Pushkin" (March 1856), 309.

You can take any microscope you like to examine Homer, Raphael, Beethoven, Goethe, or Pushkin and you won't find any such tail. But we must have that tail, and be able to justify it too. So what are we to do? It's quite simple: down with all authorities [we cry]![30]

The esthetic attack on didacticism in art was so well sustained and focused, then, that the radical critics were compelled to make concessions on the point. Thus in 1865 Maksim Antonovich proclaimed that the radicals decidedly did not require a didactic element in literature. Our theory, he wrote in that year, "demands only that art reproduce reality accurately, and then reality itself will be instructive, its moral will flow quite naturally from these reproductions of reality" (234). In this article Antonovich also needled the esthetic critics by noting that for all their disapproval of didacticism, they were always quite pleased when an artistic work preached the idea that art should *not* instruct the reader or beholder (239).

A key concept in this passage from Antonovich is that of "accuracy" (*vernost*) in the reproduction of reality. All or virtually all the participants in the discussion agreed that art ought to depict reality accurately: on this there was no dissension. But there was little agreement on the meaning of "accuracy," as a brief consideration of the contemporary reception of Aleksey Pisemsky's work over this period will demonstrate. Pisemsky was no theoretician, but rather a cynic who sought to reproduce reality as directly as he could in his short stories, novels, and plays. So long as he turned his jaundiced eye only on established society, as he did in *A Thousand Souls* (1858), the critics were relatively indulgent toward him. But when he took that same attitude toward the younger generation, as he did in *Troubled Seas* (1863), and depicted young people motivated by passions quite as

[30] Afanasii Fet, "Iz derevni," *Russkii vestnik* (January 1863), 443, 445.

unlovely as those which moved the older generation, the
critics berated him from all sides: even Annenkov, Grigorev,
and Edelson criticized the novel severely. When Pisemsky
then went on to offer a panoramic and somewhat idealized
view of the older generation to which he himself belonged
in *Men of the 1840s* (1869), Shelgunov stated the radical objec-
tion to his literary approach very clearly. Shelgunov began
by arguing that a writer must be intellectually superior to
that which he depicts. Thus as long as Pisemsky had written
of the peasant mentality as he had done in the 1850s, he was
"progressive" because his worldview stood above that of the
peasantry; but when he began analyzing the younger generation of the 1860s, as Shelgunov put it quite snobbishly,
"he simply confirmed once again the ancient truth that it is
awkward (*neudobno*) for one to judge from below that
which is going on on a higher level."[31] Philosophically more
interesting than this, however, was Shelgunov's contention
that the source of Pisemsky's deficiencies was an excessive
objectivity. "Influenced by the esthetic critics," Shelgunov
wrote,

> Pisemsky has worked out for himself a very naive view
> of a writer's role and activity. He thought that he needed
> merely *objective* depiction, and so set out to do little
> sketches which were very like reality. (47–48)

Evidently Shelgunov would have rejected a superficial interpretation of Antonovich's claim that if a writer pictured reality "accurately"—and the uninitiated might easily understand this to mean "objectively"—then its significance
would naturally flow from its depiction. Now it develops
that art is not objective but subjective: as Shelgunov wrote
at about this same time, "A literary work and any other work
of art are the result of subjectivism (*subektivnost*)" (244). This

---

[31] Shelgunov, "Liudi sorokovykh i shestidesiatykh godov," 48.

should not be taken to mean, however, that one writer's individually subjective apprehension of reality is as good as any other. There was, rather, only one correct subjective approach to reality, and it was the critic's task both to define and enforce that approach.

Dobrolyubov provided the classic formulation of the openly didactic view of art in his article "A Ray of Light in the Kingdom of Darkness" (1860), in a passage in which he not only presented literature as inferior to science but also unreservedly defended the role of didacticism within it:

> In its essence literature has no active significance: it merely either imagines what it is necessary to do, or else depicts that which is being done or has already been done. In the first instance . . . it derives its foundations and materials from pure science; in the second, from the very facts of life. Thus, generally speaking, literature is an ancillary force whose significance lies in propaganda, and whose worth is determined by what it propagandizes, and how. (6:309)

Critics like Pisarev and Shelgunov could agree wholeheartedly with that statement on the didactic role of literature, for they, too, saw literature primarily as an instrument useful for popularizing the results of contemporary scientific investigation. Other radical critics, like Antonovich, drew back before the implications of their doctrine and agreed with the esthetic critics that art should not be openly didactic. Among the esthetic critics there were those like Aleksey Tolstoy who held that art might be didactic only if it were not intentionally so, and those who maintained that art should not be didactic under any circumstances.

If the connotations of the word "didactic" worked in favor of the esthetic camp, the adjective "useful"—conceptually very close to "didactic" in the context of the 1860s—had resonances which favored the radicals. Only the most intransigent of the esthetic critics argued that art should be useless. Most accepted that requirement, but tried to redefine it to their own purposes, as did Yakov Polonsky when he wrote in 1859 that "every poet, if only he is a poet, is a *teacher of adults*."[32] Here the idea of art's didactic role (the poet as teacher) coalesces with the notion of its usefulness, though on an exalted esthetic plane.

The radical critics were unanimous in their demand that literature be socially useful, as Edelson remarked in his "On the Significance of Art in Civilization" (1867),[33] and so many writers and critics of other persuasions had accepted that demand that, as Pisarev commented in an article of 1864, the problem was now one of understanding what usefulness might mean (3:19). Antonovich took for granted the universal acceptance of the proposition that art should be useful when he wrote in his anti-Pisarevian polemic of 1865 "Pseudorealists":

> Artists and poets should not be driven out of society as useless individuals. No, instead we should demand of them that they become useful, that they serve society and its development with that powerful and active instrument they control. (286)

Antonovich implicitly agreed with Pisarev and Zaytsev that many artists were in fact "useless," but believed they could and should be compelled to become "useful" in the radical sense of the word.

The esthetic critics adopted one of two tacks in responding to radical demands that literature be useful: they could either maintain that art was by its very essence useful, or else they could simply reject those demands altogether in the name of the artist's freedom and artistic independence.

---

[32] [Polonskii], "Stikhotvoreniia Meia," 69.
[33] *Vsemirnyi trud* (February 1867), 311.

The group gathered about Dostoevsky adopted the first course, arguing that art was useful by nature. In her study of Dostoevsky's esthetic views the Soviet scholar N. V. Kashina writes that Dostoevsky agreed with his antagonists that art should have a purpose beyond itself, and even that this purpose should be "service to society"—which meant that in this area the core of the dispute between him and the radical critics became the question of "artistry as a necessary element of art."[34] In his discussion of Dobrolyubov published in 1861, Dostoevsky wrote that he parted company with the radical critic on the question of whether there could even be such a thing as "useless art," for Dostoevsky felt there could be no such art, except perhaps as a rare exception: "This is precisely the hallmark of true art, that it is always contemporary and useful for our daily needs (*nasushchno-polezno*)" (18:101). Thus Dostoevsky simply defined "useless art" as not even falling within the sphere of art, which was one way of solving the problem.

As a member of the Dostoevsky group, Nikolay Solovev in 1864 made his contribution to this discussion by pointing out that readers for some two years already had been arguing heatedly over a novel, *Fathers and Sons*: and who could maintain that such an argument was not socially useful?[35] Apollon Grigorev, on the other hand, came up with a more subtle and intermediate answer to the question of art's usefulness. In 1859 he had gone so far as to speak of art's theoretical "uselessness." "Genuine art," he wrote at that point, "does not act directly on that which it apparently chastises. Its lofty *uselessness* consists precisely in this."[36] One must interpret that formulation, however, in the light of Grigorev's general critical theory, for in 1856 he had said that "genuine

[34] Kashina, *Estetika Dostoevskogo*, 219.
[35] Nikolai Solov'ev, "Teoriia pol'zy i vygody," *Epokha* (November 1864), 5.
[36] Grigor'ev, "Neskol'ko slov," 238.

artists think of art as a higher service for the benefit of the human soul, for the benefit of the life of society."[37] Grigorev never believed in solipsistic art, art produced solely for the purpose of satisfying the artist's personal needs. Art had a social function, and should benefit society as a whole. At the same time art did not benefit society directly, as the law might, let us say: instead it acted indirectly, on the spiritual and intellectual level, working through the mysterious process of a society's organic being, in ways which the critic could not even detect. Grigorev rejected the demand that art exert a direct political influence on society, and in that sense only held that art was necessarily useless. Grigorev's view was close to Dostoevsky's idea that art was useful by its very nature, and also resembled a formulation of Katkov's advanced in his Pushkin articles of 1856:

> Do you want the artist to be useful? Then let him be an artist. . . . When his work is done, when it appears in the world, it will inevitably exert influence on all aspects of human consciousness and life.[38]

Of course, that "influence" of which Katkov spoke was too rarified for most of the radical critics, who wished artists to be straightforwardly didactic. The esthetic critics believed that art influenced a people's spiritual life, which then in turn determined its political life; whereas the radical critics either did not distinguish between these two things, or else defined its spiritual life and its political life as equivalents.

There was, however, a grouping of the esthetic critics which grasped the nettle and simply rejected the radical demand that art be useful, much as some of the radical critics accepted the esthetic complaints about didacticism in literature. In 1858 Nikolay Akhsharumov commented that "we

---

[37] Grigor'ev, "O pravde i iskrennosti," 136.
[38] Katkov, "Pushkin" (February 1856), 311.

are all *realists* [evidently this word had already circulated in ordinary conversation before Pisarev took it up for his own purposes]—a word through which our generation has defined its character quite accurately." That realistic trend in contemporary culture, he went on, denigrated the notion of "free art," seeking instead to "enslave art in the service of various objectives, purposes, and requirements of social usefulness." However, as the critic saw it, art and poetry were in their essence incapable of being enslaved to such ends. Practical individuals of that day considered poets quite "superfluous men," and with good reason: "Works of handicraft give us something necessary and needful," Akhsharumov wrote, "whereas works of free art do not do this at all, but rather provide something which is entirely superfluous in all respects."[39] And yet this did not mean society did not need art: art's value lay precisely in its freedom, in its ability to liberate man from the "stringent laws of need."[40] And if this were the essence of art, then it could not possibly accede to demands that it be directly socially useful.

Konstantin Leontev advanced similar ideas through his character Milkeev in *In One's Own Land* (1864). At one point Milkeev argues that esthetic values are superior even to the necessity of feeding, clothing, and healing ordinary people. "What is our mere physiological existence anyway?" he asks. "It's not worth a farthing! A single magnificent century-old tree is worth more than a score of faceless people, and I would never cut one down to buy peasants medicine for cholera!"[41] Ours is a practical age, Botkin had written in 1857,[42] and people like Akhsharumov and Leontev were setting their faces against a powerful intellectual current in

[39] Akhsharumov, "O poraboshchenii iskusstva," 289, 294, 300.
[40] Ibid., 299.
[41] Konstantin Leont'ev, *V svoem kraiu, Otechestvennye zapiski* (May 1864), 36.
[42] Botkin, "Stikhotvoreniia Feta," 2.

their outright rejection of social utility in art. Most of their
esthetic colleagues at least pretended to accept the idea, although they sometimes defined "usefulness" out of existence: they agreed that art did not exist in a vacuum, and
that since it was a product of human endeavor it bore certain
social obligations. But while Dostoevsky, Grigorev, and
others argued that art was socially useful by its nature, the
radical critics thought otherwise. Some, like Antonovich,
held that art could be made socially useful, while others believed either that it could not be so transformed, or else that
it could theoretically but that such a result was not worth
the necessary investment of time and energy, and thus it was
preferable to work for art's eventual abolition.

The radical critics had another phrase which they employed to good effect against the esthetic thinkers: "art for
art's sake." That set of words expressed the idea that art
should exist in an autonomous realm of its own, taking no
account of social needs. French poets such as Charles
Baudelaire and Théophile Gautier were quite prepared to
accept the doctrine that art should have no social utility, but
the Russians on the whole could not stomach such a radical
division between art and the useful. Thus most of the esthetic critics retreated in disarray when confronted with this
concept, while the radical critics were united in their contempt for "art for art's sake" just as they all supported the
notion of "utility" in art.

There were, to be sure, some among the esthetic critics
who defended the phrase "art for art's sake" and the concept
behind it. Aleksey Tolstoy, in one of his few published critical statements (1862), though maintaining that the artistic
and the social impulses should be allies rather than enemies,
spoke of himself as one dedicated to "art for art's sake," and
therefore a person who could not appeal to a wide audi-

ence.[43] In 1861 he had written a personal letter to the poetess Karolina Pavlova in which he bared his soul:

> Only with you, my dear lady, can I immerse myself in art up to my ears, if I may put it so. Goethe's "Ich singe wie der Vogel singt" might as well be Greek for some of our writers, who always want *to put over some idea* and prove something they have thought up beforehand, which gives them a more or less didactic character, may God chastise them![44]

Even so convinced a defender of artistic autonomy as Aleksey Tolstoy voiced his opinions only in private correspondence, and not all those who did defend "art for art's sake" publicly did so skillfully, as Nikolay Solovev was fond of pointing out. A good example of this may be found in a passage from Pisemsky's *Troubled Seas* in which two of his characters arrive at Dresden's Grünes Gewölbe to view the paintings of the great masters, and especially Raphael's Madonna, something of an artistic Holy Grail for the esthetically oriented generation of the 1840s. After gazing at the Madonna in rapture, Baklanov says to his companion:

> "This is no picture! . . . The heavens have simply opened up and a vision has descended! . . ."
> . . .Both of them made their way out of the gallery without speaking, under the sway of some sort of special impressions. (4:486–87)

Such descriptions or statements as these were nothing more than bare assertions of art's importance in human life, not cogent arguments on behalf of "art for art's sake." Although even assertions like Pisemsky's had a certain value, he left it

to others to mount a coherent defense of the position behind the phrase "art for art's sake."

The Soviet specialist on the literary battles of the 1850s
Boris Egorov has called Druzhinin's *Biblioteka dlya chteniya*
the "citadel of 'art for art's sake' " at that historical moment,
the platform from which Druzhinin preached what Egorov
calls an "antihistorical norm" for art.[45] Although he uses this
term, Egorov does not object to the notion of a norm or
normativeness in art generally, for the radical critics certainly applied definite norms to the literature they discussed.
Rather he objects to Druzhinin's conception of a literary
norm existing outside of history, a classical norm applicable
to all literatures of all peoples at all times, one which does
not depend upon particular historical circumstances. However, Egorov associates the concept of "antihistorical normativeness" not with Neoclassicism, as we might have
expected, but with Romanticism: "Antihistorical normativeness," he writes, "logically leads to the Romantic pathos
of that which one wished to be and which ought to be,
rather than the study of what has been and what presently
exists."[46] Though this definition requires considerable mod-
ification to be acceptable, it does point to a major issue of
the relationship between literature and the ideal which we
shall discuss in a subsequent chapter.

At any rate, Druzhinin's article "Criticism of the Gogol
Period in Russian Literature and Our Attitude to It," published in *Biblioteka dlya chteniya* in 1856, contains the classic
definition of "art for art's sake" in the entire debate of 1855–
70. It occurs in the midst of a discussion of what Druzhinin
calls the didactic theory and the artistic theory of art, and
deserves citation in full:

[45] B. F. Egorov, *Ocherki po istorii russkoi literaturnoi kritiki serediny XIX veka*
(Leningrad, 1973), 82, 83.
[46] Ibid., 92.

The *artistic* theory, which proclaims to us that art serves and should serve as its own purpose, is founded upon conceptions which are quite incontrovertible, in our opinion. The poet guided by this theory—like the poet of whom Pushkin sings—considers himself to have been created not for the difficulties of life, but for prayers, sweet sounds, and inspiration. In the firm belief that the interests of the moment are but passing, that humanity, though constantly changing, remains faithful to its ideas of eternal beauty, good, and truth alone, he finds his eternal anchor in the selfless service of these ideas. His song contains within it no predefined practical morality, no other conclusions which could be applied to the benefit of his contemporaries, for it serves as its own reward, purpose, and significance. He depicts people as he sees them, without recommending any reforms; he gives no instructions to society, or, if he does, he does so unconsciously. He lives in his exalted world and descends to earth, just as the Olympians once descended, keeping firmly in mind the fact that he has his home on lofty Olympus. Here we intentionally depict a poet dedicated to the extreme artistic theory of art, in the way the opponents of this theory are accustomed to depicting him. (7:214)

One puzzling element in this passage is the fact that at the beginning Druzhinin declares the conceptions he here sets forth to be "incontrovertible," but then at the conclusion remarks that he has cast them in an extreme form, in the way their very opponents would have done. Perhaps the explanation is that Druzhinin wished to defend his position in its most vulnerable form: anything less fragile would be that much easier for others to support. Druzhinin leans upon Pushkin's authority to define the poet as independent of the crowd, asserts that art is eternal and immutable in human society, and maintains that the artist should not instruct his audience directly. He must seek the eternal and the ideal in the world of the contingent and the temporary.

In this passage, if he did not carry the day for the artistic theory of art, Druzhinin at least framed the issue in such a manner as to inflict severe damage on the notion of didacticism in art, for, as we have seen, the radical critics fled from the accusation that they favored didacticism in art, and the esthetic critics repeated and refined Druzhinin's arguments in the years to follow. For example, in 1866 Efim Zarin mounted another detailed defense of "art for art's sake" in his essay, "Proudhon on Art." By the time he wrote, Zarin admitted, everyone professed to oppose "art for art's sake": Nikolay Kurochkin had struck a blow against it in his brief introduction to the translation of Proudhon's book under review, while Pisarev had assaulted it consistently, over a long period of time, and with "lofty fanaticism." Zarin maintained that in fact the phrase "art for art's sake" encapsulated an "entire doctrine of art" which not only had never been refuted but never would be. It expressed the idea that "there is a need for [esthetic] development in our nature" which can never be satisfied by anything but art. Just as our consciences move us to seek "good for the good's sake," and as scientists pursue truth for its own sake and not because they hope to attain certain social objectives, so the artist, Zarin argued, should dedicate himself to art regardless of its social utility. Such a viewpoint was very concisely summed up in the phrase "art for art's sake."[47]

A year later Evgeny Edelson offered his version of the position which Druzhinin and Zarin had articulated before him. We may be quite certain, he said, that Shakespeare embodied his ideas in dramatic form solely for esthetic reasons, and not because he hoped his writings might redound to the benefit of society:

[47] Incognito [E. Zarin], "Prudon ob iskusstve," 361–66.

No, the very living achievement of the ideal, i.e. the unified and artistic representation of the subject down to its finest living details, a clear contemplation of them at once in their entirety, is in itself such a difficult task, one which absorbs all a man's energies, that at that moment it positively excludes any secondary aims and considerations. This is the sense in which one should understand the famous expression *art for art's sake*.[48]

The artist's task, Edelson held, is so demanding that it requires all his energies, and thus he must ignore all other considerations, including political ones. Although Edelson shifted the emphasis slightly from the artist's subjective conception of his role to the objective requirements of his work, Edelson's central point remains the same as Druzhinin's or Zarin's.

Even though some esthetic critics thus looked at the concept behind the phrase "art for art's sake" and worked out thoughtful definitions which built upon that concept, others were so affected by the term's negative connotations as to reject it almost unthinkingly. As early as 1855 Stepan Dudyshkin not only detested the term, but even berated Annenkov for defending it: Dudyshkin thought it a "destructive theory," and could not imagine that anyone would ever take an interest in problems of artistic form alone, which is how he apparently understood the doctrine.[49] Mikhail Katkov likewise declared his strenuous opposition to the idea if adhering to it meant the artist should worry only about "elegance of execution" in his work, or if it implied that art should have no purpose beyond itself, for Katkov believed the artist should deliberately seek to mold the "consciousness" of society through his art.[50] In like manner, Grigorev

[48] Edel'son, "O znachenii iskusstva" (March 1867), 103, 105.
[49] Egorov, "S. S. Dudyshkin–kritik," 210.
[50] Katkov, "Pushkin" (February 1856), 315.

in 1861 curtly dismissed the phrase "art for art's sake" as a "pointless playing with words, sounds, or colors."[51]

Even Ivan Goncharov, long after the controversy of the 1860s had subsided, declared in an explanatory article on *The Precipice* first published in 1879 that it was silly even to speak of "art for art's sake" since a "living, that is, a truthful image, always speaks to us of life, and it does not matter what sort of life" (8:110). At first glance this comment of Goncharov's might seem puzzling, for his hero Raysky was a devotee of pure art. However, Goncharov was not entirely sympathetic to his hero: both in his contemporary correspondence and in his subsequent commentaries on the novel Goncharov consistently claimed that Raysky was but an updated variant of the slothful Oblomov. In the late summer of 1866, for example, he told a correspondent that "the entire novel is not written for the purpose of mocking Raysky, but in order to present him in all his monstrosity." Goncharov had not sympathized with his hero, as his correspondent believed, but rather had taken an attitude "not of approval but of irony" toward him: Raysky represented, he said, a "sort of artistic Oblomovism." He had originally conceived of both Oblomov and Raysky as idealists who sink into apathy after entering into irresolvable conflict with the unfeeling outside world.[52] Perhaps there is a parallel between the way Goncharov viewed his artist-hero Raysky and Turgenev's attitude toward Gagin, a character in his "Asya" of 1858, who has considerable artistic talent but lacks self-discipline or any sense of social responsibility. It was a waste of resources for such people to work in the field of art, for their artistic labors would never benefit society as a whole. Turgenev and Goncharov did not place the same value as some of their colleagues on the intrinsic worth of esthetic pursuits. Vasily

[51] Grigor'ev, "Iskusstvo i nravstvennost'," 407.
[52] Letter to S. A. Nikitenko of August 21/September 2, 1866: 8: 365–66.

Botkin was one of them: he emphasized the personal satisfaction which the artist derives from his work in his discussion of Fet dating from 1857. "Such an outpouring of the
soul," he wrote,

> whether it is involuntary, or whether it has but one pur-
> pose—to express one's feeling, viewpoint, thought, in
> some form or other—in music, painting, sculpture, in
> words—and not for some didactic or social purpose, or,
> in a word, for any mundane reason, but rather simply
> for the sake of those feelings, views, and thoughts which
> fill the artist's soul to overflowing—this has served as the
> basis for an esthetic theory under the quite confusing
> name of "art for art's sake."[53]

This formulation, however, helps us to see why the radical
and esthetic camps parted company so fundamentally on the
question of "art for art's sake." The esthetic critics emphasized first of all the artist as individual creator, and their theory stressed the production of art, while the radical critics
were concerned primarily with the consumption of works of
art by a public conceived of collectively. Since the doctrine
of "art for art's sake" revolved about the artist, it had little
appeal for the radicals, for whom the audience was of primary importance.

The radical thinkers likewise took little interest in artistry (*khudozhestvennost*) as an element of art, whereas critics
like Annenkov as early as 1856 were calling for an effort to
promote "pure artistry in art" (2:12), and later Dostoevsky
would turn the radicals' weapons against them by arguing
that artistry is precisely the element of art capable of accom-
plishing the things the radicals wished to see done (18:93).
The most intriguing discussion between the two camps in
this area, however, was over the issue of whether an artist

[53] Botkin, "Stikhotvoreniia Feta," 10–11.

had to be born, or could be made. The esthetic critics, and perhaps a few of the radical critics as well, thought an artist could only be born. As Konstantin Leontev put it through one of his characters from *In One's Own Land*, "it is quite as impossible to *make* a woman with a pleasing personality as it is to *make* a highly intelligent and educated man a writer of the sort Pushkin was. All this is inborn."[54] Pisarev, on the other hand, vigorously expounded the notion that an artist could be made, and quite easily at that. "One may *become* a poet," he wrote in "Pushkin and Belinsky" (1865),

> precisely just as one may become a lawyer, a professor, a journalist, a cobbler, or a watch repairer. A poet or generally speaking a writer, or, even more generally, an artist overall, is just the same sort of craftsman as all other craftsmen who satisfy by their labor the various natural or artificial needs of society. (3:373)

If in fact the intellect was central to a work of art and to the artist who creates it, then it should theoretically not be difficult for a person of normal intelligence to become an artist if he wished.

Perhaps it is but a quirk of etymology that the Russian word for "artistry" is *khudozhestvennost*, while the analogous derivative from the word for "art," *iskusstvo*, means "artificiality" (*iskusstvennost*). But the enemies of art were quick to seize upon that quirk for their own purposes. In the passage cited above Pisarev speaks of the "artificial needs of society," which he implicitly contrasts with its natural needs: clearly, in his eyes art was just as unnatural as artificiality. Chernyshevsky had made that connection explicit when he wrote in the *Esthetic Relations* that "art panders to our artificial tastes" (2:72). Similarly Dobrolyubov wrote in 1860 that some literary figures produced works which promoted the "natural aspirations" of society, while other works reinforced its "ar-

[54] Leont'ev, *V svoem kraiu, Otechestvennye zapiski* (August 1864), 49.

tificial aspirations": though writers of works in the second category might be entirely sincere, they were socially harmful (6:311). Thus the radical critics regularly sought to link art with artificiality in the public mind.

We see, then, that by and large the radical critics advocated the primacy of the rational intellect in art, and especially in literature. They believed that literature should be socially useful, and thought it could achieve such usefulness by conducting a species of argumentation using artistic images. The esthetic critics denied the centrality of the intellect in art, emphasized the artist's need for talent, and held that art should influence society only indirectly. Each camp had certain loaded terms which it could employ to its benefit: the radicals made good use of "art for art's sake" and "usefulness," while the esthetic critics pinned such tags as "nihilist" and "didactic" on their opponents. Though critics and journalists might have sought to resolve some of the contradictions between these two approaches on occasion, the only serious and ongoing attempt to elaborate a synthesis between the opposing viewpoints was made by Apollon Grigorev and the group about Dostoevsky's journals *Vremya* and *Epokha*. At this stage it might be profitable to look at the doctrines of "organic criticism" in more detail.

Organic Criticism and the Creative Process

Apollon Grigorev was a devotee of Schellingian philosophy, with its Romantic theory of organicism, who systematically applied that theory to Russian literary criticism. Central to this theory, of course, was the notion of an organism. In an obituary for Grigorev published in *Epokha*, his disciple Dmitry Averkiev offered the following definition:

> What is an organism? It is something complete, indivisible, finished in itself; a monad which develops according to its own laws peculiar to itself. An organism is not

shaped by outside influences, but rather develops of itself from within; external circumstances do not alter it
mechanically, but rather it adjusts itself to them; it strug-
gles against them, it strives to disclose its own laws.[55]

The major implied contrast here is that between a living organism, a coherent unit which develops according to its
own internal, largely unknowable laws, and a more or less
chance agglomeration of physical attributes subject to physical laws which may be expressed in mathematical terms.
The organic incorporates the mechanical because it is much
greater than the mechanical. In like manner the organic subsumes the intellect, but is not limited by it. That is the core
of the definition which Grigorev himself formulated when
analyzing his critical method in one of his final articles:

> Therein lies the most essential difference between the
> view which I call organic and the one-sidedly historical
> viewpoint: the former, i.e., the organic view, takes as its
> starting point creative, unmediated, inborn, vital forces;
> or, in other words: not the intellect alone with its logical
> demands and the theories necessarily generated by these
> demands, but rather intellect and its logical demands *plus*
> life and its organic manifestations.[56]

Theory, Grigorev went on, is the form logic must take, but
it is inevitably stillborn since it always derives from life
which has already receded into the past. From this one
might deduce that only an organic understanding of literature enables the artist to deal with the future as well as the
present and the past.

At the beginning of the article in question, "Paradoxes
of Organic Criticism" (1864), Grigorev declared that art was
simultaneously an "organic product of life" and its "organic

---

[55] Dmitrii Averkiev, "Apollon Aleksandrovich Grigor'ev," *Epokha* (September
1864), 3.
[56] Grigor'ev, "Paradoksy" (May 1864), 266.

expression."[57] He was hostile, he said, to all that derives solely from "nakedly logical thought."[58] Just as life was an organic phenomenon only partially subject to the laws of reason, so was art, for as life's representation it partook of its organic nature. Grigorev considered the radical thinkers wrong in seeking to found life upon rationality, for rationality was but a part of life, and by no means its whole. In like manner, the radical critics conceived of history as a linear process: that which came later in time was necessarily historically superior to everything that had gone before. But Grigorev, taking his cue from the organic world, developed a cyclical view of the history of ideas, a view from which sprang certain phrases and notions of organic criticism which his contemporaries found difficult to comprehend.[59]

One such phrase was "antediluvian talent," or "talent of antediluvian formation." If, as Grigorev believed, thought itself is an organic phenomenon and not a mechanical one, he wrote, "then it does not immediately adopt the forms which are totally suitable to it, totally well formed, totally harmonious." Viewed from the stage of its organic perfection, thought is malformed in its early development, and Grigorev applied the adjective "antediluvian" to these imperfect forms of thought.[60] This view of literature based on geology and marine development came through again, incidentally, in his final essay on organic criticism, when he spoke of how "this boiling ocean of life leaves behind the gradual sedimentation of its fermentation in the past," sedimentation which we may study in order to learn more about life.[61]

Other terms in Grigorev's peculiar critical vocabulary

[57] Ibid., 255.
[58] Ibid., 255–56.
[59] Grigor'ev, "Neskol'ko slov," 206.
[60] Ibid., 204.
[61] Grigor'ev, "Paradoksy" (May 1864), 260.

derived from biology rather than geology. One was the phrase "vegetal poetry" (*rastitelnaya poeziya*), which, Grigorev explained, referred to "folk creation, impersonal and artless, in contrast to art, personal creation."[62] Folk poetry sprang from a social collective without bearing the imprint of any single creative personality: it was an organic form of art which developed according to its own mysterious laws. Still another famous word of Grigorev's was *veyanie*, perhaps best translated as 'trend,' a spiritual development only intuitively sensed, which Grigorev preferred to the word *vliyanie*, 'influence,' because the former "expressed more precisely my conviction as to the existence of forces which I share with the poet Tyutchev, and with the teacher he and I share (quite flatteringly for me), Schelling."[63] One may conjecture that in Grigorev's mind the word "influence" denoted an excessively direct, rational impact of one person or society on another, whereas a trend may ordinarily be grasped only intuitively.

In line with his theories, Grigorev was much taken by a book of 1854 entitled *The Pilgrimages and Wanderings of the Monk Parfeny* because he thought it demonstrated the organic wholeness of the development of Russian life from the twelfth century down to the nineteenth; he saw the work as "not made, but vegetal, like a legend, a hymn, or a song."[64] It confirmed his view of a nation as an organic whole which returns repeatedly to its origins.

The radical critics had little use for a cyclical conception of history. Dobrolyubov regarded history as a process through which mankind liberated itself from one delusion after another until finally it arrived at a state of relative social perfection (6:313). And Dmitry Pisarev not only believed in

---

[62] Grigor'ev, "Neskol'ko slov," 207.
[63] Ibid., 219.
[64] Ibid., 271–72.

the linear development of history, he also denied that a national culture displayed any organic connections within that linear development. In "Pushkin and Belinsky" (1865) he berated Belinsky for accepting the Hegelian notion of the organic development of society and literature, then wrote a powerful passage deriding the very idea of organic development in the history of Russian literature in particular. Using his favorite literary work, *Woe from Wit*, as the example which proved his point, he wrote:

> *Woe from Wit* stands completely alone. It is not linked either with that which preceded it, or with that which existed along with it, or with what came after it. Before it there was Ozerov, after it there was Kukolnik; in its time there glittered the trifles in verse by Zhukovsky and Pushkin. Thus Griboedov turns out to be Ozerov's successor, Kukolnik's predecessor, and the associate of the Romantic Zhukovsky. What magnificent organic development! How much Griboedov took from Ozerov and how much he transmitted to Kukolnik! And how easy it is to guess that Griboedov and Zhukovsky were contemporaries! (3:378)

Pisarev thought, then, of history, and especially literary history, as completely devoid of logical development and causal connections. Of course in this instance he overstated his case for polemical reasons, for if he truly believed that history was entirely disjointed he could not maintain that it exhibited any linear development which was at all meaningful, not to speak of progress, which requires that the later build upon the earlier.

Those who debate the relationship between intellect and art must also grapple with the vexing question of the creative process. If art is rational, then the act of creating a work of art must be rational as well. The artist simply applies his reason to the material before him, and the work of a novelist is essentially the same as that of a scholar who arrives at an appropriate arrangement of the data reality provides. If, however, art is not the product of rational processes, then the work of an artist is quite different from that of a scholar or scientist, and in fact may not lend itself to rational analysis at all. Thus it will be instructive to examine the ways in which the participants in the discussion of 1855–70 regarded the creative process.

A poet like the Schellingian Aleksey Tolstoy was at one end of the spectrum on this issue. Tolstoy maintained that the artist had a relatively passive role in artistic creation: he simply transmitted, say, preexisting harmonies and words to which he was very much more sensitive than the average person. Tolstoy gave voice to these views, not in critical articles, but in some of his poetic works, including especially the untitled poem beginning "You are wrong, o artist, to think you create your creations!" of October 1856 (1:128–29). In this poem Tolstoy argues that such artists as Phidias, Goethe, and Beethoven simply brought into our mundane world artistic wholes which had already existed from all eternity:

> In space there are many invisible forms and unheard sounds,
> In it there are many wondrous combinations of words and
>   light,
> But they can be transmitted only by one capable of both
>   seeing and hearing,
> Who, grasping but a line of the picture, but a chord, but a
>   word,
> Can then draw the entire creation with it into our
>   astonished world.

A genuine Romantic, Tolstoy perceives the artist as one straining to catch the outlines of a work of art, then transmitting it to the best of his ability to this earthly world. As Tolstoy puts it,

No, it was not Goethe who created the great Faust; he,
In ancient German attire, but in profound and universal
    truth,
Is word for word identical with his preexistent image.

There is, of course, virtually no place for reason in a creative process so conceived. The artist is blessed with a sensitivity to harmonies and entire works which exist independently of his will, and the finest artists are those who succeed most perfectly in capturing that which exists quite independently of them.

The French scholar André Lirondelle, who some seventy-five years ago published the most detailed study of Aleksey Tolstoy in any language, remarked of this poem—much as Antonovich, who pointed up the esthetic critics' preachments against didacticism, might have—that in writing it "the poet had not been favored with divine sounds: unconscious activity had yielded to conscious activity."[65] Perhaps that is one of the paradoxes of the "esthetic" position with which we must live.

In 1856 Apollon Grigorev bolstered his case for organic criticism by proclaiming that he believed, "along with Schelling, that the unconscious nature [of the creative process] bestows upon works of art their unfathomable profundity."[66] No critic could attempt a rational analysis of the unconscious laws of creation operating through the artist's spirit. For the impulse to literary creation, Grigorev thought, was internal to the writer. There were times, he believed, when "images fill the author's soul" and simply demand expression through the prism of his personality: "for," Grigorev added, "we do not understand how images can exist without any relation to the artist and independently of

---

[65] André Lirondelle, *Le poète Alexis Tolstoï: L'homme et l'œuvre* (Paris, 1912), 491.
[66] Grigor'ev, "O pravde i iskrennosti," 197.

him." To be sure, images when they emerge from the artist's soul may be refined to a greater or a lesser degree:

> The images seek to emerge in their coarse and primary forms—and manage in any case to appear in living flesh, although insufficiently polished—or, after maturing within the artist's soul, cleansed in his internal furnace, they are elevated to pearls of creation, to types which are completed and perfect in their own way.

The critic went on to say that

> images, as visible expressions of the artist's inner world, come forth either as reflections of their creator's life, with the imprint of the character of his personality, or as reflections of pure reality, with the imprint of the viewpoint of the creating personality.[67]

In the first of these quotations Grigorev distinguishes between greater and lesser artists: though the creative process is in principle the same for both, the greater artist unconsciously accomplishes the more difficult task of perfecting his images into wholly persuasive types. In the second passage Grigorev speaks on the one hand of art drawn primarily from the artist's personal experience (probably here he has lyric poetry in mind) and, on the other, of art depicting the life of society, although even then the work of art inescapably exhibits the "imprint" of the artist's individual personality. That "imprint," however, is the result of unconscious effort rather than conscious work.

Dostoevsky's idea of the creative process as he himself had experienced it coincided very nearly with Grigorev's. Dostoevsky would start from an artistic idea, which he carefully distinguished from an intellectual idea. Thereafter the idea would be embodied within his imagination, an occur-

---

[67] Grigor'ev, "Obozrenie," 185.

rence which always took place "suddenly and unexpectedly," and therefore unconsciously. "Then" Dostoevsky wrote, "once you have received the complete image in your heart, you can set about the artistic execution of the work."[68] Thus the major components of the creative process as usually imagined at that time are present in Dostoevsky's description. Dostoevsky begins from an idea (the word recurs frequently in his correspondence, whenever he starts work on a new novel or short story); the idea is embodied in an image in inexplicable fashion; then, when all is ready "within the heart," the author undertakes the actual writing. But by that time the most essential part of the creative process has occurred within the artist's unconscious soul.

We might expect such an understanding of the creative process from a Dostoevsky or a Grigorev, but it is rather more astonishing to discover that Dobrolyubov saw it in much the same way. To be sure he paid more attention to the rational aspects of creation than did the esthetic critics, but even he stressed the centrality of the unconscious in literary creation:

> An artist is not a photographic plate which reflects only the present moment: if he were, there would be neither sense nor life in artistic works. The artist fills out the fragmentariness of the moment he has captured through his creative feeling, generalizes particular phenomena in his soul, creates a harmonious whole from scattered parts, discovers the vital link and consistency in phenomena which seem disconnected on the surface, brings together the varied and contradictory aspects of living reality and reworks them in the unity of his view of the world. Therefore, as he perfects his creation the genuine artist retains it within his soul whole and complete, with its beginning and its ending, with its concealed main-

---

[68] Letter to Apollon Maikov of December 31, 1867/January 12, 1868: 28/2:239.

springs and secret consequences which often are not susceptible of logical analysis but which reveal themselves
to the artist's inspired glance. (7:233–34)

One may add simply that Dobrolyubov thought it the literary critic's task to undertake a logical analysis of that which
the artist presented to the public for its consideration. He
was no organic critic, who believed that the laws underlying
the depiction of reality in art would always be unfathomable. But he did emphasize the unconscious aspects of artistic creation in this fairly lengthy passage.

Dobrolyubov acknowledged Goncharov's mastery in
the vivid depiction of reality, and one of the more interesting descriptions of the creative process by a practicing artist
is that found in Goncharov's commentary on *The Precipice*,
"Better Late Than Never" (1879). Here Goncharov argued
that the creative process might be either conscious or unconscious, and that within it the intellect might overbalance
the imagination, or the converse. In the first instance, Goncharov wrote, the artist's "mind may be subtle and obser-
vant, and overbalance his fantasy and heart: then the idea
may turn out more central to a work than images and the
work become tendentious." As we might expect, Goncharov
found that objectionable. "On the other hand," he continued,

> if the artist has a great deal of imagination and less intel-
> lect by comparison with his talent, the image swallows
> up its own significance, the idea; the portrayal speaks for
> itself, and the artist may himself comprehend its mean-
> ing only with the aid of a subtle critical interpreter like
> Belinsky or Dobrolyubov, for example. (8:69–70)

Since Goncharov had been accused, sometimes quite vio-
lently, of seeking to propound his own ideas in *The Precipice*,
and especially of concocting unbelievable characters like
Mark Volokhov, who allegedly hardly existed in reality,

Goncharov declared that he had contrived nothing at all. Quite the contrary: "Life itself as I had experienced it and watched others experience it flowed from my pen" (8:97). Goncharov merely observed life as it was. Under no circumstances would he approach his work with the intention of preaching to his readers, to the detriment of realism.

"Better Late Than Never" also contains a remarkable description of the manner in which Goncharov actually wrote, at least some of the time. In Goncharov's case literary creation was not only an unconscious process: it displayed hallucinatory qualities which verged on the abnormal, and which perhaps may be linked with his mental instability of later years. "When I am writing I rarely know at that moment what my image, portrait or character means," he said.

> I only see it as if alive before me, and I merely look to see whether I am depicting things accurately, or whether it is combined in action with others—consequently, I see scenes and depict these other characters who are sometimes very much yet to come in the plan of the novel, without being able to tell entirely how these portions of the whole still scattered in my head will be brought together. So as not to forget them, I hasten to set down scenes and characters on bits and pieces of paper. . . . I always have one image and a major theme in mind: this is what enables me to move forward, and on the way I grasp desperately at whatever presents itself and has a direct relationship to it. Then I work vigorously and joyfully, and my hand can scarcely keep up until I again run into a blank wall. In the meantime the work continues in my head, my characters give me no peace, they intrude upon me, pose in various scenes, I overhear fragments of their conversations—and it would often seem to me, may the Lord forgive me, that I was not creating all this but it was floating in the air about me and all I had to do was watch and interpret it. (8:70–71)

It is surely unusual even for a writer with a powerful imagination to see such scenes in the air as Goncharov did, but
this description points to a deeply vivid creative process.
Goncharov could direct it to a degree, by settling upon a
chief image and a major motif which in turn would give rise
to other characters and motifs which grouped themselves
about them in his mind's eye. The author, however, could
neither follow nor understand this process.

Turgenev lacked Goncharov's imagination, but the two
writers' experience of artistic creation was similar. In Turgenev's view the creator is to his creation much as a father is
to his son—he commented once that even quite intelligent
observers who do not also happen to be writers "are absolutely unable to understand that an artist often cannot control his own child" (5:20–21). The son is genetically linked
to his father and could not have come into existence without
him, but he is a separate being who lives an individual life
which his father can influence only partially. In much the
same way a fictional character, although obviously the off-
spring of its creator, still develops according to its own impenetrable laws. Turgenev occasionally spoke of literary creation in terms of sexual procreation, as when in a private
letter he referred slightingly to a group of radical authors as
"*infertile types (bessemyanniki)* incapable of *sowing* anything."[69] On another occasion, when responding to Afanasy
Fet's criticism that his novel *Smoke* (1867) was a failure because tendentious, Turgenev denied that it was tendentious
to any extent, and argued that if it was in fact a failure "then
it is not theory which is to blame; rather the cause of the
failure is a case of poetic impotence (*nestoyanie poeticheskogo
chlena*)" (6:316).

Nikolay Solovev followed Turgenev in linking man's es-

---

[69] Letter to Iakov Polonskii of January 2/14, 1868: 7:26. Emphasis in the original.

thetic sense to his sexual nature. In his article "Labor and Enjoyment" (1866) he wrote that man is naturally endowed with a sixth sense for beauty: "Restrained by scrupulousness and sensitivity to the beautiful," he said, "sensual feeling is transformed into esthetic feeling," which in turn then regulates our passions.[70]

Dmitry Pisarev was one of the few participants in the controversy of 1855–70 who regarded the creative process as fundamentally rational. In this connection we may note that Pisarev was only a critic, though endowed with a considerable stylistic gift. He was never tempted to write poetry, as Dobrolyubov and Grigorev did, or a novel, as did Chernyshevsky: their personal experience with art perhaps made them more cautious in issuing pronouncements on the rationality of the creative process. But Pisarev in his "Realists," in taking up the question of how an artist might be unquestionably useful to society, wrote: "I absolutely refuse to recognize such a thing as so-called unconscious and purposeless creativity. I suspect that this is simply a myth created by esthetic criticism to make itself seem more mysterious" (3:93). Here Pisarev once again remained faithful to the logic of his positions. He thought there was no substantive difference between a poet and the most ordinary of mortals. If ordinary mortals were not subject to fits of unconscious creation, as he was not himself, then poets could not be either.

Radical critics other than Pisarev found it difficult to deal with the idea of *fantaziya*, 'fantasy' or 'imagination,' a notion closely linked to the doctrine of unconscious artistic creation. As Solovev noted in 1866, the radical critics would very much have preferred to speak of content comprised of "facts or scientific ideas" instead of imagination: yielding to the temptation of a play on words, Solovev said the radicals

[70] Solov'ev, "Trud i naslazhdenie," vol. 165 (1866), 666.

wished to "replace imagination with reasoning" (*zamenit voobrazhenie soobrazheniem*).[71] And the radical critics did as a rule minimize the importance of the imagination within the creative process. In the *Esthetic Relations*, in line with his view of art's inferiority to reality, Chernyshevsky argued that "the images of poetry are weak, incomplete, and indefinite by comparison with the images of reality which correspond to them" (2:64) (we shall not attempt to decide what the phrase "images of reality" might mean in this context). Chernyshevsky was inclined to see fantasy as abnormal, a faculty which came into play only when people were in extraordinary states. A normal person does not require perfection, he maintained, but only the satisfactory; one indulges in fantastic dreams only if one is deprived excessively of the good things which reality offers. Our esthetic sense too, he added, has strict limitations and is relatively easily satisfied: it "seeks the good, and not the fantastically perfect" (2:38). In his review of the second edition of the *Esthetic Relations* Antonovich agreed with Chernyshevsky that under ordinary conditions man is content with what he has and so his fantasy remains relatively inactive (203). And Pisarev tended to link fantasy with the fantastic, for which he had no use whatever. Probably sometime in 1866 he wrote a long and interesting study of Heinrich Heine, one of the few poets Pisarev admired even though he could not accept him in his entirety (4:200): on the one hand, Pisarev would say, Heine was a utilitarian and politically highly progressive, but on the other hand his work also contained "eccentricities and internal contradictions," not to mention things which were utterly incomprehensible. Thus Pisarev is intellectually honest enough to dedicate several pages to one of Heine's more impenetrable pieces (*Ideen. Das Buch Le Grand*, part two of *Reisebilder*), pointing out all its shortcomings, though with-

[71] Ibid., 670.

out rancor. At the conclusion Pisarev pays tribute to Heine's many political strengths, but he cannot agree with Heine's apparent opinion that "a poet has the right to bring into the world certain combinations of ideas which would never enter anyone's head under any conditions," as Pisarev phrases it (4:243). In sum, Heine suffers from an excess of poetic fantasy which leads him into strange bypaths and which even his laudable political convictions cannot entirely excuse.

The esthetic critics were always mindful of the centrality of the imagination in their conception of literature. Edelson analyzed it skillfully in his "On Poetry" of 1860, where he spoke of the inborn need for fantasy in human beings: "To precisely the same degree that man by his nature wants to know the universe," he wrote, "he wishes to imagine it as well."[72] Since the intellect satisfies the first quest and the fantasy the second, intellect and fantasy should interact and work together. Our souls, Edelson maintained, seek to comprehend the laws of nature through the power of the imagination, which he regarded as superior to the rational intellect. Edelson believed that the critics of his day erred in applying the principles of logical analysis to works of the imagination and from that concluding that "the activity of the imagination in general, as the free play of a creative power, is incompatible with mature thought and the practical tendency of our time."[73] But such was the intellectual inconsistency of that day that even the imagination had become unsure of itself:

> This entire misunderstanding arises from the fact that the fantasy, being an eternal and fundamental power of the spirit and an irrefutable requirement of human nature, in our time is not granted its legitimate rights, and

[72] Edel'son, "O poezii," 9.
[73] Ibid., 30.

therefore seeks gratification by grasping at anything it
can, if only that anything be modern and recognized as
legitimate.[74]

Edelson was something of a pessimist, and it is not entirely
clear that he believed poetry as a principal manifestation of
the imagination would survive within Russian society in the
near term, but he was convinced that in the long run it
would endure, and he wished to do everything within his
power to protect it.

An Excursus: on What Is to Be Done?

One of the theoretically and practically most important
events of the debate over literature and esthetics between
1855 and 1870 was the publication of *What Is to Be Done?* in
1863, almost precisely at the period's midpoint. The esthetic
critics justifiably regarded Chernyshevsky as the fountain-
head of the antiliterary attitudes which had acquired such
dominance in Russian intellectual life by the early 1860s: not
only was he the author of the radical critics' chief theoretical
guide, *The Esthetic Relations of Art to Reality*, but he had also
published intransigent attacks on writers like Turgenev for
expending their energies on useless literary endeavors. To be
sure, he had largely abandoned literary criticism by the end
of the 1850s, devoting himself instead to producing scholarly
and philosophical essays such as "The Anthropological Principle in Philosophy" of 1860. But he had never ceased to take
an interest in literature and to write about it: in his article of
late 1861 on the short stories of Nikolay Uspensky entitled
"Is This Not the Beginning of a Change?" he called for the
appearance of a new and positively oriented radical imaginative literature. Though his reaction to *Fathers and Sons*
had been just as negative as Antonovich's, this was partly

[74] Ibid., 32.

because he recognized the impact such a work of imaginative literature could have on public opinion—in this case in a direction he considered undesirable. Thus Chernyshevsky confronted a dilemma. In theory he attached little importance to works of imaginative literature, but he realized that in practice they could very effectively implant certain ideas in the public mind: for example the term "nihilism," with all its negative connotations for the radical movement, had achieved wide currency through Turgenev's novel—which was why Chernyshevsky subtitled *What Is to Be Done?* "From Stories of the New People," for he wished to replace "nihilist" with "new man," much as Pisarev worked to supplant "nihilist" with "realist." The impact of Turgenev's book, combined with the failure of writers like Nikolay Uspensky or Nikolay Pomyalovsky to develop into first-rate literary forces and with the personal trauma of his arrest in July 1862, moved Chernyshevsky to think seriously of creating a novel which would continue the ideological battle in the literary arena.

One thing which held Chernyshevsky back was his conviction that he was totally deficient in the power of fantasy, or literary imagination, which any novelist required. When he actually undertook the writing of a novel, however, he discovered that he had been wrong about himself:

> The main thing in poetic talent is the so-called creative imagination. Since I had never dealt with anything except that which life compelled me to, I believed that this side of my capabilities was very weakly developed; and it was in fact quite unimportant for me before I thought of becoming a novelist. But while I was writing *What Is to Be Done?* I began to think I might very well possess a certain creative power. I could see that I was not depicting my acquaintances, I was not copying, that my characters were just as fictional as Gogol's. (12:682)

Chernyshevsky's discovery that he did have something of
the imaginative power necessary to write an interesting
novel indirectly and partially confirmed the arguments of
the esthetic critics on the general importance of the creative
imagination.

Though Chernyshevsky's major objective in writing
What Is to Be Done? was to make certain vital political points,
he also wished to make a statement on the nature of literature, and on the novel in particular. For this latter purpose
he worked out what may be regarded as a new form of the
contemporary novel, one which in its way contributed to
the discussion of literature and esthetics of the time. It is
true that very few of his contemporaries realized what he
was doing. Among those few was Dmitry Pisarev, who
found stimulating things to say about the book in his article
of late 1865 entitled "The Thinking Proletariat." But most
contemporary critics of whatever persuasion evaluated the
book in terms of its social and political ideas while paying
little or no attention to its artistic character, an approach
which has persisted in Soviet and Western scholarship down
to the present day.

A careful reading of *What Is to Be Done?* shows that
Chernyshevsky wished, among other things, to make an implicit statement about literature through the novel's form
and an explicit one in certain passages of the text. Grigory
Tamarchenko, author of a detailed and judicious study of
Chernyshevsky's novels, takes up the problem of the book's
genre and concludes that it should be classified as an "intellectual novel," that is, a novel which moves primarily in the
sphere of ideas.[75] And indeed the book does utilize many
devices which were unusual in the literature of that time. At
one point Chernyshevsky inserts into the text a conversation
between himself and Vera Pavlovna in which he comments

[75] Tamarchenko, *Chernyshevskii—romanist*, 247.

on the manner in which ideas spread through a society: new ideas which seem quite strange upon their introduction often become commonplace a few years later, so commonplace, he says, that Vera Pavlovna may even hear them from her decidedly unintellectual mother (11:55–57). To a degree this device of Chernyshevsky's falls into the tradition of Turgenev before him (the ideological debates between Bazarov and Pavel Petrovich Kirsanov in *Fathers and Sons*) and Dostoevsky after him, whose novels are built upon a polyphonic clash of ideas. One should note, however, that Francis Randall, one of the few Western scholars to have defended *What Is to be Done?* as a work of artistic literature, admits that it is possible even for those who disagree with his opinions to admire Dostoevsky as a novelist of ideas, while

it is difficult to work up any enthusiasm for *What Is to Be Done?* as a novel if one does not grant that the soundness and nobility of many of Chernyshevskii's views, and the effectiveness with which he preaches them, are part of his power as a writer.[76]

In short, Randall argues that one must accept Chernyshevsky's ideas in order to appreciate him as a novelist, something which is not the case with Dostoevsky, or with Turgenev either, one might add.

What Is to Be Done? has certain allegorical features, especially in Vera Pavlovna's series of prophetic dreams placed throughout the novel: Chernyshevsky did not hesitate to resort to allegory despite its "unrealistic" nature. Julia Alissandratos has dealt in some detail with the "hagiographical" elements in Chernyshevsky's book which link it to the exemplary saints' lives of Old Russia.[77] Chernyshevsky was,

---

[76] Francis Randall, *N. G. Chernyshevskii* (New York, 1967), 129.

[77] Julia Alissandratos, "Hagiographical Commonplaces and Medieval Prototypes in N. G. Chernyshevsky's What Is to Be Done?" *St. Vladimir's Theological Quarterly*, vol. 26, no. 2 (1982), 103–17.

after all, educated in ecclesiastical schools and was acquainted with medieval literature; he even explicitly entitled
section 24 of chapter 2 "Eulogy of Marya Alekseevna," using
the standard medieval locution *pokhvalnoe slovo*. It is true
that in this passage—in which the author takes leave of one
of his most negative characters—he praises Marya Alekseevna not for her virtues but for the peculiar character of
her evil, from which good may eventually spring quite independently of her volition, so that the "Eulogy of Marya
Alekseevna" is designed as an ironic distortion of the medieval tradition. But then it is also true that Chernyshevsky
presents Rakhmetov as an exemplary ideal, in the spirit of
medieval hagiography, and this genre element of the novel
certainly deserves to be recognized.

Although *What Is to Be Done?* is an intellectual novel
containing significant allegorical and hagiographical elements, it also subverts the entire genre of the novel as a
prose fiction. It does this in several ways.

The book opens *in medias res*, in the best style of a mystery novel. The setting is entirely realistic and quite specific.
The initial events described are dated precisely: Lopukhov
arrives at a St. Petersburg hotel on July 10, 1856, in the eve-
ning, and asks to be awakened promptly at eight the next
morning. At three in the morning a shot is heard on the
Liteyny Bridge, one of the chief Neva River bridges of St.
Petersburg, although nothing is discovered on it thereafter.
In the morning Lopukhov's room is broken into and found
to be empty except for a suicide note in which he speaks of
planning to take his own life in the early morning on the
Liteyny Bridge. The chapter then offers some discussion as
to whether a suicide has actually occurred, but the circum-
stantial evidence seems persuasive. Section 2 then goes back
in time to provide background on the supposed tragedy:
after discovering that his wife, Vera Pavlovna, has fallen in
love with Kirsanov, Lopukhov proposes to make it possible

for Vera Pavlovna to marry Kirsanov by removing himself from the scene through suicide.

The novel's first two sections, then, contain a concretely realistic description of a dramatic situation involving love and death and seasoned with a bit of mystery, in the established tradition of the sensationalist crime novel. Indeed the author deliberately designed the book's commencement as a hook to seize his readers' attention. Substantially past the novel's midpoint, in a brief passage filled with contempt for the implied reader (section 28 of chapter 3) (11:195), Chernyshevsky explicitly informs us that Lopukhov was the anonymous man involved in both the first and second sections. However, even at this point he does not make it clear that the suicide he had described so painstakingly and realistically was a hoax: that he does only at the novel's conclusion.

The beginning of the book is curiously arranged. The first section, numbered 1, is headed "A Fool" and describes the putative suicide; a second section, numbered 2 and entitled "The First Consequences of the Idiotic Affair," goes into the Vera Pavlovna-Lopukhov-Kirsanov triangle; and section 3 is the "Foreword." Only thereafter comes the first of six "chapters," all except the last quite lengthy and themselves divided into numerous sections. But the "Foreword"—which follows the first two sections instead of preceding them—is of substantial theoretical interest for an understanding of what Chernyshevsky hoped to accomplish through the writing of *What Is to Be Done?*

At the very start of the "Foreword" Chernyshevsky inserts himself into the novel as a participant, if not a character. Such a device was by no means unprecedented: Pushkin uses it extensively in *Eugene Onegin*, and Pisemsky employs it even more concretely in *Troubled Seas*, published almost exactly at the same time as Chernyshevsky's novel. But this device has the effect of emphasizing a work's fictional char-

acter, shifting it to a remove from reality, and underlining
the fact that it is merely an intellectual construct. Beyond
that, the author as participant plays a didactic role: he is a
mentor who tells his readers precisely what to think, comments sarcastically on their more blatant stupidities, and
generally leads his ideologically uninitiated readers by the
hand. This is linked to his famous device of direct address to
the "perceptive reader," a person judged to have extensive
experience of literature but little of reality. Chernyshevsky
grasps the nettle of literary didacticism firmly: since he believes that literature can and should be didactic, he deliberately sets out to compose a didactic novel. For that reason
alone many esthetic critics did not recognize *What Is to Be
Done?* as a genuine work of literature.

Chernyshevsky apologizes to his "perceptive reader" for
stooping to attract society's attention with the "sensationalism" (*effeknost*) of his novel, but argues that this is not
really his fault. "You [the reading public] are to blame," he
writes. "Your simple-minded naivete compelled me to lower
myself to such banality. But now you have fallen into my
trap and I may continue the story as I think I should, without any trickery" (11:10). He had been compelled, he had
said earlier, to resort to "sensational devices" because the
reading public had become so accustomed to them.

In addition to exploiting what Chernyshevsky regarded
as illegitimate sensationalism, contemporary fiction writers
also employed banal plots which the experienced reader
could predict far in advance: certain artistic clichés could
make the development of a plot quite obvious. Chernyshevsky returns to this point constantly in the course of
What Is to Be Done? Thus at the end of section 3 of chapter 2
the author addresses his reader as follows:

> Reader, you know ahead of time, of course, that at this
> evening party there will be a confession of love and Ve-

rochka and Lopukhov will fall in love? That's so, need-less to say. (11:50)

Later on, in section 8 of chapter 3, Chernyshevsky again forecasts the development of his plot:

> The perceptive reader says: I know what's happening; Vera Pavlovna is entering on a new romance in her life; Kirsanov will play a role in it; I can see even more: Kirsanov has been in love with Vera Pavlovna for a long time, which is why he stopped visiting the Lopukhovs. Oh, how perceptive you are, perceptive reader: as soon as you're told anything, you immediately respond: "I realized that," and exult in your own perceptiveness. I'm simply in awe of you, perceptive reader. (11:142)

Here, despite the thickness of the authorial irony, the "perceptive reader" does in fact understand the plot correctly. From this it follows that Chernyshevsky regards fictional situations as necessarily so banal as to be entirely predictable. In this regard art is markedly inferior to reality, which offers the most varied and unexpected "plot situations," if we may so term them.

Chernyshevsky also links the question of plot predictability with the epistemological problem of how one "knows" anything in literature:

> The reader says: "I know that this gentleman who shot himself did not shoot himself." I seize upon the word "know" and say: you don't know that at all, because you haven't been told it yet, and you know only what you'll be told; you yourself don't know anything, you don't even know that I insulted and humiliated you by the way I began my tale. For you didn't know that, did you? Then know it now. (11:10)

The only source of information in a literary work, says Chernyshevsky, is its creator himself: a reader cannot properly bring outside information to bear on the fictional world with which he is dealing. And again we should note that, for all Chernyshevsky's sarcasm in this passage, the reader is once more correct in his analysis. The intelligent author indulges in irony at the expense of his blockheaded reader, but it turns out that the reader understands the nature of his fictional enterprise quite well, precisely because such enterprises exist for dullards.

Perhaps the most interesting aspect of Chernyshevsky's demolition of the novelistic genre by means of a novel itself is to be found in his treatment of the place of "artistic talent" in literature. In this instance the outlines of Chernyshevsky's view may be a trifle uncertain. After the novel had appeared to the acclaim of the reading public, Chernyshevsky was apparently quite pleased to discover that he possessed a modicum of artistic talent. But while he was actually writing the book he had taken another approach to the question of talent in literature and art, which he discussed in a key paragraph of the "Foreword":

> I have not the slightest bit of artistic talent. I even have a poor command of language. But that's not so important: read on, good public! You will not read me without benefit (*polza*). Truth is a fine thing: it makes up for the shortcomings of a writer who serves it. And therefore I shall say to you: if I had not warned you, you probably would have thought that this story is artistically written, that its author possessed a considerable poetic talent. But I have warned you that I have no talent, and so now you will know that all my story's merits are bestowed upon it solely by its truthfulness. (II:II)

In this extraordinary passage—and even the obvious irony within it does not negate its direct meaning—Chernyshevsky argues that it is entirely feasible to replace artistry in literature with a love for truth, truthfulness, which is very close to the intellect in literature; and beyond that he contends that the substitution can be made so subtly that the ordinary reader could not tell the difference if the author himself were not honest enough to point it out. Among contemporary critics, Nikolay Solovev interpreted the book much as did its author, though he adopted quite a different attitude toward it: in 1864 he characterized the novel as an "obvious and impertinent violation of truth and art" in which "thought has undertaken to play the role of feeling."[78] Thus, though Solovev rejected the validity of Chernyshevsky's "truth," he perceptively recognized his structural objective in writing the book.

Chernyshevsky remains absolutely committed to the truth as he sees it throughout *What Is to Be Done?* For instance, when one of his rather negative female characters speaks of a velvet coat she is presenting as a gift to someone else, which she claims cost 150 rubles and has been worn but twice, and of a watch for which she paid 300 rubles, Chernyshevsky provides the correct figures in parentheses (85 rubles, more than 20 times, 120 rubles) (11:38–39). Here truth is the mathematically definable sort with which Chernyshevsky was most comfortable. On another occasion, writing in a theoretical mode, he declares:

> I am not among those artists within whose very word is concealed some sort of mainspring, I recount what people have thought and done, no more; if some action, conversation, or train of thought is needful for the characterization of a personage or a situation, why I narrate it, even though it may have no consequences for the subsequent course of my novel. (11:95)

Thus Chernyshevsky is committed to the truth of his fictional world even though it may damage the esthetic harmony of his literary work. "The first requirement of artistry

---

[78] Solov'ev, "Teoriia bezobraziia," 14.

consists in this," he wrote further on: "one must depict objects in such a way that the reader pictures them in their genuine (*istinny*) form" (II:226). Once again Chernyshevsky juxtaposes the concepts of artistry and truthfulness, and once again at least implicitly holds there is no effective difference between the two. One may compensate for a lack of innate artistic talent by a rational commitment to truth. From the point of view of the esthetic critics, to effect such a substitution was the most subversive thing Chernyshevsky could have done to the novel as an art form. As a practical matter, however, when Chernyshevsky the budding novelist fell under the sway of the literary imagination he had newly detected within himself, be became much more convinced of its importance. But that conviction found no reflection in the novel's text.

Still, Chernyshevsky did resort to the concept of artistry in justifying his introduction of Rakhmetov, that superhero among the "new people" whom unsympathetic readers at that time and since have considered wholly unrealistic. Chernyshevsky agreed that Rakhmetov was unrealistic, but only in a special sense. "The perceptive reader," he wrote with his wonted irony,

> would never see a single such person; your eyes . . . are not designed to see such people; . . . and therefore you need a description of such a person so that you may know by report what sorts of people there are in the world. (II:210)

Shortly thereafter Chernyshevsky claims to have introduced Rakhmetov for artistic reasons (II:211), but clarifies what he had in mind only quite a bit later, though in some detail. His leading characters—Lopukhov, Kirsanov, and Vera Pavlovna—are but "ordinary decent people of the new generation," he says, and by no means ideal types. Since this is not readily obvious to the average reader, Chernyshevsky provides him with a standard of artistic comparison by means of this portrait of a truly extraordinary person (11:226–28). Lopukhov embodies a quite attainable possibility, whereas Rakhmetov represents a much higher ideal.

What Is to Be Done? is, then, not only a central document in the intellectual history of modern Russia, but also a major contribution to the continuing debate over the nature of art in the Russia of the 1860s. Since he had to deal with people as they actually were, Chernyshevsky toyed with his readers by beginning the novel as an ordinary, even banal, realistic tale of intrigue and adventure, and a love story, in order to capture his readers' interest. But at the same time he used it to subvert the esthetic camp's doctrine of literature and art. By demonstrating that his unintelligent readers were quite capable of guessing the plot line far in advance, he implicitly affirmed the superiority of reality to art. He deliberately put himself forward as author and teacher in artistic and political matters to show that openly didactic novels could be quite successful. And he explicitly admitted that within it he had replaced artistic talent with dedication to truth, declaring that a novel based upon such a substitution was indistinguishable in the eyes of the ordinary reader from a novel written in accordance with all the prescriptions of the esthetic critics. That was the unkindest cut of all.

Chapter Three

◊

Art and Morality

NEARLY ALL THE PARTICIPANTS IN THE DIS-
cussion of esthetics in the 1860s were agreed that art could
not be separated from some notion of morality, or at least
from some ideal, whether it be an ideal of beauty, truth, or
the good. Only toward the turn of the century did critics in
any number begin to argue that there was no necessary linkage between art and morality, a doctrine which Konstantin
Leontev almost alone preached during the 1860s. For in that
decade almost everyone across the political spectrum agreed
that art had a moral mission, although there was deep disagreement on how that mission should be defined.

Monism and Ideals

To be sure, the radical critics were a priori disposed to be
suspicious of any connection between art and the ideal, for
they were monists who sought a single principle to unite
seemingly disparate aspects of reality. Thinkers like Chernyshevsky and Dobrolyubov rejected philosophical dualism
along with their religious upbringing: they believed there
should be no distinction between a natural and a supernatural realm, between body and soul, between the world of
the real and the world of the ideal. In "The Anthropological
Principle in Philosophy," for example, Chernyshevsky's
chief objective is to bring all the disparate phenomena he

discusses under a single grand explanatory scheme. He even sees the organic world as of a piece with the inorganic: the same processes occur, he says, within a stone, a tree, and a human being, only at different rates of speed and different levels of complexity. Chernyshevsky was more than eager to extend the monistic principle from the physical world to the realm of human intellectual and spiritual endeavor. As Norman Pereira sums up the situation in his study of Chernyshevsky:

> Černyševskij argues [that] not only are objects perceived accurately, but there is also very little variation in the nature of perception from one individual to the next. After all, what is the basis of all human communication if not the functional universality of sensory perception?[1]

If, as Chernyshevsky believed, there was little individual variation in the perception of reality, then it followed that works of art should strive for unity both within themselves ("the first law of artistry," he wrote, "is the unity of the work" [3:429]) and among themselves. Moreover, it was illegitimate, in his view, for the artist to perceive reality very differently from the critic. Much later, in a letter written from exile, Chernyshevsky offered a striking example of the monistic principle applied to human psychology when he defined the "laws of human nature" as follows: "intellect and honesty are one and the same; intellect and a good heart are one and the same."[2] There could scarcely be a more straightforward expression of belief in the essential unity of all human experience.

Although Chernyshevsky certainly maintained that literature should advance an ideal, he was legitimately fearful that the esthetic critics might take advantage of this opening to reintroduce philosophical dualism into contemporary in-

---

[1] Norman G. Pereira, *The Thought and Teachings of N. G. Černyševskij* (The Hague and Paris, 1975), 36.

[2] Letter to M. N. Chernyshevskii of March 1875: 14:598.

tellectual discourse. The radicals realized that metaphysical dualism could easily be brought back in during a discussion of esthetics, and this was precisely one of the reasons for the intensity of the esthetic debate during the 1860s. But even Chernyshevsky could not entirely avoid injecting a discussion of the ideal into *The Esthetic Relations of Art to Reality*. If he had adhered solely to his first and simplest definition— "the beautiful is life"—he could easily have been accused of advocating a Hegelian reconciliation with reality, as Belinsky had done during a period of philosophical aberration in his career. Thus Chernyshevsky had quickly introduced another concept: "That entity is beautiful in which we see life as it should be according to our conceptions." The word "should" must point to an ideal different from existing reality, even though Chernyshevsky then went on to demonstrate to his own satisfaction that an ideal rooted in reality must necessarily be *inferior* to reality. It is worth noting that in proving this point Chernyshevsky speaks of the depiction of human beauty in painting and sculpture. He does not deal either with literature or with the question of a social ideal, but if he did he would be compelled to argue that social relationships superior to those in Russia at the time existed in reality somewhere if they were to be depicted in works of imaginative literature such as *What Is to Be Done?*

As Charles Corbet, a French specialist on the Russian radical critics, has pointed out, Dobrolyubov elaborated on this point of Chernyshevsky's effectively. Whereas literature in the past had considered it quite legitimate to utilize the "discord" between reality and the ideal, Dobrolyubov and other radical critics looked for the creation of a nondualistic literary system in which theoretically such discord would no longer exist.[3]

---

[3] See Charles Corbet, "La critique de Dobroliubov: Principes esthétiques et réalités sentimentales," *Revue des études slaves*, no. 29 (1952), 39.

The radical critics were quite correct in believing that the esthetic critics promoted a dualistic view of the universe. Their suspicions could be easily corroborated, say, by a passage from Pavel Annenkov's "Criticism Old and New" of 1856 which was unabashedly dualistic in its presuppositions:

> Thus [criticism] has created two separate worlds in order to resolve the contradictions of its theory: first the world of luminous art, without error, not subject to disputes, not subjected to changes; and beyond it the world of necessity, of more or less rational chance occurrences, of all the energetic effort of our contemporary times, which does not ask for the right to exist because it is life itself. (2:5)

Some ten years later Nikolay Solovev adopted another tack in defense of philosophical dualism when he argued in an article of 1865 that materialism had every right to existence, but that it was unjustified in seeking to deny idealism's equivalent right to exist.[4]

Still, whether a critic were a monist or a dualist, he still had to cope with the question of the ideal in literature (indeed Turgenev once defined the poet implicitly as the "servant of the ideal" [Pis'ma, 5:44]). In 1867 Evgeny Edelson had expressed his belief that art, far from straggling along in the rearguard of intellectual development as some contended, would in fact always be essential "for its constant prosecution and realization of the ideal," which meant that it had a mission much more complex and difficult than the mere propagandizing of the glories of natural science.[5] And as late as 1869 Nikolay Strakhov was still vigorously affirming that art must be evaluated by the ideal. "There are various kinds of realism," he wrote in a review of *War and Peace* at that time.

[4] Nikolai Solov'ev, "Razlad (kritika kritiki)," *Epokha*, no. 2 (February 1865), 16.
[5] Edel'son, "O znachenii iskusstva" (February 1867), 322.

Art essentially can never reject the ideal and always
strives toward it; and the more clearly and vividly one
senses that striving in the creations of realism, the loftier
that realism is, the nearer it is to being truly artistic.[6]

Still, in order to make sense of such statements about art, we
must define what we understand by the ideal.

We have already noted Chernyshevsky's view that the
ideal in art must logically be inferior to reality. Writing in
late 1866, Konstantin Sluchevsky found absolutely unaccept-
able the notion that we cannot formulate an ideal loftier
than that which we have known in reality.[7] By this time
Sluchevsky had broken his former connections to the radical
camp, but some of Chernyshevsky's more faithful disciples
had difficulty with this proposition as well. For example, in
his review of the second edition of the *Esthetic Relations*
Maksim Antonovich modified that idea slightly—without
emphasizing the fact—when he wrote that the radical camp
held that literature should embody an ideal, but it should be
a "real ideal," not a "dreamy, unnatural, and unjust" one of
the sort to which the esthetic critics allegedly adhered (241–
42). Pierre-Joseph Proudhon, one of the radicals' chief foreign mentors, went further when he defined art as "an ide-
alist representation of nature and of ourselves aimed at the
physical and moral perfection of our species."[8] Dobrolyubov
also grappled with the problem of the ideal, which he
equated with the conception of reality in its "normal"
state—although to argue this was simply to shift the discussion from one plane to another and equally difficult one. "A
consciousness of the normal order of things," he wrote in
"A Ray of Light in the Kingdom of Darkness," "must be

[6] Nikolai Strakhov, *Kriticheskie stat'i ob I. S. Turgeneve i L. N. Tolstom (1862–1885)*
(Kiev, 1901), 1:194.

[7] Sluchevskii, *Iavleniia russkoi zhizni*, 2: 42–43.

[8] P.-J. Proudhon, *Du principe de l'art et de sa destination sociale* (Paris, 1865), 43.

vivid and clear within [the writer], his ideal must be simple and rational" (6:313). A bit later he came back to this question in a further attempt to explain how reality could be made to yield an ideal through rational analysis. He assumed that reality as it actually existed was somehow distorted, and that an artist was capable of discerning it as it would be in its undistorted form:

> Reality, from which the poet derives his materials and his inspiration, has its own natural sense; if that is violated, then the life of the object itself is destroyed, and there remains merely a dead skeleton of it. (6:313)

This resolved the problem in Dobrolyubov's mind: the ideal is identical with the real, but the real in its "normal" or "natural" state, a state rarely if ever encountered in actual fact because reality is constantly deformed by disease, accident, social disorder, and so forth. Through his genius the artist can as it were clear away the abnormalities afflicting reality and present us with a depiction of it as it truly should be.

Dobrolyubov applies his notion of the real and the ideal quite instructively in his discussion of Goncharov's *Oblomov* in "What is Oblomovism?" Goncharov presents Stolz as an ideal character, the critic remarked, but since Dobrolyubov did not agree with that ideal, he declared that the image of Stolz was not yet realistic: "there is no doubt," he wrote, "that many [Stolzes] will appear; but for the time being the ground is not yet prepared for them" (4:340). On the other hand, the critic did see Olga as an ideal attainable within the existing Russian society, and indeed the most lofty ideal which could at the moment be formulated (4:341).

Boris Egorov sees normativeness as the common link among all the critical theories of the 1860s. Every critic accepted the idea of an ideal in the abstract, but beyond that there was little agreement. "The normativeness of the conservatives," Egorov wrote in 1973,

drew society back, while the normativeness of the liberals, advocating reconciliation with reality or gradual development, as a practical matter also hindered society's
forward movement at a time when its steps were quick-
ening; progressive normativeness was the one which
summoned people to an ideal in advance of them and
which demanded that it be attained as soon as possible.[9]

Egorov's notion of "progressive normativeness" or "historical normativeness" locates the radical ideal in the relatively
distant future, the conservative ideal in the historical past,
and the liberal ideal either in the present or the immediate
future. This scheme is rather too neatly logical: though it
can be made to fit Dobrolyubov's and Chernyshevsky's definitions of the ideal with little difficulty, it can be applied
only very loosely to the main body of esthetic criticism.

Thus Pavel Annenkov, who in 1858 spoke of "striving toward the poetic ideal of existence" (2:165), later formulated
a conception of the ideal as located almost exclusively within
the realm of art and not in historical reality, whether past or
future:

> In the language of esthetics the word ideal denotes any
> image which contains within itself the entire sum of
> moral and poetic traits which belong to it by nature. . . .
> any moral and poetic image which is faithful to reality
> and to itself is an ideal. (2:199)

This definition of the ideal as an internally consistent artistic
image drawn from reality has affinities with Apollon Grigorev's doctrines of organic criticism. Annenkov is less concerned with the ideal's connections with reality than he is
with the internal—one might almost say organic—consistency of the image, the harmony of its "moral and poetic
traits." By this definition the laws of art, the laws of the "po-

---

[9] Egorov, *Ocherki po istorii russkoi kritiki,* 124–25.

etic ideal," are controlling. The ideal inheres in the poetic image.

Some years later Nikolay Solovev developed Annenkov's viewpoint further as he emphasized art's role in the creation of a poetic ideal. "Poetry, as a product of inspiration engendered by beauty and love," he wrote in 1867, "develops precisely the necessity that one be a human being, because it creates within the soul an ideal or a vivid representation of what one should be."[10] In another and more extensive passage written at about the same time, Solovev maintained that by thinking about life in images writers could create a more perfect ideal of life in their own minds, and subsequently in the minds of their readers. "In this way," he wrote,

> they discovered within it ideals or more perfect norms of life, more highly developed manifestations of character. . . . It goes without saying that contradictions between life and its ideals were inevitable, the more so since these ideals and higher norms of life were not yet entirely worked out, not evenly disseminated everywhere, and not accepted by everyone.[11]

There was, then, an esthetic tradition of the ideal which passed from Annenkov to Solovev and which emphasized the central importance of literature in its formulation: such esthetic critics moved, not on a metaphysical level, but on a literary one, never losing sight of the life which served as the ultimate stuff of literature. As Evgeny Edelson put it when the *Esthetic Relations* first appeared, we cannot say, with Chernyshevsky, that "poetry is life," or, with Katkov, that poetry is identical with "thought" (*myshlenie*): we require something more, "we need a striving toward the ideal, to-

[10] Solov'ev, "Printsipy zhizni," 173.
[11] Solov'ev, "Trud i naslazhdenie," vol. 167 (1866), 126.

ward that which does not exist in life."[12] Poetry formulates
that ideal as something not presently in existence but capable of existing under the proper conditions.

Apollon Grigorev devoted a great deal of thought to the
ideal in literature, but was more ambiguous about it than
many of his contemporaries. In his article of 1856, "On Truth
and Sincerity in Art," he recognized this as a major issue but
declared that he was not yet prepared to take up the "problem of the relation of art . . . to religion, to the eternal
ideal."[13] However, in this same article he did say a few things
à propos of the ideal. For instance, he averred that it was
unfortunate that each writer of his epoch was compelled to
elaborate his own individual ideal, whereas in the halcyon
days of culture from Dante through Molière writers could
simply draw their conceptions of the ideal from their society: "these conceptions live[d] in them with a firm vegetal
(*rastitelny*) life, linked to the roots of the soil on which the
artist [had] developed."[14] Nineteenth-century society suffered from such an excess of individualism that it was a simple matter indeed for artists to err in the formulation of their
individual ideals.

In this same article Grigorev also noted that true art always "strove for the *preservation* of ideals"—not the creation
of new and unheard-of ideals—and that one of its best in-
struments for the attainment of this goal was comedy.[15] Earlier he had offered an excellent definition of comedy as seen
from this perspective:

> Comedy (*komizm*) is the attitude of the higher to the
> lower, an attitude toward untruth using laughter in the

[12] Quoted by M. G. Zel'dovich in "Nesostoiavshaiasia retsenziia na 'Esteticheskie otnosheniia . . .'," *Russkaia literatura*, no. 3 (1969), 150.
[13] Grigor'ev, "O pravde i iskrennosti," 146–47.
[14] Ibid., 182.
[15] Ibid., 187.

name of a truth which it has outraged and of which the one laughing is clearly conscious.[16]

His belief in the importance of comedy as a means of upholding the ideal may explain both why Grigorev was so taken with Alexander Ostrovsky's work, which incorporated many comic elements, and why Chernyshevsky dismissed the comic so quickly in his *Esthetic Relations*: the radical critic did not sympathize with the defense of established ideals, for he promoted ideals oriented toward the future.

Furthermore, if the artist did succeed in presenting his individual ideal, the pressures of contemporary culture might well lead to its distortion. As Grigorev put it in this same article of 1856, "great artists have struggled . . . not against the higher morality . . . but . . . rather against an ideal derived from temporary, pitiful, or corrupt laws of reality."[17] He illustrates this generalization with George Sand and her *Horace*:

> The deficiencies of *Horace* lie entirely in that world which the artist *desires*: into that world she *desires* has penetrated a corruption of the heart very probably even greater than that which she criticizes in *Horace*.[18]

Grigorev was one of the few critics of either camp who maintained that an artist could quite easily fail to formulate a satisfactory ideal, and even be inferior to more ordinary persons in his moral perceptions. He returned to this point in "Nihilism in Art" (1862), where he observed that too many contemporary artists lacked an ideal altogether, or else adhered to one which was quite petty. In his next breath, however, he shifted the argument to a more affirmative and metaphysical level, saying: "The ideal is inexhaustible, and

[16] Ibid., 161.
[17] Ibid., 142.
[18] Ibid., 176.

CHAPTER THREE

therefore art is eternal."[19] Grigorev was compelled to adopt what one might term an ideal view of the ideal in art as a means of sustaining his conviction that art would survive the assaults being mounted against it at that time, for in his more sober moments he felt that artists were in fact very weak defenders of true ideals.

Dostoevsky also dealt with the problem of the ideal from time to time, and usually came forth with characteristically stimulating views on the question. In one instance he argued that the dully photographic reproduction of reality was very far from genuine artistry, and maintained that literature should be infused with an "idea":

> In poetry passion is needed, *your idea* is needed, and also by all means a passionately raised and pointing finger. Indifference and a realistic reproduction of reality, on the other hand, are worth nothing and—more important—mean nothing. Such artistry is ridiculous: a simple but just slightly observant eye will note a great deal more in reality.[20]

As Dostoevsky saw it, the artist cannot indulge in an insensible reproduction of reality: he must infuse it with an idea or an interpretation as a means of structuring his depiction of reality, and moreover his idea must possess a moral dimension (the "passionately raised finger") which makes it indistinguishable from the esthetic critics' ideal. The artist not only describes what exists, he must also point to that which should be.

In "Mr. —bov and the Problem of Art" (1861) Dostoevsky formulated a typically complex notion of the artistic ideal, which he associated with the concepts of harmony and beauty. Although the artist aspires to the image and ideal of

---

[19] Grigor'ev, "Nigilizm v iskusstve," 58.

[20] Fedor Dostoevskii, "Zapisnaia tetrad' (1876–77)," in *Neizdannyi Dostoevskii*, vol. 83 of *Literaturnoe nasledstvo* (Moscow, 1971), 610.

beauty, that very aspiration arises out of disharmony, the fact that man is "in discord with reality." Paradoxical though it may seem, man loves concord most truly at just such a time: if he in fact attains his goal of "harmony and calm" he may become dissatisfied and begin to seek unsuitable ends. Still, the ideal is correctly associated with beauty and harmony:

> Beauty is inborn in everything that is healthy, that is, the most vital, and is a necessary requirement of the human organism. It is harmony; it contains the guarantee of tranquility; it embodies the ideals of the individual and of humanity. (18:94)

This passage contains several ideas which were widely accepted at the time: the association of beauty with health; the emphasis upon the human organism, as with Grigorev and his organic criticism; the importance of beauty in the formulation of the ideal (in fact Dostoevsky claims that beauty incorporates the ideal). On this last point Dostoevsky agrees quite closely with the esthetic critics.

Beauty and the Ideal

The radical critics were obliged to discuss the concept of the beautiful in art. Although they were uncomfortable with it in theory, in practice several of them displayed a well-developed personal taste for beauty. For example the prose writer Fedor Reshetnikov (1841–71) during his Penza school days in the late 1850s was subjected to three months' confinement for stealing from the post office. When asked why he had stolen a letter, he explained that "he liked the form of the envelope, the smooth paper, and the nice handwriting on the envelope,"[21] surely an esthetic motivation for the com-

---

[21] N. Sokolov, "Tvorchesto F. M. Reshetnikova," in F. Reshetnikov, *Izbrannye proizvedeniia* (Moscow, 1956), I: viii.

mission of a crime. Another radical writer of refined esthetic taste was Vasily Sleptsov (1836–78), of whom Turgenev thought highly for a time. Korney Chukovsky begins an interesting study of Sleptsov with a section based on contemporary memoir literature to demonstrate not only that Sleptsov was an exceptionally handsome man, but that he loved to make and live among fine things as well despite his lack of personal wealth. Avdotya Panaeva, quite a beauty herself, has left us a detailed description of Sleptsov's appearance, which was so striking that, according to another observer, once when he entered a Moscow courtroom for some reason, women gathered from all around to look at him. Another woman recorded that his apartment was filled with elegant furniture and beautiful objects, and quoted Sleptsov as saying that he "absolutely needed" such things about him. That esthetic sensibility is very evident in Sleptsov's writing as well, Chukovsky holds.[22] But perhaps the most astonishing contradiction in the radical camp was to be found in the person of Dmitry Pisarev, who denounced esthetics tirelessly in his theoretical writings: we have Ivan Turgenev's word for it that Pisarev was a man of considerable elegance. Turgenev met Pisarev for the first time only in the spring of 1867 when he was passing through St. Petersburg on his way to Moscow. Turgenev found the critic "not at all stupid," and added: "the thing is that *il a l'air d'un enfant de bonne maison*, as they say, quite beautiful hands, and fingernails as long as this [insertion of a sketch of an exaggeratedly lengthy nail], which is rather strange for a nihilist."[23] Pisarev's anti-esthetic views were evidently more a matter of intellectual conviction than of temperament.

On the intellectual level, however, the radical critics

[22] Kornei Chukovskii, "Zhizn' i tvorchestvo Vasiliia Sleptsova," in Chukovskii, *Liudi i knigi*, second revised edition (Moscow, 1960), 160–62.
[23] Letter to M. V. Avdeev of March 30/April 11, 1867: 6: 213.

skirted the question of beauty whenever possible, perhaps because it was so central to the arguments of the esthetic critics. Chernyshevsky could not avoid taking up the problem in the *Esthetic Relations*, but he simply defined the beautiful as life, aiming to absorb the concept of the beautiful into the notion of life and thus eventually to eradicate it, instead of formulating a "science of the beautiful," which is what esthetics is usually understood to be. Chernyshevsky does remark that beauty exists in the three realms of reality, the imagination, and art (2:3), but then promptly inserts a long quotation from his rival Vischer on the defects of beauty in reality for the purpose of refuting his arguments and then directing the same points against beauty in art. Chernyshevsky's touchstone is always beauty in reality, and the beauty of nature in particular, for he completely rejects the notion of an ideal or metaphysical realm of beauty by which beauty in reality should be measured.

Chernyshevsky's followers had even less to say about beauty as an ideal than did he. In "A Ray of Light in the Kingdom of Darkness" (1860) Dobrolyubov remarked that no normal person would consider a famous statue of a woman esthetically superior to a living woman, and added:

> If you want to make an impression on me with a living image, if you want to compel me to love beauty—then manage to grasp within it that general sense, that breath (*veyanie*) of life, manage to point it out and interpret it to me: only then will you achieve your aim. (6:303)

For Dobrolyubov meaning, or rational interpretation, should be the core of art, and not beauty, although he did not object to beauty if it did not hinder the artist in interpreting reality properly. To his mind, though, beauty had no independent standing at all as a component of art.

In time the *Russkoe slovo* group drove the theoretical negation of beauty to its logical conclusion. Thus on one oc-

casion Pisarev attempted to define beauty of language in
such a way as wholly to incorporate it into the intellectual.
"As we understand things these days," he wrote in 1864,
"beauty of language consists solely of its clarity and expres-
siveness" (3:110). In short, language was beautiful if and
only if it transmitted its message vividly and unmistakably.
By this time, Pisarev said, language had become what it
should be: "a means for the transmission of thought"
(3:110). The critic had no use for poetic language, with its
rich connotations, and its beauty.

The following year, incidentally, in "Pushkin and Belinsky," Pisarev advanced a rather intriguing argument against
beauty. Beauty, he maintained, lacked the power to move
men's souls which other ideals possessed:

> Be it noted in praise of human nature in general and of
> the human mind in particular that up to now, appar-
> ently, hardly anyone has ever gone to his death for the
> sake of something he considered beautiful, while on the
> other hand there are infinite numbers of people who
> have given their lives for that which they considered true
> or socially useful. . . . Art never has had and never can
> have any martyrs. (3:372)

Pisarev considered this observation a striking indictment of
the cult of beauty among some intellectuals in his day, and
indeed it is worth some reflection: if beauty is an ideal of the
same order as truth or the good, then why should people
historically have been unwilling to sacrifice their lives for it
on occasion? Perhaps it is simply because questions of life
and death have rarely been formulated in terms of allegiance
to beauty alone, and so Pisarev's proposition has never been
genuinely tested.

Pisarev's ally Varfolomey Zaytsev was at least as intransigent on this subject as he was. Zaytsev found nothing of
worth in esthetic enjoyment: he maintained that it grew out

of mere "vanity," and regularly equated art with artificiality. "We negate only *esthetic* enjoyment," he wrote in a review of the 1865 edition of the *Esthetic Relations*.

> We protest only against art, and not at all against anything and everything a man may find pleasant; only against *artificial* demands, and not at all against real ones; only against trumpery and playthings for people's entertainment, and not at all against natural and legitimate human joys. (1:339)

Zaytsev was persuaded that the esthetic critics had concocted artistic criteria for the nefarious purpose of reconciling people to the dreadful reality in which they lived. He did not wish to spend time analyzing beauty, therefore, or discussing its place in human affairs, since he thought it had no such legitimate place.

By way of contrast, the esthetic critics paid serious attention to the nature of beauty. They clearly rejected any equation of the beautiful with the intelligent. Thus in 1867 Nikolay Solovev took issue with Dobrolyubov and Pisarev in their redefinition of beauty in terms of the intellect: "Beauty cannot be proven so much logically as physiologically," he wrote then. "Where beauty is, there is an end to abstraction!"[24] Some two years earlier he had maintained that beauty is always "unexpected," which means that it can be neither anticipated nor logically explained: "Everything entirely beautiful or great emerges from the soul unexpectedly and involuntarily, arousing astonishment not only in others but in the artist himself."[25] If beauty were not susceptible to logical analysis, then it had to be perceived in other ways than through the intellect.

In his discussion of Fet's poetry published in 1857, Vasily

---

[24] Solov'ev, "Printsipy zhizni," 141.
[25] Solov'ev, "Vopros ob iskusstve" (June 1865), 487–88.

Botkin seemed to agree with Chernyshevsky on the inherent beauty of nature, but in fact he did so only superficially, for he approached the question of beauty from a metaphysical viewpoint quite foreign to the radical critic. For Botkin, beauty played a fundamental role in human affairs. "Beauty," he wrote, "comprises the eternal foundation of the entire unanalyzable creative power of the universe."[26] He argued that the ancient Greeks had recognized the indwelling beauty of the natural world, for they had named it the *cosmos* (one etymology of this word links it to the word for beauty, as in the English word "cosmetics"). Indeed the Greeks had even gone as far as to deify beauty in their religion, as some esthetic critics recalled, but by the nineteenth century secularization had set in here as in so many other spheres: as Evgeny Edelson noted in 1867, contemporary man did not perceive in Greek statues any "deification of beauty," but simply derived "esthetic enjoyment" from them.[27]

Fet joined Botkin in attributing decisive importance to beauty in the artistic realm. In his piece of 1859 on Tyutchev, Fet held that art does not reproduce an object in its entirety, but rather concentrates upon a "single-faceted ideal": the artist, he maintained, is concerned solely with an object's beauty, just as a mathematician might be interested only in its outline.[28] A poet is chiefly defined by his sensitivity to beauty before all else: "In a place where the ordinary eye does not even suspect any beauty, the artist sees it, separates it from the object's other qualities, places a purely human stamp upon it, and exhibits it for the general edification."[29] The object mentioned here could even be an abstraction, for

[26] Botkin, "Stikhotvoreniia Feta," 7.
[27] Edel'son, "O znachenii iskusstva" (February 1867), 314.
[28] Fet, "O stikhotvoreniiakh Tiutcheva," 64.
[29] Ibid., 67.

Fet believed that thought could be the subject of poetry (he considered Tyutchev a "poet of thought"), though not discursive thought as such but rather its beauty. Such a view obviously placed Fet in diametric opposition to the radical critics.

Such was the pressure brought to bear against any theory of the supremacy of beauty in art that even Ivan Goncharov yielded somewhat to it. In defending his hero Raysky (*The Precipice*) against the strictures of a radical lady of his acquaintance, Goncharov made some important concessions. Thus he claimed that Raysky was based upon Botkin, Turgenev (sic), and other artistic Russians who had never accomplished very much. He could not accept the accusation that his hero was immoral, but added that, if he were, then "his immorality bordered on adoration not only of feminine beauty but beauty generally, something which has been significantly reduced lately thanks to the deficiency of esthetic training among the younger generation" (8:400). Goncharov was of the same generation as Botkin and Fet, that generation which had worked out an entire doctrine of beauty which Fet was simply adapting to the changed circumstances of the 1850s when he wrote on Tyutchev. But Raysky had remained very much a man of the 1840s, and therefore something of an anachronism in a novel of the 1860s.

Of all the esthetic critics, Konstantin Leontev went farthest in elaborating a theory based upon the primacy of beauty in the world. Leontev began with a definition of beauty very different from Chernyshevsky's: "beauty is unity in diversity." This definition was the cornerstone of Milkeev's esthetic in *In One's Own Land*, and of Leontev's as well.[30] With this definition Leontev found no necessary connection between morality as traditionally understood and

[30] Konstantin Leont'ev, *V svoem kraiu, Otechestvennye zapiski* (June 1864), 503.

the esthetic ideal. As Milkeev phrases it early in the novel: "If we must have Lady Macbeth at one end in order to have Cordelia at the other, then let's have her, but deliver us from feebleness, lethargy, indifference, banality, and a shopkeeper's caution."[31] Leontev derived his definition of beauty from observation of nature itself, which, he wrote, "adores diversity and richness of forms; if we take that as our example, then our life should also be complex and rich. The chief element of diversity is the personality, which is higher than its own creations."[32]

Leontev's doctrines had links to those advanced by his contemporaries, such as Botkin and Dostoevsky. In 1860 Leontev had written a critical commentary on Turgenev's *On the Eve* in which he upbraided the novelist for "not passing beyond the *limit beyond which beauty dwells*, or the idea of life, for which the world of [real] phenomena serves as a vague symbol" (emphasis in original).[33] If beauty was the same as the idea of life, and the idea of life was similar to the ideal, as Dostoevsky came close to saying, then beauty was the ultimate ideal and even the ultimate reality, as Botkin had argued when he said that beauty was more genuine than those temporary economic relationships on which many intellectuals based their theories. But Leontev went beyond equating beauty with the idea of life to argue that in a genuine sense beauty was identical with truth. "Taste is a transient and changeable thing," he wrote in a critical article of 1861,

> but it is founded on the laws of reason. Beauty is the same as truth (*ta zhe istina*), except that it is not clear, not bare, but concealed in the depths of some phenom-

[31] Ibid., (May 1864), 36.
[32] Ibid., (June 1864), 498.
[33] Konstantin Leont'ev, "Pis'mo provintsiala k g. Turgenevu," *Otechestvennye zapiski*, no. 5 (May 1860), section 3, 21.

Vasily Botkin

Nikolay Chernyshevsky

Nikolay Dobrolyubov

Alexander Druzhinin

Evgeny Edelson

Apollon Grigorev

Mikhail Katkov

Konstantin Leontev

Dmitry Pisarev

Nikolay Shelgunov

Nikolay Solovev

Vartolomey Zaytsev

enon. And the more complex that phenomenon is, the fuller, more profound, and less comprehensible that beauty is. In very simple phenomena (so it seems to us) beauty is the equivalent of truth and obvious legitimacy.[34]

In equating beauty both with truth and with the essence of reality, Leontev made it the core of his philosophical system, and then held that the beautiful should be the object of life. Although his system diverged from radical ideology at every major point, he developed his argument so logically that if one accepted his axioms one could scarcely arrive at any conclusions other than his:

> The beautiful is the purpose of life, and morality and self-sacrifice are of value merely as manifestations of the beautiful, as the free creation of the good (*svobodnoe tvorchestvo dobra*). The further a man develops, the more he believes in the beautiful and the less he believes in the useful.[35]

The radicals did not take up Leontev's challenge to their view of art, and therefore his doctrines did not become very widely known, but they were interesting and acquired a certain notoriety—if not influence—in Russian intellectual history. Certainly they must have buttressed the views of some of his less intransigent allies such as Nikolay Solovev.

Solovev associated beauty with the human aspiration for perfection, since he thought that beauty expressed the ideal of perfection. "The perfecting of [mankind]," he wrote in "The Problem of Art" (1865),

> cannot be attained though truths alone, no matter how profound they may be, nor by material advantages alone,

---

[34] Leont'ev, "Po povodu rasskazov Marka Vovchka," *Otechestvennye zapiski*, no. 3 (March 1861), 7.

[35] Leont'ev, *V svoem kraiu, Otechestvennye zapiski* (June 1864), 498–99.

no matter how well they may be assimilated. This perfecting is the major role of art. And for this purpose art
takes as its starting point neither truth nor nature in the
narrow sense of the word, but life. . . . A view of the
world and practical ability prepare the way for art; but
the very striving forward is conditioned within us by a
sense of the ideal of beauty; because a striving for the
beautiful is the same as the striving for perfection.[36]

If beauty represents the ideal of perfection, then human
beings will quite naturally be drawn toward beauty. Art
leaves the shackles of reality behind and holds out the ideal
to us through imagination. And that ideal is necessarily
beautiful.

Of all the esthetic critics of the 1860s, Solovev was one
of the few to deal at length with the "woman question," or
the problem of the emancipated woman who sought to live
independently in society and on an equal footing with men.
Although written by a man, *What Is to Be Done?* was among
other things a feminist novel: its heroine lived independently herself and pointed the way toward emancipation for
women in Russian society of the time, who followed her
lead with no little enthusiasm. This trend concerned Solovev, partly because he saw the family as the foundation of
society and believed the feminist movement was weakening
it, but also—and this was probably more important—because he viewed women as both the physical expression and
the philosophical repository of beauty in the real world, and
their susceptibility to radical propaganda of the 1860s upset
him. "Women must necessarily be beautiful," he wrote in
1864,

> if not physically, then morally. Just as we [men] seek
> beauty and grace in her, so she seeks strength and
> thought in us; and if our good friends [the nihilists]

should ever succeed in destroying all that is elegant, all that is poetic, all that is luminous in life, then woman would resurrect it all by her very presence, because she is the primal image of beauty.[37]

Solovev believed that nature demonstrated the centrality of beauty by the mere existence of women. Something ordained by the order of nature could not be forever destroyed by radical doctrine, though it might very well be severely damaged for a time.

Aleksey Tolstoy joined Solovev in asserting the primacy of beauty in human affairs. In his chief statement on art, entitled, "A Scene from *Don Juan* Recast: A Letter to the Editor" and published in *Russky vestnik* for July 1862, the poet complained that most of his contemporaries had abandoned "pure art" out of social motivations. "Freedom and legality," he said, were very desirable, but they remained mere surface phenomena if they did not derive from the spiritual wellsprings of a nation, wellsprings linked to the esthetic sense:

> These [spiritual] strivings manifest themselves in an instinctive feeling for the beautiful, and are inseparable from a love for art for art's sake. A sense of beauty, to a greater or lesser degree, is innate in any action, and although it may be muted and suppressed by outward circumstances, this will always occur at the expense of its moral perfection. . . . [This feeling] manifests itself only in a nation which has achieved a certain level of moral development; but it is precisely here that [this feeling] displays its superiority over the material side of humanity.[38]

To eliminate the sense of the beautiful, Tolstoy argued, is to lower man to the status of a "happy animal." The poet be-

[37] Solov'ev, "Zhenshchinam," *Epokha*, no. 12 (December 1864), 24.
[38] Aleksei Tolstoi, "Peredelannaia stsena iz Don Zhuana," 214.

lieved that a desire for social progress should go hand in hand with respect for artistic values, and not conflict with it.[39]

Dostoevsky's view of beauty harmonized with that of the esthetic critics generally. He began by defining beauty, not as "life," but as "normality, health" (18:102), from which he deduced that it must be eternal: "The ideal of beauty or normality cannot perish in a healthy society," he argued (18:102). And in one of his notebooks he seemed to agree with Leontev when he declared that "beauty is more important than bread, beauty is more useful than bread!"[40] Leontev did not have the artistic talent to advocate the primacy of "art over bread" quite successfully in a novel like *In One's Own Land*, but Dostoevsky would do it through Stepan Trofimovich Verkhovensky in *The Possessed* as the entire controversy came to a close.

Since the esthetic critics were so intrigued by the theory of beauty, we might expect them to have been equally concerned with questions of artistic form, but this in fact was not the case. A radical critic like Chernyshevsky would naturally have dismissed it, as he does in the *Esthetic Relations* when he declares rather opaquely that "feeling and form are opposed to each other" (perhaps here Chernyshevsky was thinking more of social convention: if convention prevented one from expressing one's feelings directly, it was to be condemned). Turgenev based a good portion of his critique of nihilist doctrine in *Fathers and Sons* on the radicals' contempt for form. Near the novel's conclusion, as Bazarov lies dying, he remarks that "love is a form, and my own form is already disintegrating" (8:395). The meaning of this statement is not entirely clear either, but it may be that Bazarov's passion for Odintsova has caused him to realize that love is

39 Ibid., 215.
40 Quoted in Kashina, *Estetika Dostoevskogo*, 169.

a creative emotion, and that which is created must necessarily assume some form. The nihilists wished to destroy the worthless in existing society, and destroyers are no respecters of form. As Bazarov put it, the nihilists' task was to clear the ground for those who would build after them, and thus the radicals could permit themselves a hatred for form, since that coincided with their ideological requirements. Bazarov grasps the error of this viewpoint just as his own bodily form is disintegrating and he is on the verge of nonexistence.

The radical critics did not condemn artistic form quite so forthrightly as did the fictional Bazarov in his prime, but they came close to it. Dobrolyubov occasionally allowed himself to indulge in formalistic or esthetic exercises just to demonstrate to the opposition that he could write about such matters if he chose. But Pisarev rejected any such concessions: he either totally ignored problems of form, or handled them in an exaggeratedly oversimplified manner.[41]

There were a number of writers in the esthetic grouping, however, who knew very well from personal experience that form could not be separated from content. Yakov Polonsky condemned Pisarev's device of translating Pushkin's poetry into prose in his article "Pushkin and Belinsky" as a means of denigrating the poet's ideas, affirming that "form appears together with the thought as if by itself, involuntarily." Lermontov and Pushkin, he said, would never have formulated their thoughts in prose before recasting them in verse: "As soon as the thought and the feeling and the image have come into their own, the first line of verse which emerges from his pen defines the meter in which the entire poem must be written." In the same way, a musical motif invariably occurs to a composer in a particular form: if the form is

---

[41] Konkin, *Esteticheskie vzgliady Pisareva*, 117.

unsuitable, a work will fail.[42] Goncharov, another creative artist, penned a very instructive comment on this subject in a private letter of 1866, where he combined the notions of ideas, forms, and images very effectively:

> As soon as you admit that we are people and possess bodies with five senses and that our impressions are formed and transmitted to the soul through these senses, then you must immediately agree that any notion or idea must be embodied in some form or other. From this derives the idea of beauty, and the need for beauty: this need is a lofty one found only in human nature, not among animals. And once you have admitted this . . . how can you attain one of your impassioned moods except through the imagination, which alone directs and guides all the impressions? You mean to say you arrive at this solely by the cool consciousness that this or that is good, honorable, intelligent, and so one should be attached to it! No, excuse me, these honest and intelligent things appear to you in images, and you become attached to them in the flesh. You cannot love ideas, you can only be conscious of them.[43]

Here Goncharov was expressing himself in general philosophical terms: experience shows that we conceive of things in images, and not as intellectual abstractions; a person is not a wraith, but a being of flesh and blood, and our conception of him is inseparable from his outward appearance.

Goncharov was not writing here as an artist who had to grapple with technical questions of form as he wrote. Polonsky had come closer to doing that in referring to his experience as a creative writer, as did Efim Zarin, who in an article of 1865 argued that even the most "realist" of writers must also be an esthetician since as he works he must solve a series

---

[42] Polonskii, "Prozaicheskie tsvety," 735, 736.
[43] Letter to S. A. Nikitenko of August 21/September 2 [1866]: 8: 364.

of formal problems which demand of him "a feeling of the elegant, a consciousness of measure, training through great literary examples."[44] Such problems as these may be of no interest to the general public, but they are of cardinal importance to the creative writer.

Curiously enough, Apollon Grigorev maintained that no such thing as the formalism so characteristic of twentieth-century literary criticism could ever exist. In an article of 1858 he attacked both the esthetic and radical critical camps in order to demonstrate his independence from them, and in the process rejected criticism of form. Literary criticism, he said, now encompassed psychology, public opinion, and many other areas, so that it could no longer be purely artistic:

> Purely artistic criticism . . . [which] would evaluate, for example, the plan of a work, the beauty or inappropriateness of details as they relate to the whole or the conception of the whole, or would take pleasure in the architectonics or the outlines of a work, not only does not exist at the present moment but never can exist.[45]

This comment may tell us much about Grigorev's view of criticism—and it may say quite a lot about his tendency to overgeneralize on the basis of very limited experience—but in any case the subsequent history of literary criticism has proven him quite wrong.

In addition to form, the esthetic critics also wrote of harmony and disharmony, linking them to notions of beauty and ugliness. Vasily Botkin adopted a poetic approach to the concept of harmony, as when in 1857 he defined the sense of beauty as a feeling for "the harmonious unity between concept and form, between internal feeling and external im-

---

[44] Incognito [E. Zarin], "O kachestve i kolichestve progresa v noveishem dvizhenii nashei literatury," *Otechestvennye zapiski* (February 1865), 710–11.

[45] Grigor'ev, "Kriticheskii vzgliad," 119.

age," a feeling first fully developed by the ancient Greeks who had founded the Western civilization in which Russian culture participated.[46] A few years later Nikolay Solovev would take a more scientific approach to this entire question. In 1865 he linked the "feeling we call the beautiful" with a "harmony between man and the object," although he granted that we could not fathom the "mystery of this harmony."[47] A few months later Solovev went on to maintain that "the cause of harmonious feeling is purely physical, and not psychological, as we once thought: we must seek it in the theory of sound itself"[48] (here he was speaking of music). In a series of articles published at this time and entitled "On the Relations of Natural Science to Art," relying on German authorities much as did the radical thinkers, Solovev attempted to elaborate an esthetic based on natural science and subject to experimental verification. For this purpose he introduced data from physics, mathematics, biology, and psychology. To be sure, occasionally he might slip toward the purely philosophical, as when he wrote that "that which is orderly pleases us more than the disorderly: harmony is the expression of a higher order."[49] In any case, whether the justification for harmony should be sought in metaphysical speculation, as most of the esthetic critics believed, or scientific thought, as Solovev argued, all the esthetic critics agreed that harmony was an essential element of beauty, an expression of the unity between form and content.

The esthetic critics also felt very keenly that theirs was not an age when harmony reigned supreme, that it suffered badly from discord (*razlad*). Many of them connected this disharmony to the rise of nihilism, by which they generally

---

[46] Botkin, "Stikhotvoreniia Feta," 8.

[47] Solov'ev, "Vopros ob iskusstve" (May 1865), 311.

[48] Solov'ev, "Ob otnoshenii estestvovedeniia k iskusstvu" (November 1865), 307.

[49] Ibid.

meant political nihilism. Having defined the beautiful as life, in the *Esthetic Relations* Chernyshevsky had gone on to connect "ugliness" or "formlessness" (*bezobrazie*) with "illness," although he did not dwell on this point (2:10). Nikolay Solovev dealt with it more frequently and in greater detail than most of his contemporaries. In an article of 1865 entitled "Discord" he argued that nihilism was not the cause of that "discord in life and literature" which he was analyzing, but rather that nihilism had "simply become without realizing it the blind instrument and expression of this discord."[50] Nihilism had come into existence because of this discord, but then it had in turn reinforced it. Someone like Solovev would scarcely rejoice at this development, but on the other hand he believed that this state of affairs was so unnatural that it could not long continue. The devotees of disharmony would pass from the scene without heirs. Some would die prematurely, Solovev thought, as had the talented radical prose writer Nikolay Pomyalovsky at the age of twenty-eight in 1863, of alcoholism. He had perished, Solovev maintained, because he "betrayed poetry": an inborn sense of beauty might have saved him, but instead he had dedicated himself to the propagation of ugliness.[51] Solovev developed this argument at greater length in his writings of 1865 on the "Problem of Art," where, among other things, he acutely observed that the deformed generally die without issue. "Everything which is formless and ugly," he wrote,

> has an effect which is limited in time and which for the most part passes without trace. For beauty is completed form, form capable of producing another form in its turn. Monsters do not reproduce. . . . The birth of life forms, like the birth of forms of art, is not accomplished very easily, because it must overcome barriers.[52]

[50] Solov'ev, "Razlad," 38.
[51] Solov'ev, "Teoriia bezobraziia," 14.
[52] Solov'ev, "Vopros ob iskusstve" (June 1865), 487.

Thus Solovev perceived form, harmony, and beauty as positive goods which art should seek to promote, and disharmony and ugliness as phenomena which, though temporarily ascendant in Russian life, would ultimately be overcome because they went against the natural order of things. The radical critics had little or nothing to say about ugliness in their theoretical writings, but many of the radical writers in practice developed an esthetic of ugliness by emphasizing reality's unlovely aspects in their art. Nikolay Pomyalovsky and Nikolay Uspensky provide striking examples of this, but there had always been a powerful tendency of this type in realistic fiction. Aleksey Pisemsky, for instance, though no radical, adopted a similar approach. Nikolay Leskov once recalled that when he criticized Pisemsky's writing of the 1870s for its excessive negativism, Pisemsky retorted: "I describe what I see, and I see nothing but filth."[53] Even Dostoevsky, who elaborated an explicit esthetic in which beauty and harmony occupied a central position, did not always seek such harmony in his literary practice. As Robert Jackson puts it in *Dostoevsky's Quest for Form*:

> Dostoevsky—in complete contrast to Dobrolyubov's purely historical and materialist understanding of the element of discord in human existence—views man's discord with reality as a permanent attribute of the human condition. This concept of conflict . . . has the character almost of a formal creative principle in Dostoevsky's art.[54]

N. V. Kashina is in general agreement with this assessment. She remarks that Dostoevsky regarded man as embodying good and evil simultaneously, and used this division as one of his creative literary principles.[55] Thus practicing writers

[53] Nikolai Leskov, *Sobranie sochinenii* (Moscow, 1956–58), 6: 641–43.
[54] Robert Jackson, *Dostoevsky's Quest for Form: A Study of His Philosophy of Art* (New Haven and London, 1966), 143.
[55] Kashina, *Estetika Dostoevskogo*, 83.

across the political spectrum could derive creative stimulus from a sense of discord, disharmony, even ugliness, while esthetic literary theoreticians ignored this fact. Their theoretical ideal always had to be one of harmonious beauty.

Art and Truth

If, broadly speaking, the esthetic critics were most interested in investigating the link between art and beauty, the radical critics emphasized the connection between art and truth. But this statement requires qualification. For one thing, the link between art and truth was one on which all factions agreed in principle in the 1860s: only some decades later would critics venture to break that link. Apollon Grigorev, a self-defined centrist in the critical wars, made this point as strongly as anyone could have in 1856, at the very beginning of the controversy, when he wrote: "Art, as an expression of the truth in life, does not have the right to be untruth even for a moment: in *truth* is its sincerity, in *truth* is its morality, in *truth* is its objectivity."[56] However, although all factions would connect art and truth, the radicals subordinated the former to the latter, whereas Grigorev viewed truth within the context of art. Chernyshevsky had made the radical stand quite clear at the beginning of the *Esthetic Relations*, when he wrote that "for fully developed thought there is only the true (*istinnoe*), and no such thing as the beautiful" (2:7). In the short run, though, since the radical critics were compelled to accept art as a fact of life, their position on the connection between truth and art nearly coincided with that of the esthetic critics.

The esthetic critics did analyze the relationship between truth and art in much more detail than did the radical critics. In order to follow their argument, however, we must note the distinction between the two Russian words usually

---

[56] Grigor'ev, "O pravde i iskrennosti," 200.

translated as 'truth': *pravda*, the word which Grigorev uses in the passage quoted above, is richer in connotations than *istina*, the term Chernyshevsky employs. *Istina* denotes primarily logical, scientific truth. *Pravda* incorporates much of that, but also includes the concepts of justice and of righteousness. Often enough the two words are interchangeable, but there are occasions when we must distinguish between them.

Since the radical critics regarded the demand for truth as axiomatic in their literary doctrine, they expended little effort on defining it. Pisarev, for example, simply took it for granted that a genuine writer "in each of his creations will incorporate the ideas, feelings, and aspirations of the eternal struggle for truth (*pravda*)" (3:95). A few years earlier, and much less subtly, Dobrolyubov had virtually equated the current, radical, political propaganda line with the truth of art, and conceived of the artist as a mere mechanical recorder of the truth of existence. "Writers," he argued in "A Ray of Light in the Kingdom of Darkness,"

> resemble a barometer which everyone consults, though no one cares about meteorological-astronomical calculations and predictions. Thus when we recognize that literature's chief significance is that of propaganda, we demand one thing of it without which it can have no merit at all, and this is *truth* (*pravda*). . . . In works of a historical character truth must be factual; in fiction, where events are invented, this is replaced by logical truth (*pravda*), i.e., reasonable probability and congruence with the existing course of affairs. (6:310–11)

Dobrolyubov's distinction between historical truth and what we might call "fictional truth" or "verisimilitude" intrigued several critics of varying persuasions. Some tried to preserve the unity of art and science by arguing that both shared a dedication to truth: thus Mikhail Katkov in his programmatic article of 1856 "Pushkin" promoted a unification of art and science on the basis of their common dedication to truth (*istina*):

> Ordinarily beauty is considered the foundation stone of poetry, while truth is posited as the aim of knowledge. But this is one of those formulations which are too crudely constructed. The beautiful is of course an essential trait of art, but at its foundation we should place truth, just as we do for cognitive thought.[57]

At another point in this same essay Katkov developed the notion that "art, like science, operates primarily by displaying the truth of an object,"[58] and therefore there was no essential difference between these two spheres of human endeavor. Moreover, Katkov held that truth was always socially useful: truthful art would necessarily benefit society, as the radicals urged.[59] At that stage Katkov believed that the radical critics merely had their priorities in the wrong order.

Yakov Polonsky, however, parted company with Katkov on the issue of beauty's subordination to truth in art: both were necessary, he believed, and both should coexist on an equal footing. As he wrote in 1859,

> Poetry is truth (*istina*) in beauty and beauty in truth; but not every truth is poetic and not every beauty is truthful. . . . Poetry . . . delights us as beauty and instructs us as truth.[60]

And Nikolay Solovev, after the controversy had raged for a decade, sought to distinguish between a legitimate allegiance of art to *pravda* and an illegitimate one to *istina*, which he evidently regarded as the province of scientific

[57] Katkov, "Pushkin" (January 1856), 164–65.
[58] Ibid. (February 1856), 316.
[59] Ibid., 313.
[60] [Polonskii], "Stikhotvoreniia Meia," 70, 71.

thought. "All these attacks on art, the esthetic principle, and talent," he wrote in 1865, ". . . simply increase the number of literary works depicting something presented as scientific and useful truth (*istina*), and not the truth of life (*pravda*)."[61] Solovev's demarcation line between the radical approach and the conservative one does not hold in every instance—Dobrolyubov, we recall, spoke of *pravda* rather than *istina* as important for art—but it will do as a rough approximation. Still, we are left with Pontius Pilate's eternally intractable question: what is truth?

We know that Apollon Grigorev believed strongly in abstract truth. Indeed he attached primary importance to it because at one level it was not at all subject to alteration or individual interpretation. The ideal, he wrote in 1858, is

> eternal truth (*pravda*), that changeless criterion for distinguishing between good and evil, right and wrong. Thus it is not eternal truth which is to be judged and measured by the ages, epochs, and nations, but the ages, epochs, and nations which are to be judged and measured by the extent to which they preserve the eternal truth of the human soul and by the extent to which they approximate it.[62]

Still, although Grigorev believed in the notion of eternal and unchanging truth, he also knew that the human intellect apprehends that truth in history. Consequently human beings could attain at best a partial comprehension of truth, a point which he emphasized by using the phrase "colored truth" (*tsvetnaya istina*), which helped him to distinguish between "absolute naked truth" (*istina*) on the one hand and "relative truth, colored truth" on the other.[63] Through this formulation, widespread in Romantic esthetics, Grigorev reconciled his metaphysical vision of eternal truth with

[61] Solov'ev, "Vopros ob iskusstve" (July 1865), 66.
[62] Grigor'ev, "Kriticheskii vzgliad," 135.
[63] Grigor'ev, "Neskol'ko slov," 212.

his understanding that human apprehension of it at any particular time must be historically conditioned.

Others separated the truth of reality, i.e., that truth which we apprehend directly in the reality about us, from the truth of art, a distinction of particular interest to creative artists. Thus in discussing the work of Vasily Sleptsov in his private correspondence, Ivan Turgenev maintained that the truth of reality could not be bodily transferred into art, as the radical writers of that day seemed to believe. "Realism in itself is dangerous," he declared. "Truth, no matter how powerful it may be, is not art" (Pis'ma 5:159). Dostoevsky reached much the same conclusion. It is indisputable, he held in 1861, that art must be rooted in reality and remain true to it, that by its nature it cannot be unfaithful to reality and remain genuine art. On the other hand, the truth of reality, though necessary, is not itself sufficient for art: "First one must surmount the difficulties of transmitting actual truth," he wrote in 1861, "in order thereafter to reach the heights of artistic truth" (18:100–101). This formulation makes it clear that in Dostoevsky's mind the truth of art was superior to the truth of reality, a point on which many practicing writers of that time were agreed despite the contrary views of the radical critics.

Ivan Goncharov—who displayed a gift for analyzing general critical issues very succinctly while surveying his own particular literary accomplishments—wrote an excellent brief essay on truth in literature and the relationship between truth in reality and truth in art in "Better Late Than Never" (1879):

> A scientist or scholar creates nothing, but rather discovers truth (*pravda*) which was ready and hidden in nature, while an artist creates simulacra of truth, that is, the truth which he has observed is reflected in his imagination and he transfers these reflections to his work. Precisely this is artistic truth.
>
> Consequently, artistic truth and the truth of reality

are not identical. A phenomenon transferred in its entirety from life into a work of art will lose the truthfulness (*istinnost*) of reality and will not become artistic
truth [either]. Insert two or three facts from life in series
just as they occurred, and they will come out looking
untrue and even improbable. (8:106)

Goncharov's phrase "simulacra of truth" can help us to understand the character of artistic creation: the artist actually
brings into existence imitations of reality ordinarily in other
forms (if we except staged plays, which create simulacra of
reality using the actual materials of reality), and these imitations are to be judged by the same standards of truthfulness we apply to reality itself (although there is a sense in
which anything that occurs in reality, no matter how improbable, is true).

There remains the related question of art and untruth:
how should critic and reader respond to either the depiction
of untruth in reality or the untruthful depiction of reality?
In 1867 Nikolay Solovev dealt with this problem in a discussion of ballet as a genre. He regarded ballet as a form of
"living sculpture" which could provide much esthetic enjoyment, but it also suffered by its nature from a "lack of truth
and inconsistency with reality."[64] But ballet was rather exceptional: there were few such branches of the arts which
critics were prepared to condemn in their entirety as unfaithful to reality. Untruth inhered in an individual work,
and not in an artistic genre.

The problem of untruth was most severe in literature,
which affected the intellect and the imagination directly
through the word. Pisemsky raised an intriguing theoretical
question in this connection, as we have seen, when he declared at the end of *Troubled Seas* that he had collected in the
novel a "faithful though incomplete picture of . . . all [Rus-
sia's] falsehood (*lozh*)." One may wonder in the abstract

[64] Solov'ev, "Sueta suet," 191.

whether it is even possible to make an accurate representation of lies (Pisemsky was fascinated by the phenomenon of lying, and in 1865 investigated the creative liar in Russian society in a short-story cycle entitled *Russian Liars*): probably it is, but then observers will disagree on what constitutes falsehood in reality. Thus Pisemsky's view of the false in contemporary society in *Troubled Seas* did not coincide at all with the notions of many of his critics, who accused him of creating an entirely misleading picture of existing reality. Ivan Goncharov faced similar accusations a few years later, and Nikolay Shelgunov accused him of outright lying in *The Precipice*: "Even the most imperceptive reader will recognize," Shelgunov wrote in a review of the novel, "that *The Precipice* is a concoction (*sochinenie*), that Goncharov's generalization is a lie" (250). Goncharov firmly rejected such accusations, arguing that he had honestly depicted reality as he had observed and understood it in *The Precipice*. Others might disagree with that understanding, but they had no right to accuse him of deliberate distortion. Pisemsky, indeed, at roughly this same time turned the identical accusation against the radical critics: they demanded, he said indignantly, that novelists distort the truth for the advancement of radical political objectives. Thus in April 1872 he wrote to Leskov:

> Meanwhile the novel is evidently becoming more and more a mere statistic of our time and the closest handmaid of history. Our half-bright critics constantly scream at our novelists: "Don't dare tell the truth but lie constantly so as not to damage our lofty chosen tendencies."[65]

Dostoevsky evidently experienced similar pressures during the 1860s, and yielded to them as little as did Pisemsky or Goncharov. He confronts the problem clearly in *The Idiot*

---

[65] Aleksei Pisemskii, *Pis'ma* (Moscow-Leningrad, 1936), 245.

(1868), when Prince Myshkin talks to young radicals who have published an article advancing demands against him on behalf of "Burdovsky's son." Many of the "facts" adduced in the article are correct as far as they go, but they are interpreted in a framework which makes everything come out as "untruth" (*nepravda*), to use Myshkin's word. This is especially the case with their allegations about particular sums of money which can be mathematically demonstrated to be false, in a passage which reminds us a bit of the mathematical corrections in Chernyshevsky's *What Is to Be Done?* But here the context is quite different. Now the radicals argue that strictly factual truth must be subordinated to what might generally be termed political objectives. If one's heart is politically pure, it seems, one need not be hampered by facts. "As for certain inaccuracies—hyperboles, so to say," one of the young radicals remarks to Myshkin,

> why you will surely agree that the most important thing is initiative, the most important thing is aim and purpose; the important thing is to provide a beneficent example, and then later on we can worry about particular details, and finally it's a matter of style (*slog*). (8:225)

In 1864, as a matter of fact, Pisarev had explicitly equated literary talent with political correctness: "A genuine poet born in the nineteenth century," he wrote, "cannot be either a reactionary or an indifferentist" (3:107). If it were permissible, then, to define art in purely political terms, it was but a small step to extend that political approach from art, or from factual accuracy, to the larger question of truth in general: truth is determined, not by mere facts, but by moral and political criteria. By the end of the 1860s the old notion of the objective nature of truth had begun to give way to the idea of truth politically defined, the beginning of a development which would acquire malignant intensity in our century of totalitarian movements.

As a footnote to this discussion, we might remark that

at the end of his life Dmitry Pisarev adopted a more respect-ful view of art's ability to transmit an understanding of truth than he had advanced previously. In his article "Those Who Lull Us to Sleep," first published in his collected works of 1867, he argued that the ordinary reader is frequently inca-pable of arriving at truth on the basis of discursive argument because a critic of sufficient self-confidence can formulate "new sophistries" against all refutation and thus confuse the uninitiated. But untruth, Pisarev decided, simply cannot be propagated through literature:

> Things work out entirely differently when you attempt to clothe your beloved lie in living images. Then one of two things happens: either those images drive you to de-spair and convict you of lying by their hopeless and in-curable woodenness, at which all your readers young and old will either laugh or yawn; or else these images will come to life under your pen, but not to your benefit and that of your false idea. They spring to life in order to rebel against you, to exalt that which you wished to denigrate and denigrate that which you wished to exalt.
> (4:257)

Every reader, Pisarev holds, though he may not be intelli-gent enough to follow a sophisticated logical argument, has had enough experience of life to distinguish truth from falsehood, the "probable from the improbable" in an artistic work. Thus Pisarev finally decided that the truth of art was ultimately more powerful than the truth of science. His was not a position which Chernyshevsky or Dobrolyubov would have adopted. Evidently an "esthetic" strain of the sort that Pisarev so despised in theory always remained strong within him.

Art and the Moral Good

The third large conception with which art was connected in the minds of critics and writers of the 1860s was that of the good, incorporating the moral: art must promote the beautiful, the true, and the good in the moral sense. Here again on the surface there was widespread agreement on this issue among all the participants in the discussion, with the notable exception of Konstantin Leontev. But when we analyze the notion of art's responsibility to the good in more detail, we discover great ideological fissures beneath the surface. The esthetic critics on principle separated politics from the good. Thus in 1863 Edelson criticized his old associate Pisemsky's best-known novel, *A Thousand Souls*, for failing to draw the necessary distinction between morality and politics: "In the final accounting," he said, "this or that political view is not the most essential thing in a genuinely artistic work, for its purposes are much more general and it deals primarily with the *moral* nature of man."[66] Here Edelson was thinking primarily of the moral development of the individual and of his relationship to society. The radicals, however, defined the good quite differently. As Dobrolyubov summarized his view in "A Ray of Light in the Kingdom of Darkness" (1860):

> We measure the worth of a writer or of a particular work by the degree to which they serve as the expression of the natural aspirations of a particular time and nation. And those natural aspirations reduced to their lowest common denominator can be defined in two words: "everyone should be well off." (6:307)

Although he did not use the word 'moral' in this passage, Dobrolyubov was proposing not merely a moral standard for the evaluation of literature, but a moral standard subordinated to a political one: in this instance the political objec-

[66] Edel'son, "Russkaia literatura. Vzbalamuchennoe more" (November 1863), 20.

tive is the raising of the material well-being of every member
of society to the highest possible level. In formulating this
statement Dobrolyubov was doing no more than embroi-
dering on a position which Chernyshevsky had expressed
long before, for Chernyshevsky wished to "negate the independence of art in order to subject it to the categorical im-
perative of politics and morality," as Charles Corbet sums it
up in a study of Chernyshevsky's esthetic.[67] That politicizing
strain was still very much present in the Antonovich who
reviewed the second edition of the *Esthetic Relations*, although muted and brought closer to the position of the esthetic critics. The new esthetic viewpoint, he wrote then,
demands that art "should be not only art for art's sake, but
art for the sake of thought, for the development and clarifi-
cation of our understanding, for the ennoblement of our
character and for the improvement of human relations"
(199). Moreover, Antonovich held that the artist should be
just as moral as his art: if a writer is "honest, noble, and loves
the good and other people," he declared, then his writings
will also exhibit "contempt for everything dishonorable"
(235). Antonovich here couched his opinions in moral rather
than political terms, but not all his ideological allies were so
circumspect.

In any case Dmitry Pisarev was not. In "Pushkin and
Belinsky" (1865), for instance, his entire assessment of Pushkin's place in Russian literary history is colored by politics,
and he condemns Pushkin for obviously political reasons,
saying, for example, that "no one among Russian poets can
inspire his readers with such unlimited indifference for the
sufferings of the people, such profound contempt for honest
poverty, and such systematic dislike for useful labor as Pushkin" (3:400). Pushkin's artistic achievements are of no account here: all that matters is the political impact of his writ-

[67] Corbet, "Černyševskij esthéticien," 125–26.

ing upon society in general, and in particular upon those with the fewest material advantages. In his article on Heine written a short time later, Pisarev went so far as to argue that art has always flourished at periods of political stagnation. "The more indifferent a society becomes to the great ideas of life," he said,

> the more passionately it becomes attached to beautiful forms, although its understanding of them also becomes distorted and shallow under the influence of the general intellectual stagnation. It has always been thus in Europe. Periods of political stagnation and torpor have always been the golden years of pure art. (4:214).

The problems of truth in art and the good in art are conjoined in politics. At the beginning of the discussion of 1855–70 the participants directed their attention primarily to the individual artist and the particular work of art. Even Chernyshevsky adopted this approach when he wrote in the *Esthetic Relations* that "abstract and general ideas" are not part of life for us: we can conceive of life "only in actual living beings," or in other words, in individuals (2:14). In 1863 Pavel Annenkov varied this observation in speaking of *Troubled Seas*: a novel, he said, "cannot transmit entire epochs of development except through an anecdote or an incident torn from an entire mass of events" (2:314). And Mikhail Katkov, writing at about the same time as Chernyshevsky, had this to say about the role of the individual and personal perception in works of art:

> For our thinking there is nothing more joyous than to emerge from our loneliness and find ourselves in the midst of life, and the more individual and particular the object of our consciousness is, the more profound is our enjoyment. The magic of art is founded precisely upon this feeling of individuality.[68]

[68] Katkov, "Pushkin" (March 1856), 285.

With this Katkov defined a major point of disagreement between the radical and esthetic critics. Both groups understood that the artist was an individual who created works
within society and for society. But the esthetic critics emphasized the individual, while the radical thinkers concentrated on the collective context. If one looked first to the
artist's vision, then the "truth" of an artistic depiction could
become quite relative, since individuals can see things in
quite varying ways, and moral perspectives can differ markedly from one work to another. If, on the other hand, one
adopted a collectivist, or political, view of literature, then
one might search for an objective definition of truth at least
in the commonality of individual perceptions, and one
might also believe literature should embody only one genuine moral code, one which promoted the collective's political objectives.

In the course of the debate during the 1860s the individualist perspective lost ground steadily and the collectivist
viewpoint advanced accordingly. "Instead of varied characters in society," Nikolay Solovev wrote in 1867,

> there stand out some sort of copies or reproductions of
> models created by the life of the past. . . . copies and
> masks, repeating one and the same words, holding one
> and the same little books in their hands [a reference to
> Chernyshevsky's recommendation of five or six little
> books as all one needed to read] and boasting in identical
> fashion of their intellectual and moral plagiarism.[69]

Solovev's great opponent of that time, Nikolay Shelgunov,
saw things much as he did, but considered the situation
cause for rejoicing. Shelgunov, the most plainly political of
the radical literary critics of the 1860s, did not hesitate to
damn the conservatives as individualists devoid of any understanding of history or the struggle of ideas in its social

---

[69] Solov'ev, "Idealy," 159.

context. In his valedictory to the controversy of the 1860s, "The Duplicity of Esthetic Conservatism" (1870), he denounced individualists for seeking to distract readers from the genuine problems of life through esthetic mirages. Collectivism, he declared, was the wave of the future.[70] Collectivist doctrine only began to emerge in Russian critical discussion toward the end of the 1860s, and therefore had little direct impact upon the debate for most of the period from 1855 to 1870. However, in certain of its "antediluvian" forms (to use Apollon Grigorev's term) it did make some contributions to the discussion, even though it was overshadowed by the individualist idea of morality in art.

Though they could not have agreed on its definition, the participants in the discussion of the 1860s all concurred in its importance. In 1857 Vasily Botkin argued that the practical spirit so prevalent in his day was the mere outgrowth of economics. And economics, he thought, could not alter the "basic characteristics of the human soul," which were determined by nonmaterial but nevertheless very real factors: "The human soul can never be content with material satisfactions alone . . . human society lives for and is motivated only by moral ideas."[71] Botkin clearly adhered to a rather metaphysical definition of morality as something existing on a higher level of consciousness, and a radical thinker like Mikhail Saltykov-Shchedrin could agree with him on the centrality of moral concerns to society and its art even though he adopted quite a different philosophical perspective on morality. Thus in his theoretical article of 1856, inquiring whether a writer might adopt a morally neutral stance in his depiction of life, Saltykov answered emphatically that he could not. "A man who can look upon falsehood and evil with indifferent eyes," he wrote, "not only

[70] Shelgunov, "Dvoedushie," 68, 70.
[71] Botkin, "Stikhotvoreniia Feta," 3.

does not deserve the title of a servant of art, but in the strict sense cannot even be called a man."[72] At about this same time Pavel Annenkov derived from the general need for social morality the necessity of art as a means of embodying moral ideals in forms which the ordinary person could comprehend:

> This is a constant ideal, and the more frequently it floats above our heads, the more clearly it bears witness to society's moral requirements, and the more fruitful its impact on all the moral aspects of a nation as it constantly renews them. (2:14–15)

In 1863, incidentally, Annenkov criticized Leo Tolstoy for not understanding that literature could not limit itself to reproducing the phenomena of reality "with a certain warmth and liveliness," but must "in addition define their place among all other phenomena as well as their relationship to their moral and clarified type, determine how far they fall short of their own ideal potential" (2:293). Like Saltykov, then, Annenkov held that literature was obliged to formulate a moral ideal in life and to promote the good. There could be no doubt in the minds of either of them on this point, for they both emerged from the philosophical tradition of the 1840s, which upheld the absolute supremacy of the good and the beautiful. One of the best fictional representations of the man of the 1840s, Raysky (*The Precipice*), in conversation declares that as an artist he must always be prepared to "preach . . . sincerely, and everywhere [he] may detect falsehood, hypocrisy, malice—in short, an absence of beauty" (5:40).

Nikolay Solovev, though too young to be directly influenced by the spirit of the 1840s, further developed certain ideas prominent in that decade in his esthetic writings of the

---

[72] Bograd, " 'Literaturnyi manifest,' " 292, 293.

mid-1860s. "All that is wholly beautiful is at the same time moral as well," he wrote in 1867;[73] and in an article of the following month he spoke of the "moral-esthetic development of man,"[74] thus linking linguistically two notions always intimately connected in his mind. Solovev believed that it was incorrect to tie ethics and morality to religion, for religion rightly understood dealt with the relationship between man and the divine, not with the morality of this world. Morality operates through our inborn esthetic sense, something which neither ascetics nor utopians—the adherents of extreme religious or political views, respectively— could comprehend, as Solovev maintained in an interesting passage from "Labor and Enjoyment" of 1866. People have regarded work as torture, as a heroic feat, or a number of other things, he said, but rarely as enjoyment. In fact, the very notion of enjoyment has been little analyzed:

> The views of the mystics in this area, as in many others, differ very little from the views of the utopians. Beauty, the stimulus of enjoyment, is equally incomprehensible to both of them, and the manner in which the former have forbidden that stimulus is identical to the way in which the latter have condemned esthetic enjoyment as unproductive. Neither the mystics nor the utopians have suspected that beauty exercises a lofty moralizing effect.[75]

In support of Solovev's point we may note that in his review of the second edition of *Esthetic Relations* Antonovich dismisses as an extreme "ascetic viewpoint" the opinions of those who would banish all art from society (221). Antonovich must have seen in views like Pisarev's the sort of approach to which Solovev was referring.

At any rate, as he combatted Pisarev's ideas through his

---

[73] Solov'ev, "Printsipy zhizni," 156.
[74] Solov'ev, "Sueta suet," 183.
[75] Solov'ev, "Trud i naslazhdenie," *Otechestvennye zapiski*, vol. 165 (1866), 655–56.

articles of the 1860s, Solovev resorted to science in an attempt to modernize the traditional esthetic equation of the moral and the good. As he saw it, however, the beautiful enjoyed primacy over the good ("It is not art which should learn from morality but morality which should learn . . . from art," Apollon Grigorev had said in 1861),[76] while the radical critics clearly regarded the good as superior to the beautiful.

Apollon Grigorev, though he too belonged to the generation of the 1840s, developed a more subtle doctrine of the relationship between art and morality, especially in his article of 1856 "On Truth and Sincerity in Art." Here he considered the question of the artist's relationship to morality, or the individual artist's moral duty. Up to this point, he said, the problem had always been settled by negating one in favor of the other: rejecting art in favor of morality, as Schiller and Gogol did, or rejecting morality in favor of art, as Goethe and Pushkin did.[77] But all this was on the theoretical level, and even these four writers contradicted their theory in their artistic practice. Grigorev believed that art had to be moral by its very nature: "Art is moral in its essence," he wrote, "to the extent that it is vital (*zhiznenno*), and to the extent that it evaluates life itself according to the ideal."[78] The same could be said for the artist—and here Grigorev developed the well-established notion that an evil man could not produce good art: "An artist," Grigorev argued, "as the bearer of light and truth, is . . . the highest representative of the moral conceptions of the life which surrounds him."[79] Again, though, this was theory, and reality—even the reality of art—required certain modifications in it. Thus Grigorev

[76] Grigor'ev, "Iskusstvo i nravstvennost'," 407.
[77] Grigor'ev, "O pravde i iskrennosti," 133, 134.
[78] Ibid., 145.
[79] Ibid., 143.

admitted that Byron had inflicted substantial damage on society, even though he was a great poet, because of his "lack of a moral . . . view";[80] and although in this essay he concluded that art possessed a "conserving significance . . . in relation to life and its higher moral principles"[81]—by which he meant that it should uphold and preserve the eternal ethical and moral principles which the human race had discovered over the course of the centuries—when he returned to this topic in his article "Art and Morality" of 1861, he maintained that art had always been at odds with conventional morality. Art, he claimed then, "has always and everywhere been openly or secretly hostile to the conventional morality of society . . . and indeed in this lies its higher and invigorating significance" (409). Evidently Grigorev thought of morality as something quite abstract, and believed that art owed its allegiance to this sort of morality, while at the same time he held that art should undermine that ordinary convention which the philistine considered morality.

If toward the end of his life Grigorev arrived at a more ambiguous understanding of the relationship between art and morality, Konstantin Leontev sharply divorced esthetics from morality and constructed an entire system of thought on the supremacy of esthetics in human life. His character Milkeev from *In His Own Land* is reported in the book to believe that "evil is a necessary element of the beautiful."[82] And such a conclusion did indeed follow logically from Leontev's basic premise, although most of his contemporaries recoiled from it. For if the esthetic ideal is all-encompassing, and if, as Milkeev puts it in Leontev's novel, "morality is only a small corner of the beautiful,"[83] then it

[80] Ibid., 156–57.
[81] Ibid., 164.
[82] Leont'ev, *V svoem kraiu* (August 1864), 75.
[83] Ibid., (May 1864), 16.

follows that immorality, and even outright evil, may claim a legitimate place in the house of the beautiful as well. Milkeev went on to write an article on the fashionable topic of women's emancipation in which

> he tried to demonstrate that domestic virtue should not be the objective of all women; that one should not understand the freedom of women as consisting merely of various rights and independent enjoyment; that past ages, without even thinking of emancipating women, had created Aspasia, Dido, Mary Stuart, who were just as necessary as the Vestal Virgins and virtuous mothers, and that our task consists in not falling below the level of past centuries. Before the Christmas holidays his article was returned to him, and he was told it could not be printed because it was simply permeated by indifference to evil and vice.[84]

For Leontev, then, morality was subordinate to the esthetic ideal. If life is to be esthetically rich and satisfying, then immorality must and should exist in the world on an equal footing with morality.

The controversy over art and the ideal, art and morality, art and the good, was bound up with the question of art's orientation toward future and past. Generally speaking, the esthetic critics and artists searched in the past for lessons to be applied to the present. Thus Evgeny Edelson in a discussion of *Troubled Seas* remarked that Russian society certainly needed a clear notion of where it was headed, but in order to formulate that it required a firm sense of its past and a "self-awareness" which only literature could provide through a proper interpretation of the past.[85] Konstantin

[84] Ibid., (June 1864), 481–82.
[85] Edel'son, "Russkaia literatura. Vzbalamuchennoe more" (November 1863), 4–6.

Sluchevsky mounted a stout defense of the past in his pamphlet of 1866 on Proudhon:

> Ignorance or disrespect for the past deprives us not only of the past portion of our lives but deprives us of the future portion as well, because one day the future will also be the past, and therefore nothing. . . . Poetry is fed by the past, but we trample the past under our feet.[86]

Later on Nikolay Solovev made a similar argument linking past and future with historical tradition as the connection between generations. "If we begin adopting a contemptuous attitude toward our past," he wrote in 1867, "then disrespect for the future will also involuntarily appear within us."[87]

It is worth noting that even these defenses of the past derived much of their force from a reliance upon the future, and that was a striking indication of the strength of the decade's orientation toward the future. Tolstoy, to be sure, mounted powerful opposition to that tendency by devoting most of the decade to writing a very uncontemporary historical novel, *War and Peace*, which gained acceptance from most readers by virtue of its artistic power.

The radical critics looked mostly to the future, or to a very contemporary present. Pisarev pointed this up clearly in his study of *What Is to Be Done?* when he remarked that "the author of course takes a completely negative attitude toward the past" (4:9). Again, in an unfinished essay on the same novel he attacked those literary contemporaries of his who "conceal under a collection of rhetorical sophistries their platonic, and sometimes quite unplatonic, dedication to the good old days."[88] The asperity of Pisarev's attitude is unmistakable; and he underlined the point by commenting

---

[86] Sluchevskii, *Iavleniia russkoi zhizni*, 1:38.

[87] Solov'ev, "Printsipy zhizni," 164–65.

[88] Dmitrii Pisarev, "Novyi tip," *Literaturnaia kritika*, 3 vols. (Leningrad, 1981), 2: 412.

that in his novel Chernyshevsky had unleashed "sarcasm and irony" against devotees of the past.

In his study of Chernyshevsky as novelist Grigory Tamarchenko accepts Pisarev's evaluation of *What Is to Be Done?* as a future-oriented work, then asks to what extent the novel may be termed at one and the same time "socialist" and realist, since socialism was very much a phenomenon of the future when Chernyshevsky wrote. He solves the problem by positing an "idea of the historical link between the present and the socialist future."[89] This formulation, though tempting, contains logical difficulties of the sort which even occurred to Pisarev when he criticized one of Pisemsky's shorter works on the grounds that the author "certainly does not understand the future" (3:256). This remark implies that we may define the future in much the same way as a historian defines the past through his understanding of it, and that we may therefore legitimately require of someone that he "understand the future."

On this issue Dostoevsky was very close to the radical viewpoint, if not in theory, then at least in his artistic method. He rather went along with the claim that Saltykov made in 1856 to the effect that an artist must be "a representative of a contemporary idea and society's contemporary interests,"[90] for he also believed that literature should deal with entirely contemporary phenomena, took no interest in historical writing, and cared little about anachronisms in his fiction. As Robert Jackson phrases it in his study of Dostoevsky's esthetic, the writer held that "an artist cannot know the future, but he must, artistically, *guess*, capture a social type 'on time' and 'in time' . . . he must be a historian of the future."[91] In a similar vein N. V. Kashina writes that

[89] Tamarchenko, *Chernyshevskii-romanist*, 232–34.

[90] Bograd, " 'Literaturnyi manifest,' " 294.

[91] Jackson, *Dostoevsky's Quest for Form*, 123.

in Dostoevsky's artistic world "the future (the plan, the whole) in his work exercised a powerful influence on the present."[92] In its extreme formulation, such a view might hold that the future determines the present in much the same way that the past determines the present. In a more reasonable form, it might maintain that just as the historian must identify those facets of the past which have proven vital for the formation of the present if he is not to be a mere antiquarian, so the artist must identify those elements of the present which will be reinforced in the future. In his "Preface" to *The Brothers Karamazov* (1879–80)—a novel formally set in the 1860s which deals with many issues of that decade—Dostoevsky worries that his main hero Aleksey Karamazov may strike his readers as a "strange character" (*chudak*) because he is "not yet entirely clarified," but then maintains that it is precisely such odd types which "sometimes bear within themselves the core of the whole" (14:5). And Pisarev put the matter this way in his discussion of Chernyshevsky's novel:

> All the author's sympathies lie unconditionally with the future; these sympathies are granted without stint to those intimations of the future which can already be detected in the present. These intimations have up to now been buried under a pile of social rubble from the past. (4:9)

This doctrine of the present's determination by the future—more precisely, the divination of the future in the present—might be acceptable had it not been the case that the future orientation of the radicals tended to shade into an intellectually despotic wish to determine the future singlehandedly (although this was in fact not within their power), or at least to establish the intellectual parameters for its com-

---

[92] Kashina, *Estetika Dostoevskogo*, 195.

prehension. Nikolay Solovev caught this frame of mind rather well when he accused the radical thinkers of propounding a "doctrine of frozen time."⁹³ For them history moved along predetermined tracks. At the time this point of view caused quite a division between Saltykov on the one hand and other members of the *Sovremennik* group on the other. Saltykov seems to have been distressed by Chernyshevsky's attitudes in *What Is to Be Done?*, by his tendency to indulge in "a certain arbitrary ordering of details . . . for the prevision and portrayal of which reality offers insufficient data."⁹⁴ However the link between present and future was to be understood, though, the great majority of the radical critics believed that literature should face the future and seek to divine how the best ideals of the present might be implemented in time to come.

Still, the radical critics did not view this problem all in the same way. Dobrolyubov, for instance, agreed in principle that a literary work should be judged by its relationship both to the present and to the future:

> The chief thing for criticism is to determine whether an author is keeping up with those natural aspirations which have already been awakened within the people *or which must soon be awakened at the demand of the contemporary situation*; and then by the degree to which he has proven capable of comprehending and expressing them, whether he has grasped the essence of the matter, its roots, or only the externalities, whether he has encompassed the entirety of his subject or merely certain of its aspects. (6:312. Emphasis added)

At the same time, in this very article of late 1860 "A Ray of Light in the Kingdom of Darkness," Dobrolyubov declared that although writers *should* contribute to social progress,

⁹³ Solov'ev, "Razlad," 18.
⁹⁴ Quoted in Pereira, *The Thought and Teachings of N. G. Černyševskij*, 83.

they had certainly not done so sufficiently in the past. Writers and social commentators all seek the same objective—the betterment of society—but experience has shown that the former usually lag behind the latter: "they [writers] make the masses conscious of that which has [already] been discovered by mankind's progressive activists, they reveal and clarify to people that which lives still vaguely and indefinitely within them" (6:310). Of course, Dobrolyubov wrote these pessimistic words before the appearance of such a future-oriented novel as *What Is to Be Done?* or certain works by Dostoevsky, but the same cannot be said of Nikolay Shelgunov, who flourished at the end of the decade. Perhaps he was writing carelessly, but in his article of 1870 "The Duplicity of Esthetic Conservatism," after granting that both the esthetic and radical camps believed in morality and promoting the good through literature, he went on to make the puzzling statement:

> For you [conservatives] *virtue* is the *beautiful* and the future; while for us [radicals] virtue is the present and that which facilitates movement toward what is better. Consequently, the virtuous man is one who assists people in that movement. That which does not help is immoral.[95]

Shelgunov's analysis is illogical. The radicals approved of the present only to the extent it predefined a better future, as Shelgunov evidently understood when he spoke of "that which facilitates movement toward what is better." That is precisely an orientation toward the future, and Shelgunov would no doubt have developed it had he not been captivated by the artificially neat distinction between the esthetic critics as men of the future and the radical critics and writers as men of the present. In reality the situation was almost the reverse, as Shelgunov admitted implicitly when he spoke of

[95] Shelgunov, "Dvoedushie," 52.

The Precipice and *War and Peace* as of "no significance" for
him because they were so thoroughly oriented toward the
past.

To the extent they actually followed their theories, as
Grigorev constantly maintained, the radical critics consistently looked toward the future rather than the past. One
reason for this is that the future contained no facts which
could contradict their interpretation of it: one man's assessment of the future is in a sense as good as any other's,
whereas in dealing with the past one may resort to the authority of knowledge, of facts, in a dispute, and it is at least
theoretically possible to disprove generalizations. The esthetic critics exhibited a healthy respect for reality as it actually was, and so looked naturally toward the past which
had formed it, whereas the radicals rejected much or all of
contemporary social reality and therefore understandably
yearned for the future.

Most of the participants in the controversy of 1855–70,
then, agreed that art and morality were inextricably inter-
twined, but they did not necessarily assign any priority to
one over the other. The concept of ethics, or a moral code,
was also associated with esthetics in the minds of contemporary critics, but in various ways. After reviewing the problem Norman Pereira concludes that for Chernyshevsky "aesthetics was precisely a branch of ethics,"[96] or in other words
that the radical mind saw ethics as absolutely predominant
over esthetics, which in a moral universe would be dispens-
able. Charles Corbet reaches the same conclusion about
Dobrolyubov.[97] Nikolay Solovev, however, propounded a
diametrically opposed view. He maintained that the very
similarity of the words ethics and esthetics pointed to the
"connection which exists between the ideas of morality and

[96] Pereira, *The Thought and Teachings of N. G. Černyševskij*, 40.
[97] Corbet, "La critique de Dobroliubov," 37.

the ideas of beauty."[98] In his articles of the mid-1860s devoted to esthetic questions Solovev reverted repeatedly to his theory that ethics derived from esthetics, and not from religious conviction or revelation. "The moral feelings themselves," he said in his first article for Dostoevsky's *Epokha*,

> are nothing but esthetic feelings applied to real life. If a man finds every advantage in lying or deceiving and he still does not lie or deceive, then he is guided not by some intellectual calculation, but by the fact that it seems disgusting (*gadko*) and dreadful to lie. . . . The most knowledgeable and well-established people will do rotten things if in their souls they lack a feeling of beauty and nobility, or an ideal which is the highest personal conception of that beauty and nobility.[99]

Solovev would develop variations on this basic theory over the following years, and it was probably reasonably well known in literary circles of the time even if it did not enjoy widespread acceptance, particularly among the radical intelligentsia.

We have little direct evidence at our disposal on Dostoevsky's relations with Solovev in the years from 1864 to 1870. Dostoevsky appended a note to Solovev's first article in *Epokha* (July 1864) welcoming him as a new contributor and indicating his agreement with the main outlines of his thought, though not with every one of his conclusions. From this we may suppose that Dostoevsky found his ideas powerful but not wholly persuasive. Solovev continued to publish in *Epokha* until the journal closed in 1865 and Dostoevsky went abroad for several years. We know, however, that Dostoevsky read Russian newspapers and journals regularly while he was abroad, and it is very likely that he fol-

[98] Solov'ev, "Vopros ob iskusstve" (August 1865), 651.
[99] Solov'ev, "Teoriia bezobraziia," 4, 5.

lowed Solovev's essays in the press. There was also some direct contact between them. In 1868 (probably) Solovev wrote Dostoevsky about a new journal entitled *Beseda* (Conversation), which he thought would maintain the line of *Vremya* and *Epokha*; and in February of 1868 Apollon Maykov wrote to Dostoevsky that Solovev had expressed his "delight" with the initial segment of *The Idiot* which had appeared by then.[100] Aside from this scanty information on the connections between the two men, however, Dostoevsky's great novels of the 1860s—*Crime and Punishment, The Idiot,* and *The Possessed*—provide indirect evidence of the writer's interest in the connections between esthetics and ethics, and we may adopt a fresh approach to those novels by examining them in that context.

Excursus: Esthetics, Ethics, and Dostoevsky's Novels of the 1860s

Recent scholarship both Soviet and Western has tended in effect to equate Dostoevsky's views on esthetics and ethics with Solovev's, even though specialists have paid little attention to the overt connection between the two men. N. V. Kashina, for instance, in her study of Dostoevsky's esthetics writes that Dostoevsky, like Vladimir (*sic*) Solovev, believed in the "coincidence of the ethical and the esthetic";[101] and Robert Jackson comments in a similar vein that "Dostoevsky's commitment to the notion of ideal beauty is a commitment . . . to the ideal of ethical beauty" as well.[102] William J. Leatherbarrow argues that "for Dostoevsky esthetic standards are absolute and immutable: only that which is good

---

[100] See Fedor Dostoevskii, *Pis'ma* (Moscow-Leningrad, 1928–59), 2: 500–501, 413.

[101] Kashina, *Estetika Dostoevskogo*, 170.

[102] Jackson, *Dostoevsky's Quest for Form*, 69.

can be beautiful" (the passage is taken from a section entitled "Ethics and Esthetics" of his stimulating study of Dostoevsky published in 1981).[103] In my view Leatherbarrow is
quite correct in emphasizing the importance of the esthetic
element in Raskolnikov's emotional reaction to his ax murder of the old pawnbroker in *Crime and Punishment*. And
Leatherbarrow is also right in noting that Raskolnikov is
esthetically repelled by the very thought of his crime even
before he commits it: in his mind he characterizes the entire
enterprise as "repulsive" (*otvratitelno*), and shortly thereafter
twice uses the same word—"disgusting" (*gadko*)—which
Solovev employs in his "Theory of Ugliness" (6:10). After
he has committed the crime Raskolnikov compares himself
with Napoleon, the superman capable of promulgating a
new code of laws for mankind. But his own squalid actions
literally could not stand comparison with Napoleon's "beautiful and monumental deeds":

> Napoleon, the pyramids, Waterloo—and a scruffy, vile
> old hag, a moneylender with a red box under her bed;
> what could Porfiry Petrovich make of it! Could he make
> anything of it? No, his esthetic sense would not let him.
> A Napoleon crawl under an old woman's bed? Non-
> sense! (6:211)

In discussing the murder with Dunya afterwards, Raskolnikov refuses to admit that it was morally wrong but does confess that it "lacked the esthetically proper form" (6:490). But
precisely this admission (since it implies that a crime could
have such a form), coupled with Leatherbarrow's ensuing
discussion of Svidrigaylov's repulsively evil beauty, demonstrates that the generalization "only that which is good can
be beautiful" does not hold even for this novel. Napoleon

---

[103] William J. Leatherbarrow, *Fedor Dostoevsky* (Boston, 1981), 85. See also his
article "The Aesthetic Louse: Ethics and Aesthetics in Dostoevsky's 'Prestupleniye
i nakazaniye'," *Modern Language Review*, vol. 71, no. 4 (October 1976), 857–66.

committed immense crimes against humanity, but in esthetically pleasing ways: his immorality was esthetically attractive, just as the evil Svidrigaylov is externally a very handsome man. In short, there is no necessary link between the good and the beautiful demonstrated in this, the first novel Dostoevsky wrote after his encounter with Solovev's ideas.

Beyond that, Solovev himself, perhaps under Pisarev's influence, was dissatisfied with *Crime and Punishment* when it appeared. In one of his articles of 1866 published in *Otechestvennye zapiski* he argued that the more educated a man is, the less likely he is to commit criminal acts, and maintained that in his latest novel Dostoevsky had been less than successful in demonstrating how criminal designs could germinate in the mind of an educated man like Raskolnikov.[104] And that is an important disagreement, since the central ethical issue in *Crime and Punishment* revolves about the notion of the superman, the new lawgiver, a sort of idea which could occur only to an intellectual: if a Napoleon seeks to promulgate a genuinely new set of laws, then he must inevitably be a criminal by the standards of the old law. Whether he ends as hero or criminal depends upon whether he succeeds in imposing his new code upon society. Raskolnikov wishes to discover whether he, like Napoleon, is a new lawgiver who can in the end transgress the old law with impunity.

In addition, Raskolnikov is testing the arithmetic moral code put forward by the radicals: if he can save a hundred lives by taking just one, is he not mathematically justified in killing the old woman? A major objective of *Crime and Punishment* is to show that mathematics cannot serve as a proper basis for ethics.

To be sure, the linkage between esthetics and ethics is a secondary issue in relation to the major points in dispute in

---

[104] Solov'ev, "Trud i naslazhdenie," vol. 165 (1866), 662.

Crime and Punishment. At the time he wrote the novel Dostoevsky was far from certain that the ethical sense derives from the esthetic sense, though he seemed to find this possibility intriguing. In the end, however, he decided against it. If Raskolnikov finds redemption after the novel's conclusion he will attain it through a more or less traditional religious conversion with Sonya's help, and the hope Dostoevsky holds out to him is religious in nature. There is nothing esthetic about it.

In *The Idiot*, however, Dostoevsky does pose the question of whether an ethical code may be based upon esthetic feeling, which may explain why Solovev was so pleased with its first installments. But whatever his initial intentions may have been, in the end Dostoevsky demonstrates that a code of morality founded in esthetics alone leads to destruction, and indeed that beauty in itself can be appallingly destructive if it is not bound up with religious conviction and moral principles based upon it. If we approach *The Idiot* from this perspective we can make sense of the fact that a novel whose central hero is commonly interpreted as a Christ-figure can end in hopeless catastrophe with no possibility of redemption.

If they are interpreted in the light of beauty's destructive power, certain aspects of the novel become more comprehensible than they are otherwise. For example, Pushkin, the esthetic camp's patron poet, is a major presence in the book: near its midpoint Aglaya recites his "The Poor Knight" in its entirety, and Myshkin is closely associated with both the poem and its hero. Aglaya summarizes her understanding of the poem's meaning in the following significant words:

> In this poem we have the direct depiction of a man who first of all is capable of having an ideal, and who in the second place, once he has found an ideal, can put his faith in it, and having done that, can dedicate his entire

life to it. . . . . It is not said there, in the poem, what exactly the "poor knight's" ideal consisted of, but it's obvious that it was some bright image, "an image of pure beauty." (8:207)

Whether Aglaya's interpretation of Pushkin's meaning in the poem is correct or not, her words apply very directly to Myshkin, for he is indeed enamored of all things beautiful. Very early in the novel we learn of the Prince's attraction to the beauties of calligraphy: he writes a fine hand himself and is happy to expound at length on the achievements of great calligraphic masters of the past. He ends a discourse on this topic with a revealing peroration:

> A flourish (*roscherk*) is a highly perilous thing! A flourish demands extraordinary taste; but if it should be successful, if the right proportion be found, why such a script is beyond compare, *so much so that one could fall in love with it*.[105] (8:30)

Thus it is scarcely astonishing that Myshkin is profoundly affected by Nastasya Filippovna's beauty when he first sees her portrait: the author's description of the impression that portrait makes upon the prince employs the adjectives "strange," "blinding," and—most important—"unbearable" (*nevynosimy*) attached to the noun "beauty" (8:68). Shortly thereafter, in speaking of Nastasya Filippovna's beauty, Adelaida remarks that "such beauty is power . . . with beauty like that one could transform the world!" (8:69). And Myshkin does in fact succumb to the power of Nastasya Filippovna's beauty: like Pushkin's poor knight, he dedicates himself to an ideal of pure beauty which she embodies. But there is a crucial distinction between Myshkin and the poor knight: the latter acts on the basis of religious princi-

---

[105] Italics added.

ples, while Myshkin remains on a secular plane, no matter how exalted.

Myshkin's tragedy lies in the fact that his devotion to an ideal of "unbearable beauty" is the prelude to an illness—his personal affliction—and ultimately to destruction. The famous passage in which the narrator describes the onset of Myshkin's epileptic attacks contains elements we have already noted in the description of Myshkin's reaction to Nastasya Filippovna's portrait:

> His mind and heart were illuminated with an extraordinary light; all his unease, all his doubts, all his worries were somehow eliminated at one stroke, were resolved into some sort of higher peace, full of clear and harmonious joy. . . . But these moments, these flashes were only harbingers of that ultimate second . . . which led to the attack itself. This second was, of course, *unbearable*. . . . "What difference does it make if this is an illness?" he finally decided. "Why should it matter that this tension is abnormal if its result, if the moment of sensation, recalled and examined later when I am restored to health, turns out to be *harmony* and *beauty* in the highest degree . . . ?"[106] (8:188)

Still, no matter how highly the prince may value the ecstasy of the instant before the onset of an epileptic seizure, it remains true that the attack temporarily obliterates his normal faculties, and that if the attacks continue without hindrance they will destroy them permanently.

In this connection Nastasya Filippovna's efforts to attain the apex of her beauty on the eve of her projected marriage to Myshkin become even more significant. On the morning of that day Myshkin is told that Nastasya Filippovna is "as busy as only a great beauty can be in dressing for her wedding" (8:491), and of course any woman wishes to be at her

---

[106] Italics added.

most beautiful on her wedding day. As she emerges from the house on her way to church, the narrator describes her beauty not so much directly as indirectly, by emphasizing its effect on the clownish onlookers. And a familiar word recurs in the single brief passage which speaks directly of her beauty: "her large dark eyes flashed out at the crowd like red-hot coals; and that glance was *unbearable* for the crowd" (8:493).[107] It is precisely at this moment of her supreme beauty that Nastasya Filippovna flings herself into Rogozhin's arms and sets off to her doom. Thus Nastasya Filippovna's beauty leads to her destruction, and Prince Myshkin's dedication to that beauty causes his intellectual and moral ruin.

This approach to the novel also makes sense of Myshkin's otherwise puzzling reaction to a copy of Hans Holbein's famous painting of Christ taken from the cross which he sees in Rogozhin's house. Holbein depicts the corpse of the tortured Christ with such excruciating realism that Myshkin exclaims: "Some people could lose their faith by looking at that picture!" (8:182). Furthermore, Myshkin makes this comment just after he—almost alone among Dostoevsky's major characters—changes the subject and refuses to reply when Rogozhin puts to him that central question of Dostoevsky's universe: does he believe in God? Can Myshkin—as many see him—be a genuine Christ-figure if he does not believe in God, or is at least unwilling to confess his belief? True, he is a positively good man in the ethical sense, but that is not enough. What faith in God Myshkin enjoys must be founded upon beauty and harmony, and cannot sustain a challenge from unlovely reality as depicted in Holbein's painting of the crucified Christ. Moreover, we know that Dostoevsky's own reaction to the Holbein was exactly the opposite of Myshkin's. Dostoevsky's wife has re-

[107] Italics added.

corded that when she and her husband first viewed the original painting she reacted to it much as Myshkin does, but it
filled Dostoevsky with "ecstasy," and so overwhelmed him
that he declared Holbein a "remarkable artist and poet."[108]
This is a strong indication, then, that Dostoevsky's view of
the association between religious values and esthetic feeling
diverged from Myshkin's, and that it was not at all the case,
as Leatherbarrow would have us believe, that in Dostoevsky's world "man's esthetic sense, his feeling for true beauty,
is . . . his best guide to true ethical standards."[109] On the contrary, in *The Idiot* Dostoevsky demonstrates that it is fatal to
base a moral code on a sense of beauty alone. An ethical and
moral system cannot be built upon an esthetic foundation,
for the immoral, the abnormal, even the ugly may sometimes appear beautiful under appropriate circumstances. An
esthetic sense may reinforce genuine moral conviction—a
proposition Dostoevsky would investigate in *The Possessed*—
but it cannot replace it. And that is why *The Idiot* ends in
much unrelieved gloom, without the slightest promise of
redemption for its heroes.

Dostoevsky's vehicle for investigating the notion that an
esthetic sense may reinforce and even redeem the moral
sense is Stepan Trofimovich Verkhovensky, the slightly ridiculous but still appealing representative of the generation
of the 1840s in *The Possessed*. A devoted adherent of the esthetic values of the epoch of his youth, Stepan is the only
major character to whom the author holds out the hope of
salvation at the novel's conclusion. The book by no means
ends on a note of total despair, then, even though it also
concludes with the ruin of Peter Verkhovensky's schemes
and Stavrogin's suicide.

[108] A. Dostoevskaia, "Iz dnevnika 1867 goda," in: *F. M. Dostoevskii v vospominan-iiakh sovremennikov* (Moscow, 1964), 2: 121.
[109] Leatherbarrow, *Dostoevsky*, 94.

The essence of Stepan Trofimovich's approach to life is expressed in a phrase he uses while describing his experiences as a young man in Berlin, when, as he wrote to Varvara Petrovna Stavrogina, he stayed up late at night discussing such things as the "idea of eternal beauty" (*ideya vechnoy krasoty*) (10:25). Aside from the metaphysical notion of the eternal, this phrase has two components: the intellectual (idea) and the esthetic (beauty). Although Dostoevsky's attitude toward his hero is nowhere free of irony, Dostoevsky is more skeptical about Stepan's commitment to ideas than his dedication to beauty.

Stepan views himself as an intellectual, a man of ideas, one who seeks to comprehend everything with which he comes into contact. In the process of complaining bitterly to the narrator about his son, Stepan berates his fellow Russians for their inability to produce an idea: it is "the easiest thing of all to cut people's heads off," he says, "and the hardest thing of all to have an idea!" (10:172). Stepan believes it is his duty as a "higher liberal"—"that is, a liberal without any aim," in the narrator's sarcastic gloss—to "propagandize ideas" (10:30). But, as the narrator comments elsewhere, it will not do to promote just any idea: it must be "some higher and extraordinarily noble thought" (10:9). That is why, before his death, Stepan sets out on foot along the highroad with no destination, for there is an idea in the highroad which disappears as soon as one settles upon such a practical thing as a destination (10:481).

Beyond his devotion to the life of the mind, however, Stepan possesses a fine esthetic sense. Quite early on the narrator refers (though not entirely positively) to the "artistic quality of his nature" (10:22); and near the conclusion he attributes Stepan's receptivity to religious experience to the "artistic susceptibility of his nature" (10:505). And for esthetic reasons Stepan considerably alters the structure of his autobiography as he recounts it to Sofya Matveevna during his last illness.

Although superficially it might seem that Stepan Trofimovich and the radical generation depicted in the novel should have much in common, in fact Stepan's dedication to esthetics creates a great gulf between them. When, while living in the St. Petersburg of the 1860s, he defends the proposition that "boots are inferior to Pushkin, and even very much inferior" (10:23); when he argues that the singer Elisabeth Rachel stands above any peasant, or even the peasantry as a whole (10:31–32); when he holds his own against Varvara Petrovna, who, infected by the new ideas, maintains that a simple pencil is more important than the Sistine Madonna (10:265); when he does all these things he defends an entire worldview with ramifications going far beyond the esthetic. Ordinary people may lack an explicit understanding of this, but the uproar which engulfs the fete when Stepan mounts his strenuous defense of esthetics shows that they grasp the point very well on an unarticulated level.

The much-quoted passage in which Stepan discusses *What Is to Be Done?* (the narrator tells us that he has been studying it in order to do battle with the younger generation on its own terms) sets forth an important argument:

> "I agree that the author's basic idea is correct," he would say to me feverishly. "But that makes it all the worse! It's our idea, all right, ours, to be sure; we, we were the first to plant it, nurture it, prepare it—and then what more that was new could they have said after what we said! But Lord, how all this is expressed, distorted, twisted!" he would exclaim, drumming his fingers on the book. "Were these the conclusions we sought? Who can recognize the original thought here?" (10:238)

At the core of these remarks lies a combination of the intellectual and the esthetic: the conclusions the radicals have drawn from the original idea have destroyed not just its intellectual unity but its esthetic wholeness as well (perhaps the two cannot be easily separated in any case): everything has been "distorted" and "twisted." Stepan argues that on the intellectual level the idea had been thoroughly investigated by his generation, but the younger generation's twisted esthetic sense has caused it to distort both the original thought and the conclusions which flowed from it. As Stepan puts it at the fete: "Just one thing has happened: a dislocation of purposes, a replacement of one beauty by another!" (10:372). The intellectuals have succumbed to a new but false ideal of beauty propagated by theoreticians who are by nature incapable of recognizing true beauty.

In the course of his great argument with Varvara Petrovna over radical doctrine before the fete, Stepan declares that at that event he will speak

> about that vicious slave, that stinking and degenerate lackey who will be the first to clamber up onto a ladder with scissors in hand to rip apart the divine countenance of the great ideal [the Sistine Madonna], in the name of equality, envy, and . . . good digestion (*pishchevarenie*). Let my curse thunder forth . . . . (10:265–66)

The "lackey" whom Stepan imagines as destroying the Madonna will raise his hand against the realization of an esthetic ideal. He will do so in the name of another ideal, but now one remote from any conception of beauty. He will act in the name of "equality, envy, and good digestion"—and certainly the latter two concepts, in Stepan's eyes, are squalid and ugly, very exemplars of spiritual degradation. The lackey will be motivated by an ideal which reduces man to the lowest common denominator instead of exalting him to the spiritual heights. Still, that ideal was one which moved quite intelligent and serious men in the Russia of the 1860s: for example the Soviet scholar L. A. Plotkin, in a detailed study of Pisarev's thought, remarks that Pisarev viewed "digestion (*pishchevarenie*) as the foundation of the human organism" and the "key which could resolve all the mysteries of history."[110]

In his *Esthetic Relations* Chernyshevsky had in fact redefined the esthetic ideas of the 1840s in much this same way. He reformulated the notion of the sublime in art as merely that which depicts something very large, and the beautiful as something of which we form our conceptions only through the observation of real life: in short, he shifted such ideas from a metaphysical realm to an entirely natural one. No place remained in his world for either the infinite or the eternal, two conceptions of central importance to Stepan Trofimovich.

Thus Stepan Trofimovich differs philosophically from the novel's radicals in a fundamental way. To be sure, he shares with them a devotion to ideas, and his philosophy is generally progressive and humane, but beyond that his path diverges very sharply from theirs. He believes fervently in the importance of the idea of the infinite and the eternal in human affairs, and he has an inborn sense of the beautiful which the younger generation has somehow lost. As he approaches death, it is partly his esthetic conviction that mankind requires a notion of the infinitely great which brings him to a species of religious belief, though one he formulates on his own terms. But here it is crucial to note that, through esthetic sensitivity, Stepan Trofimovich finally arrives at a religious ideal: he does not remain committed to a purely esthetic standard. Though Dostoevsky recognizes Stepan Trofimovich's many weaknesses, he thinks that ultimately he is on the right track. The younger generation in

---

[110] L. Plotkin, *Pisarev i literaturno-obshchestvennoe dvizhenie shestidesiatykh godov* (Moscow-Leningrad, 1945), 220.

the novel ends almost uniformly badly, but to Stepan Tro-fimovich it is given to renew his contact with the Russian people in the person of the Bible-seller Sofya Matveevna and to accept God. In Dostoevsky's eyes Stepan's life could scarcely have had a more satisfactory conclusion.

Chapter Four

◊

Art and Reality

THE FINAL LARGE QUESTION TO BE TREATED IN this study is one raised by Nikolay Chernyshevsky at the very beginning of the debate over art and esthetics in 1855, an immense problem which subsumes so many others: what is the connection between art and the reality which surrounds us? That there was such a connection no one doubted, but it was a difficult matter indeed to provide a satisfactory analysis of it.

Life as Reality

Where Chernyshevsky had spoken of "reality" in the very title of his *Esthetic Relations*, the esthetic critics preferred to view art as a reflection of "life." Thus in reviewing Aksakov's *Family Chronicle* Pavel Annenkov expressed his dissatisfaction with the fate of Kurolesov, that wife-beater and all-around despot. If the esthetic approach had prevailed in Aksakov's mind, Annenkov maintained, then the old Bagrov should have served as the instrument of Kurolesov's punishment, but in fact in the novel Kurolesov dies unexpectedly and quite senselessly. "We do not say," Annenkov wrote,

> that the artistic resolution of this entire story could have been better, fuller, and more satisfying than that which the course of life managed to provide: we dislike com-

paring art's virtues and strengths with the virtues and strengths of life, as that is quite useless since the two are of different origins and follow different paths. (2:119)

And yet, despite his theory, Annenkov was obviously uncomfortable when art drew so close to life as to partake excessively of life's irrationalities.

Annenkov, however, was more sensitive to this particular point than most of his colleagues among the esthetic critics, who tended to adopt a less metaphysical approach than he to the question. Thus, in a discussion of Pushkin's poetry published in 1859, Boris Almazov defined the "sphere of the poet" as "life in its entirety," holding that poetry had to be concerned with "the reflection of life in all its fullness to the degree possible"[1] and adding that "life in its unmediated form is the chief source of poetic inspiration."[2] A decade later Goncharov's artist-hero Raysky (*The Precipice*) would proclaim that "life is a novel, and a novel is life" (5:43), after explaining that "all of life, in its entirety and in its parts, is incorporated into the novel [as a genre]" (5:42). Something like this grandiose conception lay behind the attempts by several writers of that day—Pisemsky in *Troubled Seas* and *Men of the 1840s*, Goncharov in *The Precipice*, and, most notably, Tolstoy in *War and Peace*—to create vast verbal canvases which would in some sense depict the entire life of society at a given time.

Such formulations as "poetry is life" or "the novel is life" are too vague to tell us much, but they may serve as a point of departure for more detailed discussion. For example Nikolay Strakhov, in reviewing *War and Peace* upon its appearance in 1869, commented upon the remarkable clarity of the novel's representation of reality: "It is as though you are dealing with living people," he wrote, "but at the same time

[1] Almazov, "O poezii Pushkina," 150.
[2] Ibid., 157.

you see them much more clearly than you can in real life."[3]
Here the critic argued that our perception of reality through
an artistic work may be more direct than our unmediated
vision of an equivalent actual reality, or, in other words, that
art is superior to reality in a very important sense. Some
years earlier Mikhail Katkov had argued in similar fashion
that art enables us to "contemplate" life in a manner otherwise unavailable to us:

> Our attitude toward a fact reproduced through art is a
> theoretical attitude, the same sort of attitude which
> forms the essence of knowledge. Through the poet's cre-
> ation a weighty secret of the heart is raised to the liber-
> ated sphere of contemplation.[4]

Both Katkov and Strakhov, then, held that through art—
through calm contemplation or that species of unmediated
contact with other "people" which art makes possible—human beings may know reality more perfectly than they can
know it directly.

The esthetic critics believed that the artist should contemplate or depict life without condemning it morally. Indeed, they thought an artist could scarcely condemn life because he could not even understand it fully: as Apollon
Grigorev wrote, "for me 'life' is something genuinely mysterious" which overpowers "the logical conclusion of any
brilliant mind you like."[5] At least implicit in this formulation
and similar formulations by other esthetic critics were an acceptance of real life as it is and a conviction that it is good
even though we cannot entirely comprehend it. Through
the power of art we gain a greater understanding of life's
mysterious workings and appreciate its beauty, but the artist
does not seek to alter reality because he does not believe that

[3] Nikolai Strakhov, [Review of *War and Peace*], in *Kriticheskie stat'i*, 1: 188.
[4] Katkov, "Pushkin" (March 1856), 282.
[5] Grigor'ev, "Paradoksy" (May 1864), 259–60.

it ought to be or even can be substantially different than it
is. Alexander Druzhinin made this point very precisely in his
esthetic *credo* of 1856 in speaking of Homer: The Greek poet,
he said, "accepted the facts of life as he found them, without
indicating any shortcomings to us, without devising any
utopias, without offering any instructive arguments"—and
yet, despite his acceptance of life, he has remained a "teacher
of all mankind" (7:217–18).

By contrast, the radical mind generally refuses to accept
reality as it is and wishes to see it changed, often quite fundamentally. Furthermore, the utopian believes that reality is
quite susceptible to rational understanding, that in the final
analysis there is nothing "mysterious" about it. Turgenev
caught this attitude very well in Bazarov's words spoken to
Arkady after Arkady has recalled Pavel Petrovich's love affair
with the enigmatic Princess R.:

> What are the mysterious relations between a man and a
> woman? We physiologists know what they consist of.
> You just try studying the anatomy of the eye: where can
> that enigmatic glance you talk about come from? That's
> all romanticism, nonsense, rot, esthetics (*khudozhestvo*).
> (8:226)

If there is no mystery to life, if life can be entirely comprehended rationally, then it can also be judged rationally as
well, and condemned if need be. In "Pushkin and Belinsky"
(1865) Pisarev with intense disapproval quoted a passage
from Belinsky praising Pushkin for his love and devotion to
everything that exists, or, in short, for his acceptance of reality as it is. "In these humble and kind words," Pisarev wrote
indignantly,

> we find the most complete and merciless condemnation
> not only of Pushkin's poetry alone, but of all pure art in
> general. He who loves everything loves nothing at all;
> he who loves equally the plaintiff and the defendant, the

offended and the offender, the truth and prejudice, the blockheaded reactionary and the brilliant thinker, cannot wish for the plaintiff to win his case, for the offended to overcome the offender, for truth to eliminate prejudice, or for the brilliant thinker to achieve a decisive victory over the blockheaded reactionaries. . . . With such attitudes toward life there can be neither love for people, nor an accurate and profound comprehension of their aspirations and sufferings. (3:374–75)

For Pisarev and other radical thinkers of utopian bent, then, reality was not to be accepted, much less adopted as a standard of beauty. They thought life should be appraised very carefully and then rationally reoriented and modified, primarily through the instrumentality of science.

In this attitude toward reality lay the root of the dispute between the esthetic and the radical camps. The esthetic critics rightly saw Pushkin as their champion: Pushkin recognized that life was full of contradictions and irrationalities but did not believe they required any resolution: they were simply to be accepted. The radicals for their part rightly regarded Gogol as their standard-bearer, even though his political views were very different from theirs: Gogol regarded reality as rife with anomalies which not only should but could be altered. In short, the radicals rejected the notion that reality was simply a given to be accepted and even esthetically enjoyed.

The radical rejection of reality was quite obvious in Chernyshevsky's *Esthetic Relations*, for he took as his standard "life as it should be according to our conceptions," which implied a negation of reality as it was at the moment. Maksim Antonovich offered an interesting formulation of this point in his review of the 1865 edition of the *Esthetic Relations*. In view of the definitions Chernyshevsky utilizes in his essay, Antonovich wrote at the end of his review, "it is not the ideal which should soften and make concessions to a given reality, but the opposite: reality must change and approach the ideal as much as possible" (241). It would be difficult to compose a much clearer statement of the nonacceptance of reality as it actually is and the belief that it may be molded almost at will. This is not to say, of course, that the esthetic critics saw reality as immutable while the radical critics saw it as infinitely malleable, but the emphasis of the esthetic camp was placed on the stability of life. And that helps explain the radical intolerance for their conservative opponents. If the radicals are persuaded that reality can be altered quite readily but if in fact it changes only slowly or not at all, then evil men must be to blame: the conservatives, the esthetes, those who deliberately defend routine and the unjust existing order of things.

Among the esthetic critics Apollon Grigorev devoted a great deal of thought to the relationship between art and life. He understood art always to be founded upon life, and even to be something like an analogue of life. "Works of art," he wrote in 1856, "are just as living and original as the phenomena of life itself, they are born and not made just the same way that everything alive is born and not made."[6] At another point in the same article from which the preceding passage was taken, Grigorev defined art as the "ideal expression of life,"[7] where we should understand the word "expression" in an organic sense. Two years later Grigorev would substitute "reflection" for "expression." "Reflection" is a more mechanical concept than "expression," but Grigorev remained true to his organic approach when he wrote then that art "always remains that which it is predestined to be on this earth, that is, an ideal reflection of life, *positive* when there is no disunity in life, *negative* when there is."[8] Grigorev

---

[6] Grigor'ev, "O pravde i iskrennosti," *Sochineniia*, 1:140.
[7] Ibid., 142.
[8] Grigor'ev, "Kriticheskii vzgliad," 124.

also criticized the radical esthetic thinkers for taking "life as a phenomenon (*iavlenie*) as the norm of art." By "phenomenon" here Grigorev evidently meant life as it was actually realized in reality. In his view, though life might superficially appear to lack all rationality, art was obliged to make some sense of it. "Art must give meaning to life," he said in 1856, "must define the sense of its phenomena—positively or negatively, for which it has two weapons: the tragic—or rather the lyric—and the comic."[9] Still, however much he argued that art should infuse reality with meaning, he also knew that reality would resist. That is why, in composing Grigorev's obituary, his colleague Dmitry Averkiev emphasized Grigorev's "belief in life and belief in art as one of life's principal expressions," but recalled that the critic had possessed a strong sense of the "irony of life" as well,[10] that irreducibly mysterious element of life which could never be rationally comprehended.

The idea that reality can be at least partially grasped by the reason, or else that there is an "idea" in its manifestations, occurred to nearly all the participants in the debates of 1855–70: perhaps only Fet in certain of his wilder moments would have denied that life made sense. Mikhail Katkov wrote about this rather intriguingly in his article of 1856 on Pushkin. "Without doubt there is an idea here," he said in speaking of Pushkin's lyric "For the Shores of a Distant Fatherland,"

> but it is difficult to extract it from these sounds and images without destroying their enchantment. There is an idea in a beautiful human face, there is an idea in a beautiful landscape, but how can you express this idea using abstract concepts and general words? The artist catches it in his depiction.[11]

[9] Grigor'ev, "O pravde i iskrennosti," 142.
[10] Averkiev, "Apollon Aleksandrovich Grigor'ev," 1,2.
[11] Katkov, "Pushkin" (March 1856), 286.

Katkov's argument that reality contains an indwelling idea which cannot be interpreted in the terms of abstract philosophy but only transmitted through images and pictures is akin to the notion that Dostoevsky advanced in *The Possessed* when he said there is an "idea" in the open road that one cannot define in rational terms. Perhaps we might dub it an "arational idea," one transmitted directly and without the intervention of discursive expression, as the novelist put it in his article on Dobrolyubov:

> Artistry . . . is the ability to express your thought in personages and images so clearly that a reader after reading the novel understands the writer's thoughts precisely as he did himself while creating his work. (18:80)

However, Dostoevsky—and no doubt Katkov as well—would have denied that a writer could successfully depict reality in accordance with some "preconceived idea." Even Dobrolyubov, a leading proponent of propaganda in literature, was in accord with that. "An artistic work may be the expression of a certain idea," he wrote in "A Ray of Light in the Kingdom of Darkness" (1860), "not because the author set out to preach this idea at the beginning, but because the author has been struck by certain facts in reality out of which this idea flows of its own accord" (6:312). In the abstract, indeed, this view of art is rather similar to Katkov's: the artist transmits through his depiction of reality particular ideas which somehow inhere in that reality so that his readers may grasp them as well.

Among the radical critics Pisarev dealt consistently with literature in terms of its ideas, and as the years passed he moved ever closer to viewing the writer and his creation solely in terms of the ideas to be found in them. He spoke approvingly of Dobrolyubov as a "fanatic for an idea" (*fanatik idei*) (3:280), and at another point defined a writer as a "fabricator of ideas" (3:258), a phrase which placed writers in close proximity with scientists, or discursive thinkers generally. Only three years earlier, however, he had argued that Turgenev had wished to promote preconceived doctrines in *Fathers and Sons* but had simply been unable to do so:

> [Turgenev] wanted to say that our younger generation was proceeding along a false path, but instead he said: all our hope is in our younger generation. Turgenev is not a debater, not a sophist, he cannot attempt to prove a preconceived idea through his images, no matter how correct that idea may seem to him in the abstract or useful in practice. He is first of all an artist, a man who is sincere, unconsciously and involuntarily. (2:48)

Pisarev thus claimed to discern, not merely the points that Turgenev actually made in his novel, but other arguments that he did not succeed in making because his artistic sensitivity would not permit him to contradict the truth of life and art. At the height of his ideological commitment in the mid-1860s Pisarev evidently deserted this position temporarily, but returned to it over the last year or so of his life, as we have seen in the preceding chapter.

In 1867 Evgeny Edelson offered an interesting observation on thought or ideas as the central ingredient of literature. He pointed out that if the idea is truly the main content of any work of art, then contemporary art should surely be incomparably superior to the art of previous ages, since rational thought easily builds cumulatively upon the achievements of earlier times.[12] But it was clear that this was not so, the critic believed, unless one adhered to an extremely narrow view of historical progress. That frame of mind was at least implicit, however, in the approach of many radical critics, who denigrated the art of the past and, like Saltykov, demanded that literature be as up-to-the-

---

[12] Edel'son, "O znachenii iskusstva" (January 1867), 240–41.

minute as possible. In their eyes, the art of bygone times had nothing to say to the contemporary age.

The Nature of Reality

Still, in the final accounting, a central question from which many others flowed in the discussion of the 1860s was that of the link between the physical and social reality surrounding human beings and the art human beings created on the basis of it. Was art in some way superior to reality, or was it inferior, nothing more than its surrogate, as Chernyshevsky had argued forcefully in his *Esthetic Relations*?

The classic formulation of the Chernyshevskian view was the assertion that "a painted apple is [worse] than an actual apple."[13] To be sure, sometimes painted apples seemed excessively passive, and the radical critics resorted to comparisons with women instead. Pisarev put the radical case powerfully, as usual, in his "Realists" (1864):

> Pygmalion prayed the gods would transform his marble Galatea into a living woman, and that is understandable; but to exchange a living and loving woman for a piece of canvas or marble is so absurd that not one of our wild-eyed idealists has yet made an attempt along these lines. (3:91)

Of course the esthetic critics did not agree that the only choice was between the depiction of an apple and a genuine one, or between a living woman and her portrait. They dealt rather with esthetic values where the planes of reality and art did not intersect directly. "Yes, you are perfection, cousin," Raysky (*The Precipice*) says to a woman he is courting at the moment. "But the Venus of Milo, heads painted by Greuze, or Rubens's women are still more perfect than you" (5:29).

---

[13] See Antonovich, "Sovremennaia esteticheskaia teoriia": 201.

Through Raysky Goncharov maintains that the reality of art may be emphatically superior to the reality of nature on the esthetic plane, which is where they must be compared.

The radical critics were on the whole agreed that art was inferior to reality. During his most radical period (1864–65) Dmitry Pisarev was a vigorous proponent of this viewpoint. In speaking of drama, Pisarev in 1865 argued that the fact that different actors may interpret the same role quite differently demonstrates that the text of a play can provide only "pale and indefinite hints at reality" (3:431), things far less impressive than reality itself; and in "Pushkin and Belinsky" Pisarev denounced Pushkin for creating in *Eugene Onegin* a "vivid and brilliant apotheosis of the most joyless and senseless status quo" and for depicting reality as splendidly as if the golden age were scheduled to arrive on the morrow (3:357). The poet had totally disregarded the dreadful social injustices of his day such as serfdom, the critic complained.

These remarks of Pisarev's point up a strong tendency on the radical intelligentsia's part to concentrate on the unlovely aspects of existing reality. As Evgeny Edelson said in an essay of 1864, the new critical school demanded "first of all a malicious attitude toward reality."[14] The writers of this school in particular strove to eliminate all barriers whatever between themselves and reality:

> Social pathologies, genuine and concocted or exaggerated, faults, the filth and banality of life, all this—not artistically reworked or purified, but in its raw state—has begun to be presented to the public for its consideration; and the public is a bit taken aback by such a quantity of filth discovered in its depths, in its pools and backwaters, and now brought out into the light.[15]

[14] Edel'son, "Russkaia literatura. Sovremennaia natural'naia shkola," *Biblioteka dlia chteniia*, no. 3 (March 1864), 18.
[15] Ibid., 10.

Certain apparent contradictions within the radical view of reality may be eliminated if we distinguish between the reality of nature and social reality. The radicals accepted the reality of nature, and argued that nothing our imagination could create could be more beautiful than a forest or a lake, a mountain or a stream, or a lovely woman. Man could not improve in the slightest upon the beauty of nature thus understood. But the radical critics thought it a waste of time to reproduce such beauty except as a surrogate: one might purchase a seascape if one could not live by the sea, but one would certainly not give up the opportunity to live at the shore in exchange for a seascape, even by the most brilliant of artists. But the radical attitude toward social reality was entirely different: since social reality was created by man, it could also be altered by man, they thought. The radical critics regarded existing social reality as quite unsatisfactory and worked to change it through all available instrumentalities, including art. As Edelson put it, for example, Antonovich held that art should work for the "creation of dissatisfaction with the present and a passionate aspiration for the future."[16]

If one begins with this general dichotomy—it is not absolute, of course, for man can alter natural reality too, and there are obvious limits to the changes which might conceivably be introduced into social reality—then one can eliminate a seeming contradiction in the radical view of art: the belief, on the one hand, that reality is superior to art against the conviction, on the other, that reality stands much in need of improvement. "Reality," Dobrolyubov wrote, "from which the poet takes his materials and inspiration, has its natural sense (*naturalny smysl*); if this is violated the very *life* of the subject is destroyed, and there remains only its lifeless carcass" (6:313). Existing social reality thus had a particular "natural sense"—a phrase close to what others might

---

[16] Edel'son, "O znachenii iskusstva" (January 1867), 229.

term an "idea"—and indeed only one such sense. It was that
sense which each artist had to discover and to proclaim in
order to help raise reality to its ideal state. "Evidently it is
clear that now we do not need people who would 'raise us
even more above our surrounding reality,'" Dobrolyubov
wrote in "When Will the Real Day Come?" (1860), "but
rather people who will raise—or teach us to raise—reality
itself to the level of these rational demands of the sort which
we have already formulated" (6:103). Art could transform
social reality if and only if it correctly analyzed the "natural
sense" of that reality and moved it along that trajectory. In
this theory of the superiority of reality over art there is no
place for either individual perceptions of reality in the present or generally accepted perceptions of reality which have
receded into the past.

The esthetic critics had their own difficulties at the theoretical level with the relationship between reality and its
perception. Thus in 1859 Fet wrote that poetic activity in-
volves both the objective and the subjective, but that only
the latter is really of interest since all artists deal with the
same objective reality.[17] The problem of the subjective interpretation of an objective reality puzzled such esthetic critics
as Evgeny Edelson.

In his essay of 1867 on art and civilization Edelson argued that reality as a conception has no meaning until and
unless reality is interpreted by human consciousness, and
that this consciousness changes and develops throughout
history.[18] "Strictly speaking," he wrote,

> we see, we contemplate with rational clarity all of living
> reality only to the extent it has passed through our own
> artistic reworking or else has been reworked by artists of
> the brush, chisel, pen, or word before our time.[19]

[17] Fet, "O stikhotvoreniiakh Tiutcheva," 65.
[18] Edel'son, "O znachenii iskusstva" (February 1867), 324.
[19] Ibid., 325.

In another place he asserted that the "only facts in human experience" are our "impressions,"[20] or, in other words, that the only way we can apprehend reality is through the spirit: indeed he maintained that we perceive ourselves only through the spirit as well.[21] The artist depicts reality as he understands it, to be sure, and only as he understands it, but he seeks to arrive at a "unified comprehension of the universe," as Edelson phrased it in his article of 1860 "On Poetry." While developing this thought Edelson sustained the legitimacy of individual modes of perception as opposed to the radical ideal of the single mode by the observation that our souls wish to assimilate the laws of nature, and although we may accept violations of the laws of perspective in, say, Hogarth's pictures, we could not sustain them in reality[22]— which may be interpreted to mean that we are more flexible in our interpretations of reality through art than in our unmediated perception of it. And indeed reality may be perceived not only by individuals but by entire cultures as well: "Poetic and other works of the imagination," he wrote in the same article, "are the chief living monuments of the worldviews of the past, and in this sense they are powerful movers of civilization."[23]

Other critics and writers advanced variant views as to what art does to the reality with which it deals, and how it is sustained by that reality. Apollon Grigorev held that art transforms an ever-changing reality into motionless forms capable of transmission through time and space: "Art catches life, which is eternally flowing, pours its moments out into lasting forms while linking them, through a process which still remains mysterious, to the common idea of the human soul."[24] At the same time the ideal, though closely

[20] Ibid. (March 1867), 119.
[21] Ibid., 118.
[22] Edel'son, "O poezii," 13.
[23] Ibid., 30.
[24] Grigor'ev, "Obozrenie," 187–88.

related to reality, was by no means identical to it. In "Realism and Idealism in Our Literature" (1861) Grigorev criticized both Tolstoy and Pisemsky for displaying what he called "negative realism," and declared that "neither of them has a definite ideal in the face of which certain phenomena would seem false, except for the negative ideal of 'reality' " (437). Reality as it was fell too far short of the ideal to be employed as a standard of judgment, Grigorev thought.

Most esthetic critics held that reality fell short of the ideal because it was replete with apparently or actually random occurrences, events which lacked logic or consequence and therefore could not be part of an "idea" of reality. On this issue Mikhail Katkov adopted a minority view among the esthetic critics. In his article of 1856 he maintained that seemingly chance events were in fact connected, and that it was the task of art to display those connections. He argued that in art the logical not only could, but should, be constructed from the apparently random:

> A phenomenon depicted by a poet should not appear to be the work of abstract thought, but of reality; it should express its idea entirely freely; every element of it taken separately should be absolutely fortuitous, and only in their overall effect should all these chance occurrences become an essential expression of their truth.[25]

A page later Katkov rephrased his argument. "The more fortuitous the subject of poetic depiction apparently is," he wrote, ". . . the higher it is in the artistic sense."[26] Katkov evidently thought that ultimately there was no such thing as a chance occurrence, and that art could demonstrate that even random reality was subject to reason.

Other esthetic critics, however, maintained that reality

[25] Katkov, "Pushkin" (March 1856), 283.
[26] Ibid., 284.

did suffer from accidental accretions which art must simply
eliminate in order to demonstrate its underlying rationality.
In a thoughtful review of Sergey Aksakov's *Family Chronicle*
Pavel Annenkov declared that novel truly artistic because
the events it described, while obviously drawn from reality,
had been cleansed of those "chance occurrences" which
often make life seem senseless. "Life, of course, should have
the same meaning overall [as its depiction in literature]," he
wrote,

> but in its course and in its details it is not so clear and
> consistent, and is remarkable for its greater variety, quite
> frequent arbitrariness, caprice, and vivid, though tem-
> porary, contradictions of its own purpose. (2:119)

Life's fortuitous events have no place in art, which should
be informed by rationally developed thought.

Evgeny Edelson adopted a view much like Annenkov's
in his essay of 1863 on Pisemsky's *Troubled Seas*, when he
declared that "strict and serious artistic work in itself cor-
rects all that could be fortuitous and inessential in the author's attitude toward his subject."[27] And even Dobrolyubov
agreed with Annenkov and Edelson that theory could properly demand that the chance events which form so prominent a part of life be eliminated from works of art. His opponents, he wrote in "A Ray of Light in the Kingdom of
Darkness," claimed that he believed a dramatist should include random events in his plays simply because they occur
in real life—but that was not so, since he held neither to the
"daguerrotype" view of art nor the old esthetic theory
(6:305, 307). He, too, believed that the true sense of reality
could be much better discerned if the fortuitous were re-
moved through the power of art.

---

[27] Edel'son, "Russkaia literatura. Vzbalamuchennoe more" (December 1863),
12.

This does not exhaust the possible ways in which critics could see the relationship of art and reality. For example, at the end of a lengthy review of Dobrolyubov's works entitled "The Problem of Art," Nikolay Solovev elaborated an ambitious notion of poetry as the artist's "second life":

> In spasms of unsatisfied longing human genius produces poetry, in which man finds satisfaction of his aspiration toward the infinite, in which he feels completely free, morally bettered, comforted and even happy, and in which, finally, he places all his most cherished thoughts and hopes. Poetry is something like a second life in which the phenomena of reality are presented transformed and perfected. Only poetry can give us a notion of what higher happiness is.[28]

Thus in Solovev's conception the poet uses the materials of reality to recreate reality in his imagination for the purpose of showing how it could adhere more closely to an ideal also derived from that reality.

The biographer of Efim Zarin ("Incognito"), after praising him for his defense of the traditional verities, in summarizing his esthetic makes the point that in Zarin's mind a "fact" reproduced in art was not an actual fact but "rather the artist's conception of reality." However, when this fact enters art it becomes part of a changed reality: "In a work of fiction, in his opinion, the artistry of the depiction of a fact amounts at the same time to its introduction into reality."[29] Zarin himself had written in an early review of Dobrolyubov's collected works that a novel after all does not even claim to reflect reality as it actually exists: that is done by "reports, denunciations, notes, and court transcripts." Lit-

---

[28] Solov'ev, "Vopros ob iskusstve" (August 1865), 655.
[29] See the article by A. Nikolaev on Zarin in *Russkii biograficheskii slovar'*, 25 vols. (St. Petersburg, 1896–1918), 7:234.

erature, he said, deals with "the entire content and direction of [society's] intellectual and moral powers."[30]

As a practicing novelist, Dostoevsky accepted some of the esthetic camp's theoretical ideas. Like Grigorev, he sensed the fleeting quality of reality, and used to speak of "flowing reality" (*tekushchaya deystvitelnost*).[31] For him reality was ever in flux. The very nature of his craft compelled him to fix that flux in permanent forms, though he came closer to preserving a sense of its instability than perhaps any other writer ever has. Yet Dostoevsky did not hold with the interpretation of reality on the basis of preconceived schemes. Dostoevsky thought Dobrolyubov ("a theoretician . . . and in many cases . . . poorly acquainted with reality" [18:81]) suffered extensively from that shortcoming. To Dostoevsky's mind a theory was legitimate only if it emerged naturally from the study of accurate factual material:

> But a writer's views and ideas derived on the basis of an analysis of the material he has accumulated are quite another matter; this is not at all a preconceived and idealistic view, but a realistic (*realny*) view, expressing—depending on the writer's ability—sometimes a complete contemporary social conception of the life of the people at a particular moment. (19:179)

Still, if we consider the sort of reality Dostoevsky analyzed in his novels, we discover that for him the interesting aspects of reality were not necessarily the social pathologies of the time (as they usually were for the radicals), but the unusual and the extraordinary as distinct from the typical and the everyday. In this area Dostoevsky's journalistic background affects his fiction:[32] journalists look for "news,"

---

[30] Z- [E. Zarin], [Review of Dobroliubov's *Sochineniia*], *Biblioteka dlia chteniia*, no. 7 (July 1862), 86–87.

[31] See, for example, Dostoevskii, 11:73.

[32] On this topic see Charles A. Moser, "Dostoevsky and the Aesthetics of Jour-

those highly contemporary and unusual events which are
quite "real" because they have actually occurred. A passage
of great significance for an understanding of Dostoevsky's
view of art occurs in a letter of his written to Nikolay Strakhov in 1869:

> I have my own special view of reality; what most people
> term almost fantastic and exceptional for me comprises
> the very essence of the actual. The ordinariness of an
> event and a standard view of it is not realism, in my opin-
> ion, and even quite the opposite. In every issue of the
> papers you will find accounts of the most actual facts and
> the most puzzling ones. Our writers consider them fan-
> tastic, and pay no attention to them; but indeed they are
> reality because they are facts. Who will note them, elu-
> cidate them and write them down? They happen every
> minute of the day, they are not exceptional.[33]

In Dostoevsky's mind a genuine artist perceives the fantastic
element in reported reality (the "news" of journalism) and
formulates, if only intuitively, the laws governing that fantastic reality. If the artist can then apply these laws successfully to imaginative literature, his writing may possess great
predictive power, as Dostoevsky thought his fiction did.

Dimitry Pisarev devised a rather startling view of the relationship between art and reality in dealing with the figure
of Rakhmetov, that ideal of ideals in Chernyshevsky's *What
Is to Be Done?* In his novel Chernyshevsky admitted that he
had met very few examples of such a man as Rakhmetov in
reality. He also considered it unlikely that his readers had
ever met such persons, or that they would be capable of
"seeing" them even if they should encounter them (11:210).

---

nalism," *Dostoevsky Studies: Journal of the International Dostoevsky Society*, vol. 3
(1982), 27–41.
    [33] Letter to Strakhov of Febrary 26/ March 10, 1869: 29/1:19.

Leskov, a sympathetic reader of Chernyshevsky's novel in the summer of 1863 and a reviewer, also confessed that he had never run across anyone like the heroes of *What Is to Be Done?*[34] But Pisarev, confronted with this situation, argued that the very existence of such people as Rakhmetov in actuality was guaranteed by the vividness of Chernyshevsky's literary images. Pisarev's was an extraordinary assertion of the power of art:

> Chernyshevsky has seen . . . many phenomena of a sort which speak quite persuasively of the existence of the new type and of the activity of extraordinary people like Rakhmetov. If these actual phenomena did not exist, then the figure of Rakhmetov would be just as pale as Insarov. And if these phenomena actually exist, then perhaps the bright future is not at all so immeasurably distant from us as we have come to think. (4:49)

Thus as Pisarev sees it, the existence in reality of certain types of people is either demonstrated or strongly indicated by the vividness of their images in literature: in his future-oriented world literary creations may call particular types of actually existing individuals into being.

The controversy over whether art was inferior or superior to reality was never definitively settled. In theory there was a neat dividing line between the radical and the esthetic critics, with the former asserting the supremacy of reality over art while the latter upheld the superiority of art over reality. But at the same time the esthetic critics never denied the importance of reality for art, even in their most extreme theories, and the radicals behaved and sometimes spoke as though art could in fact affect social reality, which was, after all, created just as much by the mind of man as was art.

Linked to this overarching problem was the lesser one

[34] Nikolai Leskov, "Nikolai Gavrilovich Chernyshevskii v ego romane 'Chto delat'?'," *Sobranie sochinenii* (Moscow, 1956–58), 10:21.

of exactly how the artist was to "reproduce" the reality that he presented to his audience, a question of especial importance for literature. Pierre-Joseph Proudhon had held that "in the beginning was the Thing," and not, as St. John would have it at the great opening of his Gospel, the Word.[35] It was relatively easy to apply such an approach to sculpture or especially drama on the stage, which used the materials of reality to create a representation of it; but what are we to do with literature, which not only relies upon the word as its medium but which could also be extraordinarily ambitious in presenting a broad panorama of social reality?

The discussion of this point during the period from 1855 to 1870 offered nothing very startling. Chernyshevsky had decreed from the beginning, in the *Esthetic Relations*, that art's primary task was the "reproduction (*vosproizvedenie*) of nature and life" (2:77). He did not consider the problem of how that "reproduction" might best be accomplished, which gave his antagonists such as Nikolay Solovev the opportunity to chide him for demanding that art merely "copy" reality and to quote Belinsky to the effect that the ability to copy from nature, though a necessary condition for becoming a poet, was by no means a sufficient one.[36] In his review of the second edition of the *Esthetic Relations* (1865) Maksim Antonovich defended Chernyshevsky's position, at considerable length, by drawing a detailed distinction between "imitation" of nature—which he equated largely with photography, the mechanical reproduction of that which is before the eye—and the creative "reproduction" of reality. "The reproducing artist," he wrote,

> takes a conscious and rational approach to his work; he reproduces with greatest accuracy the most important

---

[35] See Edward S. Hyams, *Pierre-Joseph Proudhon: His Revolutionary Life, Mind and Works* (New York, 1979), 267.
[36] Solov'ev, "Kritika kritiki," 293.

and essential traits, depicts others not so clearly, and still others he omits altogether; in the most essential traits he does not transmit everything down to the finest details, but only those aspects of it which to his mind are especially characteristic of the object. The artist makes a copy of nature too, and the closer it is to nature the better; but this is a conscious and rational copy, one which does not follow every detail of the original slavishly, but reproduces only the predominant details. (219)

Antonovich thus argued that the artist had to pass judgment on reality: he decided which aspects of reality were especially "characteristic" in order to emphasize them. And yet the notion of a "copy" is still at the core of this view. The artist, far from creating a "simulacrum" of reality, merely chooses among the details that reality presents to his consciousness.

In discussing this topic, Ivan Goncharov resorted primarily to the word "reflection," used in association with the traditional notion of a mirror or similar object which provides an image of the substantial reality about it. "If images are typical," he wrote in "Better Late than Never" (1879),

then they necessarily reflect within themselves—more or less powerfully—the epoch in which they live, for which reason they are typical. That is to say, within them will be reflected, as in a mirror, the phenomena of social life, and morals, and general way of living. And if the artist is himself profound, then there is a psychological aspect to them as well. . . .

I myself, and the milieu in which I was born, brought up, and lived—outside my own consciousness, all this has been mirrored by the power of reflection in my imagination, as a landscape seen through a window may be reflected in a mirror, or as occasionally in a small pond there may be reflected an enormous reality: the sky inverted above the pond with its tracery of clouds, trees, a mountain with some buildings, people, animals, vanity, and immobility—all this is a miniature likeness. (8:72)

The idea of "reflected" reality contains a certain mechanical element too, to be sure, but Goncharov stresses the unconscious character both of the absorption of surrounding reality by the artist and his later recreation of it, whereas Antonovich underlines the consciously rational nature of the artist's decisions as he reproduces the reality before him.

Turgenev's doctrine of artistic reproduction was similar to Goncharov's. In 1862 Fet had declared *Fathers and Sons* a failure because, in his opinion, Turgenev had approached his subject with a preconceived tendency. Turgenev rejected Fet's opinion entirely: he still did not know, he said, whether he "loved Bazarov or hated him," whether he had wished to "exalt Bazarov or condemn him." "I'll tell you one thing, though," he went on in a letter to the poet:

> I sketched all those characters the very same way I would sketch mushrooms, leaves, or trees; they caught my eye and I set about drawing them. But it would be a strange mockery to reject my own impressions simply on the grounds that they resembled tendencies. (4:371)

Thus Turgenev sees reality as an objective entity which an inner artistic urge compels him to reproduce. Not by chance does he speak of natural reality ("mushrooms, leaves, or trees") in the same breath with social reality. If we are to believe Dostoevsky or Katkov, there can be "ideas" within natural reality just as there can within social reality, and it is the artist's task to reproduce that reality in such a way as most effectively to transmit those ideas ("impressions which resemble tendencies") to his audience. Turgenev was within the Pushkinian tradition: he accepted reality with all its ironies, paradoxes, even injustices, and found it beautiful.

Dostoevsky was on the other side of that divide; or at

least he believed that reality was highly unstable, even if he did not consider that it could be remolded quite so easily as did the radicals. He even displayed certain links to Pisarev in his critique of a realism (Dostoevsky called it naturalism) which simply viewed the good and evil of reality as givens. As N. V. Kashina phrases it after a detailed study of Dostoevsky's esthetic views,

> Naturalism, reducing the role of subjective creation to that of a photograph, eliminates the correction [of reality] by an ethical ideal within the creative process and transforms art into an immoral phenomenon.[37]

And Dostoevsky himself once reportedly said to a young acquaintance of his that it was "rubbish" to demand that "an artistic work reflect life" since "the writer (the poet) [*sic*] creates life, a life in such full amplitude as did not exist before him."[38] Such an understanding fits well with Dostoevsky's artistic practice. In his fiction he sought not only to create a "fuller" life than reality afforded by drawing upon the extraordinary—not to say the pathological—for his material, but he also sought to define and extrapolate the laws of contemporary reality to be tested against the future "facts" of social reality. There was, however, this difference between the radical approach to a future-oriented literature and Dostoevsky's, that the radicals sought as it were to predefine the future from the vantage point of the present, whereas Dostoevsky respected the unfathomable laws of life and attempted merely to comprehend them intuitively, and then check them against the future development of actual reality.

Logically we might expect that those who took a prescriptive view of reality and literature should also demand that literature judge existing reality in some form, while

[37] Kashina, *Estetika Dostoevskogo*, 104.
[38] E. Opochinin, "Besedy s Dostoevskim," *Zven'ia*, no. 6 (1936), 472.

their opponents would either oppose such judgment or be quite ambiguous about it.

Here again Chernyshevsky's *Esthetic Relations* furnishes the foundation of the radical position with its statement that art must concern itself not only with the "reproduction" of life but with its "explanation" as well, followed by the remark that any artist must pronounce "judgment (*prigovor*) on the phenomena he depicts" (2:85). The more consistent of Chernyshevsky's followers accepted this doctrine with no difficulty, especially since they shared his negative view of existing social reality, but there was also a certain middle ground upon which some esthetic and radical critics could meet. Members of both groups believed, for instance, that art must pass some sort of moral judgment on reality, but the esthetic critics argued that this must not be done consciously. "The great significance of any disciplined and accurate narration," Pavel Annenkov wrote in his study of the *Family Chronicle*, "consists in this, that conclusions which it did not seek at all and of which it had not even thought, unavoidably appear in the reader's mind of themselves" (2:114). Annenkov no doubt thought this an entirely desirable situation, but Dobrolyubov had a great deal more difficulty with it even though he made a major point of seemingly accepting it in what remains perhaps his most famous single article, "What Is Oblomovism?" of 1859. "The life [Goncharov] depicts," Dobrolyubov wrote at the outset of his discussion, "does not serve for him as a means of abstract philosophizing, but as a direct aim in itself. He cares nothing for his reader or for the conclusions you may draw from his novel: that is entirely your affair" (4:399). Precisely this interpretation, of course, justified Dobrolyubov in going on to draw extraordinarily wide-ranging conclusions about the Russian reality that Goncharov had depicted in his novel, to provide interpretations that Goncharov had not only not offered his reader but that quite possibly had never even entered his mind.

For Goncharov was persuaded that art should not judge the reality it depicts. In a letter of 1869 to a radical friend Goncharov defended his image of Mark Volokhov (*The Precipice*) on the gounds that he had dealt honestly with reality as he understood it: "A work of art is not a speech for the prosecution, not a speech for the defense," he argued, "and not a mathematical proof either. It does not condemn, justify, or prove anything, but depicts."[39] Some ten years earlier Goncharov had placed similar sentiments in the mouth of Oblomov in conversation with a writer, Penkin, who visits him at home. Penkin specializes in producing "literature of exposure" condemning the moral filth of Russian society, and Oblomov objects strenuously to that literary approach. "Depict a thief, a fallen woman, a conceited idiot," he exclaims, "but don't forget the human being! Where is humanity? You want to write with your head alone!" He later argues that one may condemn a "usurer, a hypocrite, or a corrupt official," but one must remember they are nonetheless human beings, and therefore still entitled to respect (4:30). Goncharov thus answered affirmatively and well in advance the question an indignant Pisarev would ask some years later: are we to love the offender as well as the offended, the blockhead as well as the brilliant thinker?

On the other hand, when Pisemsky adopted an analogous literary approach, Evgeny Edelson found it objectionable. Edelson felt that Pisemsky did not meet his requirement that every writer possess a moral ideal which that writer could transmit to any reader through his depiction of reality:

> However, even as he depicts a type who unquestionably emerges from observation of a particular reality, as he yields to the historical necessity of this type, an author with a certain sensitivity of moral feeling—while remaining wholly an artist and without resorting to didacti-

---

[39] Letter to E. P. Maikova of April 1869: 8:401, 402.

cism—cannot avoid pronouncing moral judgment. It is precisely this absence of a moral ideal obligatory for any soul which lives with full force which one senses in Pisemsky's novel [*A Thousand Souls*].[40]

A writer of any worth by Edelson's definition simply could not help passing judgment on reality in the process of describing it: this necessity sprang from the very nature of art. And yet Edelson and others, unlike the radicals, held that the passing of that judgment should not be a conscious process.

Nature, Man, and Society

The participants in the debate of 1855–70 did not have much to say about nature. The world of nature was essentially a given, and so the critics spent little time analyzing its description in, say, Turgenev's works. Nature plays a very important role in Aksakov's fiction, including the *Family Chronicle*, but even in this instance Annenkov merely noted briefly that in Aksakov "nature is displayed . . . only in her eternal aspects" (2:111), and quickly moved on. The radical critics raised no strenuous objections to nature description, but neither did they regard it with much esteem: one of their *bêtes noires* was Fet, whose masterful nature descriptions in lyric verse had no social effect at all. There were occasional attempts to popularize phrases such as the "physiognomy of nature," a notion Nikolay Solovev advanced in 1865 in an article in which he claimed that nature spoke to us in a langage consisting of "colors, forms, and sounds" and which provided an entirely natural foundation for our esthetic sense.[41] However, Solovev's attempt at constructing a

---

[40] Edel'son, "Russkaia literatura. Vzbalamuchennoe more" (November 1863), 21–22.

[41] Solov'ev, "Ob otnoshenii estestvovedeniia k iskusstvu" (November 1865, book 2), 305.

scheme of esthetics founded on natural science attracted little attention or support.

Much more controversy arose, however, over the literary depiction of individuals rather than general social phenomena, especially when that depiction was connected with the vexed problem of the "typical." As Pavel Annenkov put it in 1858, although literature may seem on the surface to depict individuals, in fact those personages must express something of the larger social order about them if they are to be truly literary. "Exceptional and isolated phenomena," he wrote in "The Literary Type of the Weak Man," "belong to history, biography, or the anecdote, and only in very rare instances to artistic literature" (2:162). Grigorev had made an analogous point two years earlier, when he commented that "for true art chance occurrences are unworthy of elevation to types."[42] The individual, the fortuitous, the eccentric, all these things which play so large a role in life, have no place in literature, which must offer images of individuals which are simultaneously statements about the larger society in which they live.

One of the better discussions of the literary type at that time came from Pisarev. To be sure, he approached the subject a trifle mechanically, and believed a type should be created on the horizontal and not the vertical (i.e., a type should represent as many facets of contemporary society as possible, but need not have deep historical roots), but his doctrine is still of some interest. "A writer in society often meets with a number of personalities," Pisarev wrote in his study of *What Is to Be Done?*

> who possess similar characters and almost identical views of life. These common features come to interest the writer, he looks at them more closely, he meditates on them, and in his mind there is formed, little by little,

[42] Grigor'ev, "O pravde i iskrennosti," 142.

246   CHAPTER FOUR

an ideal person usually called the representative of a
type.[43]

If this understanding is correct, then, clearly the discovery and creation of types—the general exemplified in the individual—are among the chief tasks of the artist. In 1863
Edelson implicitly defined art as the "depiction of types,"[44]
and Grigorev said something similar about the artist's dedication to the typical in his article of 1859 "A Few Words on
the Laws and Terminology of Organic Criticism," when he
wrote: "A love of types and a striving to create them are a
striving for life and the vital, and a turning away from that
which is dead, rotten, and stagnant, whether in life or in
logic."[45] Thus one of the artist's principal duties was to formulate definitions of typical individuals, for in so doing he
would also define the society surrounding that individual.
Edelson made it clear that the artist should follow certain
unwritten laws in creating a type. One was that the artist
could not be arbitrary: the reality surrounding him re-
stricted his imagination to a high degree, so that he could
not simply bring into being at his whim eccentric characters
lacking in general resonance. In 1863 Edelson found precisely this fault with *Troubled Seas*: some of Pisemsky's characters, he said, bore the "stamp of the author's arbitrari-
ness."[46] A second unwritten law—and rather more
controversial—was that a truly typical character could not
be morally depraved. A personage like Pisemsky's Basardin,
Edelson wrote, "was not typical if only because he is a positively repulsive person, a moral monster, and exceptions are

[43] Pisarev, "Novyi tip," *Literaturnaia kritika*, 2:405. This article was never completed.
[44] Edel'son, "Russkaia literatura. Vzbalamuchennoe more" (November 1863),
25.
[45] Grigor'ev, "Neskol'ko slov," 230.
[46] Edel'son, "Russkaia literatura. Vzbalamuchennoe more" (December 1863),
10.

never typical."[47] Here the problem of the typical—and especially the question of the typical within the antinihilist novel, of which *Troubled Seas* was an example—became interwoven with the question of morality and the novel, and especially morality as politically defined. *Troubled Seas* contains one of Pisemsky's best-known characters, the utterly depraved Iona-Cynic; Chernyshevsky had created Marya Alekseevna, Vera Pavlovna's evil mother in *What Is to Be Done?*; and the list of such characters could be greatly lengthened even if one limited oneself to the literature of the 1860s. But such characters as these were accepted as "typical," because the reading public and even esthetic critics like Edelson felt that their individual traits were not only widespread among the older generation, but also somehow characteristic of it. But when Pisemsky asserted that in the area of personal morality the younger generation was just as bad as the older, he encountered stout resistance from the critics. Yes, they said, there may be corrupt or evil individuals among the younger generation, but they are not "characteristic" or "typical" because they do not define its fundamental nature, and it is illegitimate for a writer to claim they do. The question was not capable of a mathematical solution. Even if it could have been shown statistically that the younger generation contained a higher percentage of corrupt individuals than did the older, it would not have altered the critics' overall evaluation of the two generations, it would not have shifted their opinion that the Lopukhovs and the Vera Pavlovnas, even extraordinary figures like Bazarov and Rakhmetov, somehow defined the essence of the younger generation, no matter how few of them there might be in reality.

Here the notion of the ideal intertwines with the "typical" in a complex fashion. The critics saw venality and evil

[47] Ibid., 11.

as a function of age: people almost invariably lose their ideals and succumb to corruption as they grow older. There were individuals who upheld the "ideal" among the older generation, true, but they did not represent its basic line of development: rather the self-seekers did, if only because—as Chernyshevsky thought—the social order rewarded corruption in such a way that it was in people's interests to be evil. There were also egoists among the younger generation, but they diverged from its generally positive outlook, especially if the social order were altered to reward "good" behavior, as Chernyshevsky advocated: thus the idealists were the "typical" representatives of the younger generation. Ultimately this understanding of the "typical," just as of the "ideal," was political.

Occasionally critics noted that literary types might have their own literary genealogy: earlier literary types engendered later ones, as Goncharov remarked in "Better Late Than Never" (8:104, 105). But most critics of whatever camp were so persuaded of art's dependence upon contemporary life that they would not seriously contemplate the possibility that literary phenomena might have a vitality of their own. Instead they debated whether the creation of a literary type required some historical distance between the author and his creation, or whether a literary type should be delineated just as soon as he appeared in society. Goncharov, that genius of reminiscence, naturally adopted the former view.

Goncharov believed that it was very difficult to depict a type that had not yet settled out in historical reality. When he had sought to present a contemporary hero in Tushin (*The Precipice*), that "representative of a new force and a new cause," he had failed to a large degree because this positive personality had still been too new:

> One may in general terms hint at the idea and the future character of these new men, as I did in Tushin. But it is

impossible to describe the actual process of fermentation: while it is going on personalities alter practically
every day, and the pen cannot keep pace with them.
(8:101)

Although he saw eye to eye with Goncharov on very few
issues, Shelgunov did accept Goncharov's viewpoint in this
case. He, too, believed that a particular type required time
to develop within social reality before it could properly serve
as a model for a literary image. In his study of Pisemsky's
novel *Men of the 1840s* Shelgunov argued that Bazarov—
whom he rejected, as the *Sovremennik* group had earlier—
had wrought great damage because Turgenev had created
him prematurely and on the basis of insufficient knowledge.
Had Turgenev made a thorough study of Bazarov, the critic
thought, then the entire antinihilist movement in literature
which *Father and Sons* stimulated might never have come
into being (191–92). In fact, Shelgunov maintained, even at
this late date (1869) writers had still not created an appropriate image of the "new man." Why?

> Simply because this type has not yet revealed itself in a
> form worthy of ideal depiction. On can hardly picture a
> man pacing back and forth in his room with his hands
> behind his back, lost in thought! A writer does not con-
> trive anything, but rather depicts that which life itself
> gives him. The man of the 1860s now is not Proskriptsky,
> not Bazarov, not Rakhmetov or Rayner or Liza. These
> characters embody the first phase of the intellectual de-
> velopment of the man of the 1860s, but he has not yet
> reached the final stage, either in his intellectual develop-
> ment or in the form of his external behavior.[48] (208)

Such a conclusion follows logically from the assumption
that the artist creates nothing, but simply draws upon the

[48] Proskriptsky is a character from Pisemsky's *Troubled Seas*, Rayner and Liza
characters from Leskov's *No Way Out*.

materials supplied him by reality, a theoretical position to which Shelgunov adhered loyally even after his mentor Chernyshevsky had in practice abandoned it in writing *What Is to Be Done?*

Dostoevsky, by way of contrast, agreed in theory with Chernyshevsky's practice, and not with Goncharov: he evidently disliked Goncharov's greatest creation, Oblomov, as a type, and felt that an author not only could but should depict social types in the process of their emergence. "Only a writer of genius," Dostoevsky said, "or at least a very powerful talent can divine a type *contemporarily* and transmit it *contemporarily*" (11:90). As Robert Jackson holds in his study of Dostoevsky's esthetics, it is precisely by creating accurate types on the basis of still incomplete information that the writer influences society. Indeed, Dostoevsky maintained at that time, he created a Nechaev type in Peter Verkhovensky (*The Possessed*) as an act of artistic intuition by means of which he could examine larger social problems.[49]

Thus the question of whether a type should be depicted in literature before it was fully formed in social reality was answered in accordance with the subjective viewpoints of particular authors. As a matter of fact, it is difficult to discover a writer who worked either entirely in the past or entirely on the basis of a future-oriented intuition. We may place in the former category a number of historical novelists who wrote in detail about a more or less complete and distant past: Tolstoy in *War and Peace*, for instance, or Aksakov in *The Family Chronicle*. The radicals took a dim view both of history and of historical novels. As their opponent Nikolay Solovev put it in 1867, after noting that the past does not exist solely in order to be destroyed by the present,

> Therein lies the deficiency of our generation, that it is excessively miserly and calculating with regard to every-

[49] See Jackson, *Dostoevsky's Quest for Form*, especially 97–103.

thing linked to its temporary benefit, and totally spend-
thrift and improvident with ideas developed over the
ages![50]

We may find abundant confirmation of Solovev's generalization in the writings of the radical critics themselves. In his
article "Realists" Dmitry Pisarev advanced the antihistorical
viewpoint with great vigor when he declared that the historical novel was entirely useless, proclaiming that "in our
day . . . it is shameful and disgraceful to withdraw in
thought into the dead past, with which all decent people
should long since have broken all ties" (3:114). And a few
years later Shelgunov would condemn Nikolay Solovev for,
among other things, the "endless paeans" he had sung to
War and Peace.[51]

Not all the radical thinkers of that day adopted such an
unremittingly hostile attitude toward the historical novel
and history generally. Mikhail Saltykov-Shchedrin had a
deeper historical sense than most of his allies, so that even
in his programmatic piece of 1856 in which he demanded
that writers be wholly "contemporary," he agreed that writers of historical novels could meet this demand, for "history
can also have very contemporary interest in explaining the
present to us as the logical outcome of that life now in the
past."[52] On the whole, though, the radical critics exhibited
little interest in the historical roots of a contemporary reality
which they considered wholly undesirable.

The esthetic critics were much more favorably disposed
toward history and the historical novel, even though they
often shared the radicals' commitment to contemporaneity,
and sometimes wondered whether an author could legitimately write of times and peoples he could not possibly

[50] Solov'ev, "Idealy," 158.
[51] Shelgunov, "Dvoedushie," 48–49.
[52] Bograd, " 'Literaturnyi manifest,' " 295.

know at first hand. Thus Grigorev set out to write "On Truth and Sincerity in Art" in response to a question from Aleksey Khomyakov as to whether a writer could accurately recreate states of mind and historical circumstances that were foreign to him. Grigorev considered the query entirely appropriate, and answered it affirmatively, pointing to the example of Goethe, who wrote on ancient themes while remaining very much a man of his age.[53] Nikolay Solovev defended the study or the depiction of the past on the grounds that the "esthetic or the ideal" became more and more nearly perfect as mankind moved through history,[54] and Konstantin Leontev argued that full esthetic development could only occur in the fullness of historical time. "Genuinely poetical works," he wrote in his "Letter of a Provincial to Turgenev" (1860),

> detach themselves more and more fully from surrounding trivia in the course of time; the flame of historical and temporary aspirations dies down, while beauty is not only eternal but even intensifies with the passage of time, as it adds to its own inner power the entrancing thought of the no longer extant forms of another full and vital life.[55]

Thus Leontev saw poetic works of the past as more—not less—satisfying in the present than they were at the time of their creation.

In addition to the dispute over literature and the past, there was also, as we have seen, a considerable controversy over literature and the future, or art as prophecy. Dobrolyubov seems not to have been entirely consistent on this score: sometimes he claimed that art lagged behind reality, but at other times he argued that it could fulfill a prophetic role.

---

[53] Grigor'ev, "O pravde i iskrennosti," 127–29.
[54] Solov'ev, "Idealy," 161.
[55] Leont'ev, "Pis'mo provintsiala," 27.

In "The Kingdom of Darkness" (1859), he wrote that an artist differs from a thinker in his ability to discern emerging social phenomena very early. When an artist notes a particular fact,

> he may yet have no theories that would explain this fact; but he realizes that he is dealing with something unusual, something that deserves attention, and so he investigates the fact itself with eager curiosity, takes it in, bears it in his soul at first as a unique representation but the adds to it other facts and images of the same character, and finally creates a type expressing within itself all the particular phenomena of this sort that the artist has taken note of earlier. (5:22)

In 1858 Annenkov had said something rather similar to this. In "The Literary Type of the Weak Man," Annenkov began by noting that literature instructs us, then added that

> Instruction through literature acts upon us more freely and more independently than a scholarly investigation: it often sees over the phenomena of life and far beyond them, engraving its prophetic words upon the distant and still empty horizon. And God grant we never doubt the great utility of this work of instruction. (2:51)

Apollon Grigorev emphasized this point even more strongly than Annenkov, for he attributed to literature, as he said in 1861, "powers of foreseeing, foretelling, and predefining life" on a basis at once rational and organic (407). On another occasion a few years earlier he had asserted that art could intuitively perceive that which was still immanent in the social order, and claimed that "everything *new* is introduced into life only through art."[56]

Dostoevsky agreed with Grigorev's opinion in this area almost entirely, and indeed made it a major tenet of his ar-

[56] Grigor'ev, "Obozrenie," 187.

tistic practice: as N. V. Kashina puts it in her study of Dostoevsky's esthetic, he conceived of the artist as "prophet."[57] Dostoevsky thought that in the 1840s he had discovered Golyadkin (*The Double*) as the type of the psychological double, and become his prophet in Russian literature; in the 1860s he considered his Underground Man a similar sort of type.[58] Dostoevsky formulated an intriguing variant of this argument in a letter to Nikolay Strakhov of 1869 in which he discussed Prince Myshkin as a type. Dostoevsky admitted he had never encountered a Myshkin in reality, but his general observations of society convinced him that such a man must exist, and he believed that one day he would encounter him. "Do you mean to say," he wrote,

> that my fantastic Idiot isn't reality, and the most everyday reality at that! It is precisely now that there must exist such characters among the layers of society which have been torn away from the soil—layers of society which are in reality becoming fantastic.[59]

To the best of my knowledge, Dostoevsky never found journalistic confirmation of the accuracy of his reading of social reality as embodied in Myshkin from *The Idiot*, but he thought he did for *Crime and Punishment* and *The Possessed*. In a much-quoted letter to Katkov of October 1870 on *The Possessed*, Dostoevsky reported that he had based his plot on the murder of a student named Ivanov in Moscow by the terrorist Sergey Nechaev and his associates in November 1869, though he knew of the crime only through the newspapers. He began from the fact of the murder, he said, and could not at all guarantee that his fictional hero would resemble the actual Nechaev, but he did believe he had succeeded "in creating in my imagination the person, the type,

---

[57] Kashina, *Estetika Dostoevskogo*, 108.
[58] See Jackson, *Dostoevsky's Quest for Form*, 93–94.
[59] Letter to Strakhov of February 26/March 10, 1869: 29/1:19.

who corresponds to this evil deed."[60] Roughly half the novel had already been published serially by the time the Nechaev trial opened in July 1871 and detailed reports of Nechaev's activities started to appear in the press. His reading of these accounts satisfied Dostoevsky that reality had indeed confirmed his artistic assessment of the fantastic and fanatic type who was Sergey Nechaev.

Some years before Dostoevsky had received what he considered even more striking confirmation of his artistic intuition. *Crime and Punishment* was the work involved in this instance. The Soviet scholar V. V. Danilov records that while he was completing the novel Dostoevsky worried lest his readers consider his topic eccentric, and therefore he was in a sense relieved when, according to Strakhov's memoirs, he learned a few days before the book began to appear that a Moscow student had killed a moneylender in reality: "F. M. [Dostoevsky] made quite a note of this, often spoke of it, and was proud that he had accomplished such a feat of artistic perception," Strakhov recalled some twenty years later.[61] It is quite possible that Strakhov's memory betrayed him here, and that he was referring to an incident of this sort reported in the press in August 1865, when Dostoevsky was only beginning *Crime and Punishment*, but the important thing (as the young radicals tell Myshkin when discussing their article with him in *The Idiot*) is not so much the facts as their interpretation.

Dostoevsky is an extreme instance of the "writer as prophet," but other writers exhibited traces of this attitude as well. Turgenev, for example, ordinarily depicted more or less well-defined historical types, but once in a while he suc-

---

[60] Letter to Katkov from Dresden of October 8/20, 1870: 29/1:141.

[61] V. Danilov, "K voprosu o kompozitsionnykh priemakh v 'Prestuplenii i nakazanii' Dostoevskogo," *Izvestiia Akademii nauk SSSR, Otdelenie obshchestvennykh nauk*, 3 (1933), 263.

cumbed to the temptation of creating a "positive hero" who would be dominant in the future, as Solomin in *Virgin Soil* (1877). Even Goncharov, for all his strong orientation toward the past, considered Raysky a new type difficult to define (8:71), although he surely must have meant by that that no one had ever sought to depict a Raysky in Russian literature before, and not that he was undeveloped within society. Goncharov also was so bold as to picture ideal positive heroes of the future in Stolz (*Oblomov*) and Tushin (*The Precipice*), types which he hoped were emerging in contemporary society. But the radical critics rejected these figures for political reasons, and denounced them roundly. When the radical writers offered images of the man of the future such as Rakhmetov, the esthetic critics found them equally unbelievable.

Dostoevsky was also characteristic of his time in his orientation toward journalism, especially newspapers, which attained unprecedented prominence in the 1860s. And journalism purports to deal with reality as it is. Reality must, however, be interpreted in some way: as Nikolay Solovev wrote in Dostoevsky's *Epokha* in 1865,[62] life teaches society primarily through the press. The term "press" covers imaginative literature, literary criticism, and journalism proper, however, and as time passed the three tended to merge. Both literature and journalism dealt with social reality, though in different ways, and literary criticism frequently analyzed social reality under the pretense of discussing literature. Consequently there were those—especially among the radical critics—who looked forward to a unification of all three modes of discourse under the banner of journalism. In the *Esthetic Relations* Chernyshevsky had claimed that poetry's only advantage over a "precise account" of an event or phenomenon lay in "rhetorical elaboration" (2:68). In 1870

[62] Solov'ev, "Razlad," 2.

Shelgunov asserted that it was "impossible to separate criticism from journalism";[63] and in 1865 Varfolomey Zaytsev declared that in principle one should not distinguish between
literature and journalism or scholarly writing:

> There exist certain poetic works which deal with various
> contemporary social problems and in fact teach people
> to regard them correctly; these works are without doubt
> useful, and provide the only instance in which works of
> art are not only tolerable, but even deserving of respect.
> However, it is not difficult to see that here it is not art
> which deserves respect, but the accurate and honest
> thought expressed by its aid. And that thought would
> have deserved just as much respect even if it had been
> expressed in the most artless and prosaic manner. (1:337)

The esthetic critics, however, though they did not reject
the links between journalism and imaginative literature, hesitated to ally them too closely. In 1865 Nikolay Solovev iden-
tified the confusion between journalism and criticism as the
root of the radicals' intellectual difficulties.[64] He admitted
that the two fields were related, but still he believed they
should be kept quite separate: "Criticism is linked, of
course, to journalism just as it is to philosophy," he wrote,
"but it must not be subordinated to either of them."[65] Evgeny Edelson had warned of a similar danger the year before, when he remarked that society is too often drawn into
journalism's artificial existence and the quarrels it manufac-
tures for itself, so that if one journalistic current emerges
triumphant over others, it imposes itself upon society as
well.[66] Thus in this instance of the interrelation between
criticism, journalism, and literature, as in so many others,

[63] Shelgunov, "Dvoedushie," 51.
[64] Solov'ev, "Vopros ob iskusstve" (July 1865), 60.
[65] Ibid. (August 1865), 417.
[66] Edel'son, "Russkaia literatura. Sovremennaia natural'naia shkola," 14–15.

we find the esthetic critics striving to maintain distinctions and the radical critics seeking to blur or eliminate them.

There remains, finally, the problem of the general connection between literature on the one hand and society or social reality on the other. At the start of the discussion, in 1856, Pavel Annenkov had upbraided his fellow critics for their failure to investigate what he called the "mysterious link between literature and society" (2:12), although one may wonder how one could investigate something that is ultimately unknowable. Katkov sought to define the problem further when, at about the same time, he wrote that "literature is the same thing in relation to society as consciousness in an individual";[67] and in the same essay he maintained that the "elegance of forms and nobility of social relations" to be discovered among advanced and civilized nations are ultimately the result of art's influence, for art's "beautiful images and sounds insert into [the social] consciousness the essence of beauty which distinguishes them."[68] Some ten years later, having passed through what he regarded as bitter experience, Nikolay Solovev reverted to this notion. In 1865 he maintained that the theater does not supply specific information, but simply promotes what he here terms "self-consciousness."[69] Two years later he would speak of it as the "social mood" (*nastroenie*), "that internal esthetic movement which is the chief result of art."[70] Solovev agreed with Katkov in principle that art promoted social harmony, and attributed what he saw as society's moral breakdown in the mid-1860s to its rejection of art. He concluded his series of articles entitled "Labor and Enjoyment" (1866) with a peroration on the sorry condition of

[67] Katkov, "Pushkin" (January 1856), 155.
[68] Ibid. (February 1856), 312–13.
[69] Solov'ev, "Razlad," 28.
[70] Solov'ev, "Printsipy zhizni," 155.

contemporary society, which suffered from family disinte-
gration, corruption, and all other possible social pathologies: "Society, like a pile of materials or an immense con-
glomeration, presents itself in the form of a dead mass,
without principles, without ideals, without higher norms of
life," he wrote.[71] This situation, of which we catch a glimpse
in, say, the condition of Marmeladov and his family in
Crime and Punishment, in Solovev's view clearly arose from
the contempt for art and beauty so widespread in contemporary society.

Since he belonged to the literary generation of the 1840s,
Pavel Annenkov tended to believe that literature should emphasize the personal and individual rather than the political
and broadly social. In his review of Pisemsky's *A Thousand
Souls*, for which he did not particularly care, he wrote:

> The distinctive feature of a novel in which civic affairs
> comprise the mainspring of the action is a certain dry-
> ness. It is capable of evoking the most varied sensations,
> with the sole exception of the feeling of poetry. (2:81)

However, in that very same year of 1859 Annenkov praised
Turgenev's *A Nest of Gentlefolk*, with its powerful social component, declaring that Turgenev was without peer in his
"understanding of the invisible streams and flows of social
thought which intersect our contemporary life in all sorts of
directions" (2:81): in short, Annenkov here praised Turgenev for his mastery of social psychology, an area which he
had earlier condemned Pisemsky for venturing upon. And
by 1863 even such a convinced supporter of art's autonomy
as Evgeny Edelson was assigning a primarily social role to
literature. "The chief and most essential task of contemporary artistic literature," he wrote in a discussion of *Troubled
Seas*,

[71] Solov'ev, "Trud i naslazhdenie," vol. 167 (1866), 148–49.

is a genuinely accurate and intelligent reproduction of social phenomena, of the current life of society; in this very way literature provides direct and powerful encouragement for the further development of life along conscious and rational lines.[72]

In the next year Edelson followed up on this by concluding one of his critical articles with a summons to literature "to become the faithful and true expression of all society's interests."[73] On this point Edelson had little disagreement with Dobrolyubov, who in his discussion of *On the Eve* had called upon writers to seize upon the "most essential features" of "social thought and morality" as a means of analyzing society as a whole (6:98).

Thus on this question, too, there was widespread consensus among critics and theoreticians of all persuasions. Literature was indeed, they believed, the nervous system of society; it provided the channels of society's consciousness or self-consciousness, and therefore it was obliged to deal primarily with social and political relationships, social reality, and not the intricacies of individual psychology unless they clearly had social ramifications. The prominence of this viewpoint helps to explain lyric poetry's low estate during the 1860s: by nature lyric poetry is best suited to the transmission of very personal experience. Nearly everyone believed that social reality defines literature because it provides the materials upon which literature draws for its very existence. On that point there was next to no disagreement, either in theory or in practice. But there was a division on the question of whether literature could in its turn influence or even determine reality on the theoretical level, though in practice most writers, including radical writers, acted as

[72] Edel'son, "Russkaia literatura. Vzbalamuchennoe more" (November 1863), 3–4.
[73] Edel'son, "Russkaia literatura. Sovremennaia natural'naia shkola," 21.

though they believed it could. We address that point in a final brief excursus.

Excursus: Social Reality and Some Novels of the 1860s

From our twentieth-century vantage point it is obvious that the interaction between society, or social reality, and literature is a complex, two-way process. Literature may strongly influence reality by defining or altering our perceptions of it, and therefore what we expect of it; and that changed social reality will in turn be reflected in new literary works. Fiction once published becomes an integral part of social reality: surely the history of Russian society in the 1860s would have been perceptibly different if, say, *Fathers and Sons* or *What Is to Be Done?* had never been written. These novels' very real influence illustrates the importance of literary works for the development of social reality.

Fathers and Sons, in fact, supplied an entire intellectual framework for the debate on the radical movement of that decade. In his explanatory article of 1869 "On the Subject of *Fathers and Sons*" (14:97–109), Turgenev commented that while writing the novel he had closely observed social reality, especially as it was embodied in the personality of an unnamed "young provincial doctor," a "remarkable man" he once knew who died evidently in late 1859. In him Turgenev discerned that "still fermenting phenomenon" (*nachalo*) which later came to be known as "nihilism"—after Turgenev had named it, of course. Turgenev began planning the novel in August 1860 while vacationing on the Isle of Wight, where, he recalled, he spoke with an intelligent (but also unidentified) Russian associate about the social current that the provincial doctor seemed to exemplify. To his astonishment, his associate pointed out that he had already created a similar type in Rudin. Thus Bazarov, the central figure of *Fathers and Sons*, was born from an inextricable intertwining of literary image and social reality: after observing a certain social type in reality, Turgenev links him to a literary image to produce a new literary creation which diffuses into social reality once more, for, as Turgenev recalled a few lines later in that same article, when he returned to St. Petersburg in May of 1862, shortly after his novel's publication and just at the time of the mysterious fires in the capital, the first acquaintance he met on the Nevsky Prospect declared that *his* nihilists were burning the city to the ground. The continuing interaction between literary image and social reality is clearly demonstrated in this remark.

The literary image of Bazarov is central to an understanding of the nihilist movement of the 1860s: all thinking Russians had read *Fathers and Sons* and thus "knew" him well enough to argue endlessly over him and what he represented. Turgenev also defined the terminology of the period. The *Sovremennik* critics rejected Bazarov as a true image of the radical while the critics of the *Russkoe slovo* group accepted him, but both circles objected strenuously to the terms "nihilism" and "nihilist" which Turgenev had given such currency through his novel. What is beyond dispute is that the image of Bazarov determined Russian society's vision of the radical younger generation of the 1860s at the time, and indeed ever since. Chernyshevsky's *What Is to Be Done?* presented a powerful paradigm of radical social and marital relationships as well as an influential personal model for young women in Vera Pavlovna, but Lopukhov and Kirsanov, not to mention the unattainable Rakhmetov, could do nothing more than marginally alter the public perception of the radical created by Bazarov. They could not eclipse it, for Bazarov had seized upon society's imagination too vigorously for that. Alexander Herzen badly underestimated Bazarov's influence on the younger generation in a passage which otherwise makes some excellent points on the relationship between fiction and reality:

It is an odd thing, the mutual interaction of people and books. A book takes all its material from the society in which it appears, generalizes that material while making it sharper and more obvious, and thereafter is bypassed by reality. The originals become caricatures of their sharply delineated portraits, and actually existing people coalesce with their literary shadows. At the end of the last century all German men reminded one a bit of Werther, and all the women of Charlotte; . . . Russian young people who arrived in Europe after 1862 were nearly all out of *What Is to Be Done?*, with the addition of a few Bazarovian traits.[74]

Other observers agreed with Herzen's assessment at the time. Pisarev (who consistently used the world "realist" instead of "nihilist") wrote in 1864 that "society is acquainted with our realists through the novel *Fathers and Sons*": the man on the street, who often may not have known many young radicals personally, had formed his conception of them through that book (3:83). Nikolay Leskov, writing a year after the publication of *Fathers and Sons*, maintained that it was not *Sovremennik* but Turgenev's novel which had loosed the nihilists upon Russian society: "These freaks of Russian civilization," he wrote, "began making their mark (*nadyuzhatsya*) after the appearance of *Fathers and Sons*," as young people everywhere copied Bazarov.[75] In 1864 Evgeny Edelson commented that before *Fathers and Sons* came out there were only vague radical theories floating about, but Turgenev had brought them into a system, to the benefit of the radicals themselves:

The so-called nihilists who have recently received such extensive publicity actually were not exposed by Turgenev's novel, as many think, but are essentially indebted

[74] Aleksandr Gertsen, *Sobranie sochinenii*. 9 vols. (Moscow, 1955–58), 8:38In.
[75] Leskov, "Nikolai Gavrilovich Chernyshevskii," 10:17.

to him both for their name ("nihilists") and for their
well-articulated and consistent doctrines.[76]

In 1865 Nikolay Solovev made a similar point when he
claimed that the radicals of his day had taken as their "first
commandment" the "negation of art and of theoretical science" which Bazarov had preached and simply developed
these things further: "Accepting Turgenev's benediction,
they have surged forward to become our imaginary realists."[77] Still another conservative critic at mid-decade, Efim
Zarin, discussing the dispute over *Fathers and Sons* in which
Sovremennik and *Russkoe slovo* had long been engaged, declared that the two factions behaved as though the younger
generation would follow "those who come up with the best
interpretation of Turgenev's *Fathers and Sons*, or else write
the greatest number of articles on this subject,"[78] In sum,
critics of all possible political persuasions agreed that Turgenev's novel had had a profound impact upon Russian life
as well as Russian literature.

The dimensions of Bazarov's influence upon social reality may be gauged from his effect upon Dmitry Pisarev. In
an interesting article of 1978 Edward J. Brown has persua-
sively argued that the leading radical critic of the mid-1860's
consciously sought to "fashion *himself* as an image of Bazarov."[79] For example, Bazarov was famous for his hostility to
art and esthetics, and Pisarev, taking Bazarov as his model,

[76] Edel'son, "Russkaia literatura," *Biblioteka dlia chteniia*, no. 4–5 (April–May
1864), 2.
[77] Solov'ev, "Vopros ob iskusstve" (August 1865), 424. A considerable portion
of this article is dedicated to demonstrating the influence of Turgenev's fiction on
contemporary reality.
[78] Incognito [E. Zarin], "Verba novissima," *Otechestvennye zapiski*, no. 7 (July
1865), 148.
[79] Edward J. Brown, "Pisarev and the Transformation of Two Russian Novels,"
in *Literature and Society in Imperial Russia, 1800–1914*, ed. William M. Todd III
(Stanford, 1978), 164.

promulgated Bazarov's anti-esthetic ideas among large segments of Russian society. And thus, Brown writes, *"Fathers and Sons*, a work of art, contributed under Pisarev's ministrations to the anti-esthetic movement of the sixties."[80] Surely no greater esthetic irony than this could be imagined; and Pisarev at the time perceived a very similar irony when—in a review of *What Is to Be Done?* published in *Russkoe slovo* in late 1865—he remarked that "Chernyshevsky, the destroyer of esthetics, has turned out to be the only writer of ours whose artistic work has exerted direct influence upon our society" (4:26). By so saying Pisarev merely acknowledged a rather obvious fact, one which Herzen had observed and on which Chernyshevsky had obviously counted when he set out to write his novel. For Chernyshevsky had perceived the influence that *Fathers and Sons* had exercised upon society, and had realized that it could effectively be countered only in the esthetic realm, through another novel, and not through literary criticism, even the intemperate variety practiced by Antonovich in "An Asmodeus of Our Time."

Still, for all his genuine sensitivity to ideological currents and his understanding of art's role as the "consciousness" of society, Turgenev conceived of social reality as quite stable. As he does in most of his works, he provides *Fathers and Sons* with a specific historical and geographical setting which gives the reader a clear sense of a particular reality. He firmly roots such personages as Nikolay Petrovich Kirsanov and Pavel Petrovich Kirsanov within that reality by means of the thumbnail biographies of which he was so fond. True, Bazarov lacks any such background, but we learn a good deal about his origins nevertheless. More important than this is the fact that when Bazarov mounts a relentless ideological assault on the institutions of society, declaring them with-

[80] Ibid., 165.

out exception worthy of condemnation and destruction, that society passively but stoutly resists his onslaught, and in the end destroys him. Shortly before he dies, Bazarov muses in Odintsova's presence: "Russia needs me . . . no, evidently she doesn't" (8:396). He had hoped to accomplish much through his theories and doctrines only to realize that they did not fit reality, whether physical, biological, or social: in Turgenev's universe reality does not yield to theory, but the reverse. The unbending ideologue disappears, partly as a result of his own inner contradictions, while social reality remains, specific and firm.

Though Chernyshevsky evidently hoped to alter social reality substantially through his novel, he conceives of it as perhaps even more stable than does Turgenev, although for different reasons. Like Turgenev, Chernyshevsky places *What Is to Be Done?* in a very concrete historical and temporal setting. To be sure, he presents his book as a verbal artifice: he inserts himself into its fabric, addresses his "perceptive reader," predicts the development of the plot, and so forth, as we have already seen. But he does this because he wishes to degrade literature as an element of reality, to make sure that his reader does not interpret the novel as anything other than a fiction. But when he dealt with physical or social reality—and especially the former—Chernyshevsky believed more than firmly in its solidity. His view of reality derived from his absolute belief in the authority of science: reality was an objective entity which in the end would be entirely comprehended through the mathematical methods of natural science. He extrapolated the certainties of axiomatic mathematics out through physics and chemistry as far as physiology, and he was persuaded that eventually they would reach even to the realms of ethics and morality. All aspects of human social life would one day, he was convinced, be subject to a single, true, and mathematically determined interpretation.

Chernyshevsky lived at a time when natural science was making great strides on all fronts and reaching entirely new areas of understanding, but it was also a time—unfortunately for him—when some scientists had begun to question the certainties of mathematical axioms. Indeed a Russian mathematician, Nikolay Lobachevsky, pioneered in the field of non-Euclidian geometry, which questioned the geometrical axioms purporting to define the physical space in which we live, particularly the axiom that parallel lines extended to infinity will never meet. Chernyshevsky reacted with unbridled fury against the very idea of non-Euclidian geometry, and well he should have, for if non-Euclidian geometry were in some sense true, then his entire philosophical viewpoint was threatened. That is why he mounted intemperate attacks on people such as the physicist Hermann Ludwig Helmholtz, or Lobachevsky, or anyone else who worked with non-Euclidian geometry. Here is what he said of Lobachevsky, for example:

> Everyone in Kazan knew Lobachevsky [who lived there]. Every last person in Kazan used to say he was an absolute idiot. . . . What is the "curvature of a ray" or a "curved space"? What is "geometry without the axiom of parallel lines"? Can one write Russian without verbs? You can, as a joke. A certain Fet did this. Once upon a time he was a well-known poet. He was a truly rare idiot. He wrote this quite seriously, and people laughed at him until they got stitches in their sides. (15:192–93)

Chernyshevsky had similarly uncomplimentary things to say of Helmholtz, for Chernyshevsky exemplified the split in the radical intellect which had formed its views of social reality on the basis of the seeming certainties of early nineteenth-century natural scientific thought, just before leading scientific theoreticians began to realize how problematical their interpretations of reality actually were. That dichotomy still persists in the minds of Chernyshevsky's intellectual descendants.

It remained for Dostoevsky to write the novel which not only summed up Russia's historical experience with the nihilist movement since the appearance of *Fathers and Sons*, but also conveyed as does no other nineteenth-century Russian novel a sense of the fragility of social reality: *The Possessed*. Its setting is an anonymous and generalized Russian town; the time is the later 1860s, but no explicit year. The narrator, artistically central to the book, masterfully employs rumor, report, and contradictory information to undermine the reader's confidence in the fictional "reality" presented to him; and yet the verisimilitude of those very uncertainties recalls our own attitude toward reality. The social structure of the town turns out to be quite brittle: headed by a governor who ends up insane, local society is so uncertain of itself that its continued existence is threatened by the distribution of leaflets notable primarily for their stupidity, and by small groups of people, themselves of unstable mind, bent on fomenting disorder. Even the town's physical existence is problematical, for much of it is destroyed by a fire that Governor Von Lembke correctly connects with a conflagration in men's minds: the stability of even the physical environment rests upon the ideological and spiritual steadiness of the individuals who comprise the social structure. Their stability is not very great, or even their hold on life itself in the presence of murderers like the convict Fedka, not to mention Peter Verkhovensky, who regards assassination as a legitimate political instrument.

Among other things, then, *The Possessed* is a supreme statement on the uncertainty of social reality, a statement which emerged from a Russia that had experienced unprecedented political and ideological instability during the 1860s, and that in turn gave unsurpassed expression to the uncertainty principle which has remained a hallmark of the modern mind down to our day. Starting from his interpretation of social reality, Dostoevsky extrapolated through Peter Verkhovensky into the future the character traits of the extreme political radical, and through the very artistic structure of his novel he expressed the fragility of the social order that the radical generation had exposed as no one had ever done before them. Dostoevsky dealt with the most momentous contemporary issues in both the personal and the social areas, and also capped the development of the "antinihilist novel," which after *The Possessed* declined into insignificance. *The Possessed* is the most profound treatment of the relations between art and social and physical reality to emerge from the 1860s. In it the controversy over literature and esthetics which had raged since 1855, that esthetic nightmare of both sides in the dispute, culminated in a political nightmare of the collapse of a provincial Russian society.

Bibliography

◊

I. Primary Sources: Collected Editions

Annenkov, Pavel. *Vospominaniia i kriticheskie ocherki. Sobranie statei i zametok.* 3 vols. St. Petersburg: Stasiulevich, 1877–81.

Antonovich, Maksim. *Literaturno-kriticheskie stat'i.* Moscow-Leningrad: Gosudarstvennoe izdatel'stvo khudozhestvennoi literatury, 1961.

Chernyshevskii, Nikolai. *Polnoe sobranie sochinenii.* 16 vols. Moscow: Goslitizdat, 1939–53.

Dobroliubov, Nikolai. *Sobranie sochinenii.* 9 vols. Moscow-Leningrad: Gosudarstvennoe izdatel'stvo khudozhestvennoi literatury, 1961–64.

Dostoevskii, Fedor. *Polnoe sobranie sochinenii.* Projected for 30 vols. Leningrad: Nauka, 1972–.

Druzhinin, Aleksandr. *Sobranie sochinenii.* 8 vols. St. Petersburg: Imperatorskaia akademiia nauk, 1865–67.

Goncharov, Ivan. *Sobranie sochinenii.* 8 vols. Moscow: Goslitizdat, 1952–55.

Grigor'ev, Apollon. *Literaturnaia kritika.* Moscow: Izdatel'stvo 'Khudozhestvennaia literatura,' 1967.

Pisarev, Dmitrii. *Sochineniia.* 4 vols. Moscow: Goslitizdat, 1955–56.

Pisemskii, Aleksei. *Polnoe sobranie sochinenii.* 8 vols. St. Petersburg: A. F. Marks, 1910–11.

Shelgunov, Nikolai. *Literaturnaia kritika.* Leningrad: 'Khudozhestvennaia literatura.' 1974.

Tolstoi, Aleksei Konstantinovich. *Sobranie sochinenii.* 4 vols. Moscow: Izdatel'stvo khudozhestvennoi literatury, 1963–64.

Turgenev, Ivan. *Polnoe sobranie sochinenii i pisem.* 28 vols. Moscow-Leningrad: Nauka, 1960–68.

Zaitsev, Varfolomei. *Izbrannye sochineniia.* [Only one volume appeared of a projected two]. Moscow: Izdatel'stvo Vsesoiuznogo obshchestva politkatorzhan i ssyl'no-poselentsev, [1934].

II. PRIMARY SOURCES: JOURNAL PUBLICATIONS

Akhsharumov, Nikolai. "O poraboshchenii iskusstva," *Otechestvennye zapiski,* no. 7 (July 1858), 287–326.

Almazov, Boris. "O poezii Pushkina," *Utro: Literaturnyi sbornik* (Moscow, 1859), 139–92.

Botkin, Vasilii. "Stikhotvoreniia A. A. Feta," *Sovremennik,* no. 1 (January 1857), section 3, 1–17 (part 1 only).

Edel'son, Evgenii. "O poezii," *Biblioteka dlia chteniia,* no. 10 (October 1860), [1]–32.

———. "Russkaia literatura. Vzbalamuchennoe more. Stat'ia pervaia," *Biblioteka dlia chteniia,* no. 11 (November 1863), 1–26; "Stat'ia vtoraia" no. 12 (December 1863), [1]–21.

———. "Russkaia literatura. Sovremennaia natural'naia shkola," *Biblioteka dlia chteniia,* no. 3 (March 1864), 1–21.

———. "O znachenii iskusstva v tsivilizatsii," *Vsemirnyi trud,* no. 1 (January 1867), [213]–55; no. 2 (February 1867), 310–28; no. 3 (March 1867), 98–124.

Fet, Afanasii. "O stikhotvoreniiakh F. Tiutcheva. A. A. Grigor'evu," *Russkoe slovo,* no. 2 (February 1859), 63–84.

Grigor'ev, Apollon. "Obozrenie nalichnykh literaturnykh deiatelei," *Moskvitianin,* no. 15–16 (August 1855), 173–209.

———. "Nigilizm v iskusstve," *Vremia,* no. 8 (August 1862), Kriticheskoe obozrenie (critical survey), 51–59.

———. "Paradoksy organicheskoi kritiki (Pis'ma k F. M. Dostoevskomu)," *Epokha,* no. 5 (May 1864), 255–73; no. 6 (June 1864), 264–77.

Katkov, Mikhail. "Pushkin," *Russkii vestnik,* no. 1 (January 1856), 155–72; no. 2 (February 1856), 306–24; no. 3 (March 1856), 281–310.

[Leont'ev, Konstantin]. "Pis'mo provintsiala k g. Turgenevu," *Otechestvennye zapiski*, no. 5 (May 1860), section 3, 18–27.

[Polonskii, Iakov]. "Stikhotvoreniia Meia," *Russkoe slovo*, no. 1 (1859), section "Kritika," 66–81.

———. "Prozaicheskie tsvety poeticheskikh semian," *Otechestvennye zapiski* (April 1867), book 2, 714–49.

Shelgunov, Nikolai. "Dvoedushie esteticheskogo konservatizma," *Delo*, no. 10 (October 1870), [41]–70.

Solov'ev, Nikolai. "Teoriia bezobraziia," *Epokha*, no. 7 (July 1864), 1–16.

———. "Teoriia pol'zy i vygody," *Epokha*, no. 11 (November 1864), 1–16.

———. "Besplodnaia plodovitost'," *Epokha*, no. 12 (December 1864), [1]–14.

———. "Zhenshchinam," *Epokha*, no. 12 (December 1864), [15]–24.

———. "Razlad (kritika kritiki)," *Epokha*, no. 2 (February 1865), [1]–40.

———. "Vopros ob iskusstve," *Otechestvennye zapiski*, no. 5 (May 1865), section 1, 307–34; no. 6 (June 1865), 468–92; no. 7 (July 1865), 58–86; no. 8 (August 1865), 416–44; no. 8 (August 1865), 626–55.

———. "Kritika kritiki," *Otechestvennye zapiski*, no. 9 (September 1865), 283–313.

———. "Ob otnoshenii estestvovedeniia k iskusstvu," *Otechestvennye zapiski* (November 1865), 132–46, 302–26; (December 1865), 435–54, 679–702.

———. "Trud i naslazhdenie," *Otechestvennye zapiski*, vol. 165 (1866), 655–78; vol. 166 (1866), 562–83; vol. 167 (1866), 125–49.

———. "Printsipy zhizni," *Vsemirnyi trud*, no. 1 (January 1867), [137]–77.

———. "Sueta suet," *Vsemirnyi trud*, no. 2 (February 1867), [167]–202.

———. "Idealy," *Vsemirnyi trud*, no. 3 (March 1867), [157]–93.

Tolstoi, Aleksei Konstantinovich. "Peredelannaia stsena iz Don Zhuana: Pis'mo k izdateliu," *Russkii vestnik*, no. 7 (July 1862), 213–27.

[Zarin, Efim]. [Review of *Sochineniia N. A. Dobroliubova*], *Biblioteka dlia chteniia*, no. 7 (July 1862), 62–98.

———. "Predislovie k literaturnomu obozreniiu. O kachestve i kolichestve progresa v noveishem dvizhenii nashei literatury," *Otechestvennye zapiski*, no. 2 (February 1865), 694–715.

———. "Verba novissima (Posviashchaetsia vsemu zhurnal'nomu miru)," *Otechestvennye zapiski*, no. 7 (July 1865), 145–74.

———. "Prudon ob iskusstve," *Otechestvennye zapiski*, vol. 168 (1866), 123–44, 361–79.

III. SECONDARY LITERATURE

1. GENERAL WORKS

Egorov, Boris. *Ocherki po istorii russkoi literaturnoi kritiki serediny XIX veka (Uchebnoe posobie)*. Leningrad: Leningradskii gosudarstvennyi pedagogicheskii institut imeni A. I. Gertsena, 1973.

———. *Bor'ba esteticheskikh idei v Rossii serediny XIX veka*. Leningrad: "Iskusstvo," Leningradskoe otdelenie, 1982.

Genereux, George. "The Crisis in Russian Literary Criticism: 1856 —The Decisive Year," *Russian Literature Triquarterly*, no. 17 (1982), 117–40.

Ivanov, I. I. *Istoriia russkoi kritiki*. Four vols. St. Petersburg: "Mir bozhii," 1898–1900.

Terras, Victor. *Belinskii and Russian Literary Criticism: The Heritage of Organic Aesthetics*. Madison, Wis.: University of Wisconsin Press, 1974.

Wasiolek, Edward. "Nineteenth-Century Russian Criticism and Soviet Literary Policy," *Modern Age*, vol. 14, no. 2 (Spring 1970), 190–98.

2. STUDIES OF SMALL CLUSTERS OF CRITICS

Bel'chikov, N. "P. V. Annenkov, A. V. Druzhinin, i S. S. Dudyshkin," in A. Lunacharskii and V. Polianskii, eds., two vols. *Ocherki po istorii russkoi kritiki*, Moscow-Leningrad: GIZ, 1929–31, I: 263–304.

Egorov, Boris. " 'Esteticheskaia' kritika bez laka i bez degtia (V. P. Botkin, P. V. Annenkov, A. V. Druzhinin)," *Voprosy literatury*, vol. 9, no. 5 (1965), 142–60.

Lampert, Evgenii. *Sons Against Fathers: Studies in Russian Radicalism and Revolution* [on Chernyshevskii, Dobroliubov, and Pisarev]. Oxford: Clarendon Press, 1965.

Offord, Derek. *Portraits of Early Russian Liberals. A Study of the Thought of T. N. Granovsky, V. P. Botkin, P. V. Annenkov, A. V. Druzhinin and K. D. Kavelin.* Cambridge: Cambridge University Press, 1985.

Prutskov, N. I. " 'Esteticheskaia' kritika (Botkin, Druzhinin, Annenkov)," in V. P. Gorodetskii et al., eds., *Istoriia russkoi kritiki*, 2 vols. Moscow-Leningrad: Akademiia nauk SSSR, 1958, 1: 444–69.

Wellek, René. "Social and Aesthetic Values in Russian Nineteenth-Century Literary Criticism (Belinskii, Chernyshevskii, Dobroliubov, Pisarev)," in Ernest Simmons, ed., *Continuity and Change in Russian and Soviet Thought*. Cambridge, Mass.: Harvard University Press, 1955, 381–97.

———. "The Russian Radical Critics" (Chernyshevsky, Dobrolyubov, Pisarev), in Wellek, *A History of Modern Criticism 1750–1950*, 5 vols., New Haven and London: Yale University Press, 1955–86, 4:238–65.

———. "The Russian Conservative Critics" (Grigorev, Dostoevsky, Strakhov), in ibid., 4: 266–91.

3. STUDIES OF INDIVIDUAL CRITICS

Pavel Annenkov

Egorov, Boris. "P. V. Annenkov—literator i kritik 1840-kh-1850-kh gg.," *Uchenye zapiski Tartuskogo gosudarstvennogo universiteta*, no. 209 (1968): *Trudy po russkoi i slavianskoi filologii. XI. Literaturovedenie*, 51–108.

Zel'dovich, M. G. "Esteticheskii traktat N. G. Chernyshevskogo i obshchestvenno-literaturnoe dvizhenie ego vremeni (N. G. Chernyshevskii i P. Annenkov v spore o problemakh khudozhestvennosti)," *Osvoboditel'noe dvizhenie v Rossii*, no. 9 (Saratov, 1979), 39–52.

Maksim Antonovich

Shishkina, A. N. "Antonovich," in V. P. Gorodetskii et al., eds., *Istoriia russkoi kritiki*, 2 vols. Moscow-Leningrad: Akademiia nauk SSSR, 1958, 2: 182–203.

Tamarchenko, Grigorii. "M. A. Antonovich—literaturnyi kritik i polemist," in M. A. Antonovich, *Literaturno-kriticheskie stat'i*. Moscow-Leningrad: Gosudarstvennoe izdatel'stvo khudozhestvennoi literatury, 1961, iii–[lii].

Vasilii Botkin

Egorov, Boris. "Botkin—kritik i publitsist," in V. P. Botkin. *Literaturnaia kritika, Publitsistika, Pis'ma*. Moscow: Sovetskaia Rossiia, 1984, 3–[22].

Nikolai Chernyshevskii

Bursov, Boris. *Chernyshevskii kak literaturnyi kritik*. Moscow-Leningrad: Akademiia nauk SSSR, 1951.

———. *Masterstvo Chernyshevskogo-kritika*. Leningrad: Sovetskii pisatel', 1959.

Corbet, Charles. "Černyševskii esthéticien et critique," *Revue des études slaves*, vol. 24 (1948), 107–28.

Fridlender, Georgii. "Estetika Chernyshevskogo i russkaia literatura," *Russkaia literatura*, vol. 21, no. 2 (1978), 11–35.

Lavretskii, A. "Chernyshevskii," in V. P. Gorodetskii et al., eds., *Istoriia russkoi kritiki*, 2 vols. Moscow-Leningrad: Akademiia nauk SSSR, 1958, 2: 42–89.

Lukács, Georg. "Einführung in die Aesthetik Tschernyschewskiis," in Lukács, *Beiträge zur Geschichte der Aesthetik*. Berlin: Aufbau-Verlag, 1954, 135–90.

Pereira, Norman. *The Thought and Teachings of N. G. Černyševskij*. The Hague and Paris: Mouton, 1975.

Solov'ev, Gennadii, *Esteticheskie vozzreniia Chernyshevskogo*. Second edition. Moscow: "Khudozhestvennaia literatura," 1978.

Woehrlin, William. "Aesthetics and Literary Criticism," chapter 6 in Woehrlin, *Chernyshevskii: The Man and the Journalist*. Cambridge, Mass.: Harvard University Press, 1971, 144–86.

Nikolai Dobroliubov

Corbet, Charles. "La critique de Dobroliubov: Principes esthétiques et réalités sentimentales," *Revue des études slaves*, no. 29 (1952), 34–53.

———. "Dobroliubov als Literaturkritiker," *Zeitschrift für slavische Philologie*, vol. 24 (1956), 156–73.

Kozhinov, V. V. "Teoriia literaturnogo tvorchestva v rabotakh Dobroliubova," in G. V. Krasnov, ed., *N. A. Dobroliubov: stat'i i materialy*. Gor'kii: Gor'kovskii gosudarstvennyi universitet imeni N. I. Lobachevskogo, 1965, 3–17.

Lebedev-Polianskii, P. I. *N. A. Dobroliubov: Mirovozzrenie i literaturno-kriticheskaia deiatel'nost'*. Moscow: Academia, 1933.

Tunimanov, V. " 'Real'naia kritika' N. A. Dobroliubova. Kriterii narodnosti i zhiznennoi pravdy," *Russkaia literatura*, no. 1 (1986), 36–55.

Zhdanov, V. V. "Dobroliubov," in V. P. Gorodetskii et al., eds., *Istoriia russkoi kritiki*, 2 vols. Moscow-Leningrad: Akademiia nauk SSSR, 1958, 2: 90–145.

Fedor Dostoevskii

Fridlender, Georgii. "Dostoevskii-kritik," in V. P. Gorodetskii et al., eds., *Istoriia russkoi kritiki*, 2 vols. Moscow-Leningrad: Akademiia nauk SSSR, 1958, 2: 269–87.

Gural'nik, U. A. "F. M. Dostoevskii v literaturno-esteticheskoi bor'be 1860-kh godov," in N. L. Stepanov et al., eds., *Tvorchestvo F. M. Dostoevskogo*. Moscow: Akademiia nauk SSSR, 1959, 293–329.

Jackson, Robert. *Dostoevsky's Quest for Form: A Study of His Philosophy of Art*. New Haven and London: Yale University Press, 1966.

Kashina, N. V. *Estetika F. M. Dostoevskogo*. Moscow: Vysshaia shkola, 1975.

Lapshin, I. I. *Estetika Dostoevskogo*. Berlin: Obelisk, 1923.

Leatherbarrow, William. "The Aesthetic Louse: Ethics and Aesthetics in Dostoevsky's 'Prestupleniye i nakazaniye,' " *Modern Language Review*, vol. 71, no. 4 (October 1971), 857–66.

Moser, Charles A. "Dostoevsky and the Aesthetics of Journalism,"

Dostoevsky Studies: Journal of the International Dostoevsky Society, vol. 3 (1982), 27–41.

Stammler, Heinrich. "Dostoevsky's Aesthetics and Schelling's Philosophy of Art," *Comparative Literature*, vol. 7, no. 4 (Fall 1955), 313–23.

Aleksandr Druzhinin

Offord, Derek. "Druzhinin and the 'Pushkin School' of Russian Literature," in William Harrison and Avril Pyman, eds., *Poetry, Prose and Public Opinion: Aspects of Russia 1850–1970. Essays Presented in Memory of Dr. N. E. Andreyev*. Letchworth, England: Avebury Publishers, 1984, 19–42.

Skatov, N. N. "A. V. Druzhinin—literaturnyi kritik," *Russkaia literatura*, no. 4 (1982), 109–21.

Stepan Dudyshkin

Egorov, Boris. "S. S. Dudyshkin–kritik," *Uchenye zapiski Tartuskogo gosudarstvennogo universiteta*, no. 119 (1962): *Trudy po russkoi i slavianskoi filologii*, 5:195–231.

Afanasii Fet

Bukhshtab, Boris. "Esteticheskie vzliady Feta," *Literaturnaia ucheba*, no. 12 (1936), 35–51.

Gustafson, Richard. "The Imagination of Spring: The Aesthetics of Pure Poetry," chapter in Gustafson, *The Imagination of Spring: The Poetry of Afanasy Fet*. New Haven and London: Yale University Press, 1966, 11–36.

Ivan Goncharov

Ehre, Milton. "Ivan Goncharov on Art, Literature, and the Novel," *Slavic Review*, vol. 29, no. 2 (June 1970), 203–18.

Lavretskii, A. "Esteticheskie idei I. A. Goncharova," in Lavretskii, *Esteticheskie vzgliady russkikh pisatelei: Sbornik statei*. Moscow: Gosudarstvennoe izdatel'stvo khudozhestvennoi literatury, 1963, 49–82 [article written in 1940].

Tseitlin, A. G. "Goncharov-kritik," in V. P. Gorodetskii et al., eds., *Istoriia russkoi kritiki*, 2 vols. Moscow-Leningrad: Akademiia nauk SSSR, 1958, 2: 288–302.

Apollon Grigor'ev

Egorov, Boris. "Apollon Grigor'ev—literaturnyi kritik," in A. Grigor'ev, *Literaturnaia kritika*. Moscow: Izdatel'stvo "Khudozhestvennaia literatura," 1967, 3–39.

Gural'nik, U. A. "Apollon Grigor'ev–kritik," in V. P. Gorodetskii et al., eds., *Istoriia russkoi kritiki*, 2 vols. Moscow-Leningrad: Akademiia nauk SSSR, 1958, 1: 470–87.

———. "Literaturno-kriticheskoe nasledie Apollona Grigor'eva," *Voprosy literatury*, vol. 8, no. 2 (1964), 72–91.

Lehmann, Jurgen. *Der Einfluss der Philosophie des deutschen Idealismus in der russischen Literaturkritik des 19. Jahrhunderts: Die "organische Kritik" Apollon A. Grigor'evs*. Heidelberg: Carl Winter, 1975.

Rakov, Valerii, *Apollon Grigor'ev—literaturnyi kritik*. Ivanovo: Ivanovskii gosudarstvennyi universitet imeni Pervogo v Rossii Ivanovo-Voznesenskogo obshchegorodskogo soveta rabochikh deputatov, 1980.

Terras, Victor. "Apollon Girgoriev's Organic Criticism and Its Western Sources," in Anthony Mlikotin, ed., *Western Philosophical Systems in Russian Literature*. Los Angeles: University of Southern California Press, 1979, 71–88.

Konstantin Leont'ev

Gaidenko, P. P. "Naperekor istoricheskomu protsessu (Konstantin Leont'ev—literaturnyi kritik)," *Voprosy literatury*, vol. 18, no. 5 (1974), 159–205.

Dmitrii Pisarev

Brown, Edward J. "Pisarev and the Transformation of Two Russian Novels," in William Mills Todd III, ed., *Literature and Society in Imperial Russia, 1800–1914*. Stanford: Stanford University Press, 1978, 151–72.

Coquart, Armand. *Dmitri Pisarev (1840–1868) et l'idéologie du nihilisme russe*. Paris: Institut d'études slaves, 1946.

Gural'nik, U. A. "Pisarev," in V. P. Gorodetskii et al., eds., *Istoriia russkoi kritiki*, 2 vols. Moscow-Leningrad: Akademiia nauk SSSR, 1958, 1:470–87.

Konkin, Semen. *Esteticheskie i literaturno-kriticheskie vzgliady Pisareva*. Saransk: Mordovskii gosudarstvennyi universitet imeni N. P. Ogareva, 1973.

Plotkin, L. *Pisarev i literaturno-obshchestvennoe dvizhenie shestidesiatykh godov*. Moscow-Leningrad: Akademiia nauk SSSR, 1945.

Tunimanov, V. "Printsip real'noi kritiki: Evoliutsiia Pisareva v 1860-e gody," *Voprosy literatury*, vol. 19, no. 6 (1975), 153–85.

Mikhail Saltykov-Shchedrin

Goriachkina, M. S. "Saltykov-Shchedrin—kritik," in V. P. Gorodetskii et al., eds., *Istoriia russkoi kritiki*, 2 vols. Moscow-Leningrad: Akademiia nauk SSSR, 1958, 2:146–81.

Nikolai Shelgunov

Kupreianova, E. N. "Shelgunov," in V. P. Gorodetskii et al., eds., *Istoriia russkoi kritiki*, 2 vols. Moscow-Leningrad: Akademiia nauk SSSR, 1958, 2: 226–42.

Slabkii, Aleksandr. "Esteticheskie i literaturno-kriticheskie vzgliady N. V. Shelgunova," chapter in Slabkii, *Mirovozzrenie N. V. Shelgunova*. Khar'kov: Izdatel'stvo khar'kovskogo gosudarstvennogo universiteta imeni A. M. Gor'kogo, 1959, 129–83.

Ivan Turgenev

Lavretskii, A. "Literaturno-esteticheskie vzliady I. S. Turgeneva," in Lavretskii, *Esteticheskie vzgliady russkikh pisatelei: Sbornik statei*. Moscow: Gosudarstvennoe izdatel'stvo khudozhestvennoi literatury, 1963, 5–48 [article written in 1938].

Moser, Charles. "Turgenev and the Esthetics of the Whole Man," *Transactions of the Association of Russian-American Scholars in U.S.A.*, vol. 16 (1983), New York, 19–30.

Nazarova, L. N. "Turgenev-kritik," in V. P. Gorodetskii et al., eds., *Istoriia russkoi kritiki*, 2 vols. Moscow-Leningrad: Akademiia nauk SSSR, 1958, 1: 509–30.

Index

ety, 258; opposes "art for art's sake," 119; on relation between art and science, 100–101; on truth in art, 180–81; on useful art, 112; mentioned, 16, 30, 106, 157, 240, 254. Article: "Pushkin," 181
Khomyakov, Aleksey, 252
Konkin, Semyon, 34
Krestovsky, Vsevolod, 78
Kukolnik, Nestor, 127
Kurochkin, Nikolay, 62–63, 82, 118

Leatherbarrow, William, 205–6, 212
Leontev, Konstantin: on beauty in art, 167–69; biography, 47; on historical novel, 252; on morality in art, 196–97; opposes usefulness in art, 113; mentioned, 50, 122, 150, 172, 188. Article: "Letter of a Provincial to Turgenev," 252
Lermontov, Mikhail, 17, 173
Leskov, Nikolay: on *Fathers and Sons*, 263; mentioned, 33, 53, 178, 185, 237
Library for Reading. See *Biblioteka dlya chteniya*
Lirondelle, André, 129
Lobachevsky, Nikolay, 267

Manfred, 65
Markevich, Boleslav, 83, 94
Maykov, Apollon, 23, 205
Men of the 1840s, 108, 219, 249
Mérimée, Prosper, 74
Mey, Lev, 90
Mickiewicz, Adam, 78
Minaev, Dmitry, 17, 82
Mlikotin, Anthony, 22n
Molière, 158
Molotov, 95
monism, philosophical, 6–10, 150–61
"Monument, The": analyzed by Pisarev, 55–56
moral good in art, 187–97
Morning. See *Utro*
Moser, Charles, 32n, 47n, 235n

Moskvityanin, 11, 21, 30
Murillo, Bartolomé Esteban, 78
Muscovite, The. See *Moskvityanin*

Napoleon Buonaparte, 17, 206, 207
Nechaev, Sergey, 250, 254–55
Nekrasov, Nikolay, 12, 17, 20, 34, 65
Nest of Gentlefolk, 24, 259
Neue Lehre von den Proportionen des menschlishen Körpers, 84
Nicholas I (tsar), 3
Nikitenko, Alexander, 4, 5
Notes from the House of the Dead, 33
Notes from Underground, 47
No Way Out, 53

Oblomov, 27, 29, 155, 256
Offord, Derek, 19n
Olkhovsky, Yuri, 10n
On Creative Force in Poetry, 4
Onegin: Pisarev on, 54
On the Eve, 28, 168, 260
organicism in literary criticism, 123–27
Ostrovosky, Alexander, 26–27, 28, 29, 30, 159
Otechestvennye zapiski, 25, 30, 35, 37, 47, 61, 64, 65, 66, 67, 207
Ozerov, Vladislav, 127

Panaeva, Avdotya, 162
Panurge's Herd, 78–79
past and future: attitude toward, 197–203
Pavlova, Karolina, 115
Pereira, Norman, 151, 203
Phenomena of Russian Life Under Esthetic Criticism, 66–67
Phidias, 128
Pilgrimages and Wanderings of the Monk Parfeny, 126
Pisarev, Dmitry: on art and life, 221–22; on art and reality, 227, 228, 236–37; on art and scientific thinking, 99; attacks Solovev, 51–52; on beauty in art, 162, 164; biography, 34–35; on